The First Islamic Classic in Chinese

The First Islamic Classic in Chinese

Wang Daiyu's *Real Commentary on the True Teaching*

Translated with an Introduction and Notes by
SACHIKO MURATA

Cover art from iStock by Getty Images.

Published by State University of New York Press, Albany

© 2017 State University of New York

All rights reserved

Printed in the United States of America

No part of this book may be used or reproduced in any manner whatsoever without written permission. No part of this book may be stored in a retrieval system or transmitted in any form or by any means including electronic, electrostatic, magnetic tape, mechanical, photocopying, recording, or otherwise without the prior permission in writing of the publisher.

For information, contact State University of New York Press, Albany, NY
www.sunypress.edu

Production, Diane Ganeles
Marketing, Kate R. Seburyamo

Library of Congress Cataloging-in-Publication Data

Names: Wang, Daiyu, active 17th century, author. | Murata, Sachiko, 1943– translator.
Title: The First Islamic Classic in Chinese : Wang Daiyu's "Real Commentary on the True Teaching" / translated, with an introduction and notes, by Sachiko Murata.
Other titles: Zheng jiao zhen quan. English | Wang Daiyu's "Real Commentary on the True Teaching" | 1st Islamic Classic in Chinese: Wang Daiyu's "Real Commentary on the True Teaching"
Description: Albany : State University of New York Press, 2017. | Includes bibliographical references and index.
Identifiers: LCCN 2016031430 (print) | LCCN 2016032698 (ebook) | ISBN 9781438465074 (hardcover : alk. paper) | ISBN 9781438465081 (pbk. : alk. paper) | ISBN 9781438465098 (e-book)
Subjects: LCSH: Islam—Essence, genius, nature. | Islam—Doctrines.
Classification: LCC BP163 .W26513 2017 (print) | LCC BP163 (ebook) | DDC 297.2—dc23
LC record available at https://lccn.loc.gov/2016031430

10 9 8 7 6 5 4 3 2 1

Contents

Acknowledgments	vii
Introduction	1
Wang Daiyu	7
Tawḥīd Chinese Style	9
Cosmic Hierarchy	13
Moral Perfection	18
Observing Propriety	24
The Contemporary Relevance	26
The Text and Translation	32
Notes	33
The Real Commentary on the True Teaching	35
Self-Narrative	35
Record of Questions and Answers	37
Book One	41
1.1. The Real One	41
1.2. The Original Beginning	49
1.3. Predetermination	59
1.4. Universal Compassion	64
1.5. The Real Solicitude	70
1.6. The Real Sage	74
1.7. Similarity to the Real	79
1.8. Changing the Real	83
1.9. Darkening the Real	88
1.10. The Outstanding Differences	95
1.11. Nature and Mandate	101

1.12.	The Real Heart	108
1.13.	Life and Death	112
1.14.	The Level of the Human	116
1.15.	Husband and Wife	121
1.16.	Immortals and Spirits	124
1.17.	The True Teaching	129
1.18.	The True Learning	133
1.19.	*Huihui*: The Returning Returners	139
1.20.	Bearing Witness	141

Book Two		145
2.1.	The Five Constants	145
2.2.	Real Loyalty	154
2.3.	Utmost Filial Piety	158
2.4.	Listening to the Mandate	162
2.5.	The Chief Leader	166
2.6.	The Way of Friendship	171
2.7.	Taking and Putting Aside	176
2.8.	Preparation	179
2.9.	Observing the Moments	186
2.10.	Wakeful Reflection	188
2.11.	Name and Profit	193
2.12.	Living up to the Measure	195
2.13.	Sacrificing Animals	201
2.14.	Meat and Vegetables	206
2.15.	Gambling and Drinking	209
2.16.	Interest and Hoarding	212
2.17.	Wind and Water	219
2.18.	The True Mandate	223
2.19.	This World	229
2.20.	The Afterworld	233

Cited Works	241
Index	245

Acknowledgments

I owe a major debt of gratitude to my friend Tu Weiming, who guided me in reading Wang Daiyu when I first discovered his works twenty years ago. The several years we then spent together working on *The Sage Learning of Liu Zhi* were invaluable preparation for my recent return to Wang Daiyu. As always, I owe a great deal to my editor (and husband), William Chittick. I extend my special thanks to Dr. Wang Xi 王希 of the Chinese Academy of Social Sciences in Beijing. During a research year spent at SUNY Stony Brook, he took time off to read my translation of the *Real Commentary* and make numerous helpful suggestions for its improvement. I am especially grateful to the John Simon Guggenheim Foundation, which awarded me a fellowship for the academic year 2011–12, without which it would have impossible to find the time to finish the translation.

Introduction

In *Chinese Gleams of Sufi Light* (2000) I translated one short treatise by each of two major Muslim scholars, Wang Daiyu 王岱輿 and Liu Zhi 劉智. Wang announced in the title of this short treatise, *The Great Learning of the Pure and Real* (*Qingzhen daxue* 清眞大學), that he was drawing from both the Islamic and the Confucian traditions. *Great Learning* refers to a Confucian classic much studied and cited by Neo-Confucian scholars. *Pure and Real* is an expression that Muslims have used to designate their own tradition, so it is commonly translated as "Islam."

It is worth noting at the outset that the term *zhen* 眞 or "real" plays a prominent role in Muslim writings as an indicator of things Islamic. The word has a long history in Chinese thought, especially in Daoism, but never had the same favor it was to gain among Muslims, for whom it is the Chinese equivalent of the Arabic word *ḥaqq*, which means real, true, right, appropriate, and worthy. In the Qur'an *ḥaqq* is used to name God, to designate the content of prophetic revelation, to describe God's activity in the world, and to indicate the nature of ideal human activity.

When I finished *Chinese Gleams* with the help of my two collaborators, Tu Weiming and William Chittick, we decided that despite Wang Daiyu's historical priority, Liu Zhi was the more significant philosopher/theologian and that he would provide greater insight into the manner in which Muslims were able to synthesize Chinese and Islamic thought. We spent several years studying and translating *Nature and Principle in Islam* (*Tianfang xingli* 天方性理), which appeared as *The Sage Learning of Liu Zhi: Islamic Thought in Confucian Terms* (2009). I then turned my attention back to *The Real Commentary*, which proved to be more difficult to decipher than Liu Zhi's book, no doubt because of its relative lack of system and its pioneering quality. In any case, it provides a remarkable window into the worldview and ethos of Muslims in seventeenth-century China.

Over the past thirty years China has seen a great revival of interest in Chinese-language writing on Islam. Hundreds of books and treatises that originally appeared from the seventeenth through the nineteenth century have been republished.[1] Most of them pertain to the school of thought that has come to be called the Han Kitab 漢克塔補, a Chinese-Arabic compound meaning literally "the Chinese books."[2] This literature was produced by scholars commonly known as the Huiru 回儒, that is, Muslim scholars trained in Confucian learning, or "Confucian Muslims."[3] Despite all the new research and ongoing discoveries, it still seems safe to say that the first significant text published by the Huiru was Wang Daiyu's *Real Commentary on the True Teaching* (*Zhengjiao zhenquan* 正教眞詮), which appeared in 1642. Other works had already been printed, including two that Wang criticizes in chapter 1.8, but this book overshadowed earlier writings and became the benchmark of Islamic learning.

English readers have a fine survey of the school of thought that produced Wang Daiyu in Zvi Bendor Benite's *Dao of Muhammad*. Benite explains how the Huiru appeared as the result of the efforts of a number of significant scholars, beginning with Hu Dengzhou 胡登洲 (d. ca. 1597), who established a madrasah in Xianyang 咸陽 in Shaanxi province in the middle of the sixteenth century. Hu Dengzhou broke with the practices of traditional Islamic learning by teaching not only Islamic but also Chinese classics. His students established schools in four different cities, among them Nanjing, where Wang Daiyu was trained and subsequently taught, though in later life he moved to Beijing where he remained until his death. Wang's students praised his ability to answer questions in a clear and logical manner. It is likely that much of *The Real Commentary* was composed precisely to answer the questions that he was constantly being asked, not only by Muslims but also by non-Muslims curious about Islamic teachings.[4]

Wang tells us in the introduction to *The Real Commentary* that he compiled notes on his scholarly conversations and eventually organized them as this book. He divided the material into two sections, theory and practice. The first part explains the Islamic worldview and the manner in which it is distinct from the Three Teachings, which are Confucianism, Daoism, and Buddhism. The second part deals not, as one might expect, with the details of Islamic practice, but with the spiritual and ethical underpinnings of practice. Wang clearly assumed that his readers already knew how to practice their religion, so he wanted to explain the rationale for that practice, not least in cases that would meet strong objections in Chinese society, such as dietary rules, the prohibition of alcohol and gambling, and burial customs. He has almost nothing to say about the typical issues that come up in books of jurisprudence (*fiqh*), the field of Islamic learning that sets down rules and regulations as established by the jurists on the basis of the Qur'an and the tradition. Given the lack of attention to practice per se, Muslims and non-Muslims who imagine that Islam is basically a set of instructions may have a difficult time recognizing the thoroughly Islamic character of the book.

In Arabic, Persian, and other Islamic languages, discussion of the social and spiritual rationale for practice takes place primarily in works that the secondary literature classifies as "Sufi," even though many of the authors so classified would not have used the term in reference to themselves. I use the word for want of a satisfactory alternative.[5] I understand it to mean an approach to Islamic learning that looks for inner meaning when dealing with outward forms and that emphasizes the need to undergo transformation of the soul to achieve a constant personal engagement with God. When texts of this nature address ritual observance, they explain how practice brings the soul into harmony with God and the cosmos. In the process of undertaking such explanations, Sufi teachers have produced some of the greatest and most profound books of the Islamic tradition. To cite but one example, Ghazālī's famous *Iḥyā' 'ulūm al-dīn*, "Giving life to the sciences of the religion," announces in its very title the role that Sufism has played in Islamic civilization.

Given the constant attention of Sufi authors to the inner meanings of external forms, it should not be surprising that Wang and other Huiru drew heavily from Sufi writings. Among all Muslim scholars, the Sufi teachers were most adept at penetrating the received mode of expression and explaining its significance to their audience, often without recourse to the standard expressions in the transmitted learning. The Sufis stood in marked contrast to the jurists, whose role has been to clarify the precise details of activity as delineated by the Qur'an and the Sunnah and who always insisted on exact conformity with the received modes of expression. For the jurists, the basic issue has always been how to do things correctly. For Sufi teachers, correct activity is necessary, but they also insisted that activity brings about the transformation of the soul only in proportion to the practitioners' understanding of the reality of correctness itself and the rationale for conforming to it. Jurists explain how, and Sufis explain why. As Islam spread to regions more distant from the center, the need to explain why became more pronounced. It was especially strong in China, where Muslims were faced with a civilization possessing great powers of assimilation while they themselves found it more and more difficult to master Persian and Arabic, the two main languages of Islamic learning.

If I mention Persian before Arabic, it is not because I have forgotten that Arabic is Islam's sacred language, but because Persian tended to be the language of instruction in what is often called the Persianate realm—which extends from Eastern Europe through Turkey to Iran and Central Asia, the Indian subcontinent, and China. Arabic continued to be the language of ritual, but Persian was likely to be used in the classroom, even when Arabic texts were being studied. In China itself, Arabic did not begin to replace Persian as the primary Islamic language until the late nineteenth century, with the decline of Huiru learning and an influx of "reformers" trained in Arab countries. Today Persian learning is preserved mainly in a few women's mosques; in China as in many other places the women are more attached to the ancestral ways than the men.[6]

The number of books translated from Persian and Arabic into Chinese before the twentieth century is not known, though scholars have suggested as many as twenty-five titles, including texts on grammar (the Qur'an was not translated in its entirety until the 1920s).[7] A great deal of research remains to be done before the details of these translations can be established with any certainty. Of the translated books, four are known to have been used by the Huiru as sources for their thought, but only one can be identified as a source for Wang Daiyu (Liu Zhi, in contrast, used all four). This is *Mirṣād al-ʿibād min al-mabdaʾ ilaʾl-maʿād* (The path of the servants from the origin to the return) by Najm al-Dīn Rāzī (d. 1256), a teacher affiliated with the Kubrawī Sufi order. This long Persian book, available in a good English translation, provides an overview of basic Islamic teachings about God, the cosmos, the human role in creation, and the path of achieving human perfection. It was extremely popular in the Persianate lands of Islam, and indeed, it is arguably the best summary in any language of the overall Islamic worldview as understood before modern times. It was also the first Islamic book to be translated into Chinese, by Wu Zixian 伍子先 in 1670, twenty-eight years after the appearance of Wang's *Real Commentary*. The translation remained a basic textbook of Chinese Islam into the twentieth century.

It is likely that Wang also studied a second book that was later translated into Chinese, that is, *Maqṣad-i aqṣā* (The furthest goal), by 'Azīz Nasafī (d. ca. 1300). Nasafī, like Rāzī, was affiliated with the Kubrawī order. His short and lucid Persian text explains basic Islamic learning in a straightforward but rather philosophical style. Its manner of presentation is quite different from that of Rāzī, who employs relatively little technical terminology and speaks to those not trained in the Islamic sciences. Parts of Nasafī's book are popularizations of the teachings of the school of Ibn al-'Arabī (d. 1240), perhaps the most influential theologian in later Islamic history. In contrast to Liu Zhi, however, Wang shows little evidence of being familiar with teachings specific to Ibn al-'Arabī's school of thought.

In *The Real Commentary* Wang outlines Islamic teachings on God, the universe, the human self, and the manner of living properly in the world. In doing so he uses the language at his disposal, that is, the literary Chinese of the day. This was dominated by the Neo-Confucian synthesis, so it brought together terminology and concepts from all Three Teachings. Nonetheless, like many Confucian authors, Wang is harshly critical of both Daoism and Buddhism. At the same time he is inclined to appreciate the Confucian classics as explained by the Neo-Confucians, though not to the same degree as Liu Zhi, for he does not hold back from highlighting the inconsistencies and shortcomings that he sees in the Confucian canon.

One needs to keep in mind that Wang was addressing Chinese-speaking Muslims of the seventeenth century. He does not display the modern inclination to search for religious harmony and brotherly love, so he makes no attempt to downplay differences or to stress similarities. His stance is often polemical. Addressing readers immersed in Chinese culture, he is aiming to lead them back to their Islamic roots using the resources of Chinese thought. He is not engaged in an outward dialogue with representatives of other traditions, even though his use of Confucian terminology makes it inevitable that the Chinese and Muslim worldviews are constantly interacting in his soul and his writings. In *The Dao of Muhammad* Benite has a good deal to say about the manner in which the Huiru were able to harmonize their Chinese and Muslim identities.[8]

Given that Wang spent a number of years studying the Three Teachings, he was surely aware that many of his arguments against them were oversimplifications. In fact, he notes in his introduction that one of the criticisms he met when he showed his manuscript to readers was that he had not given due credit to Neo-Confucian thought. "You have quoted only superficial and extraneous arguments. You have certainly not sought deeply after their subtleness." In response he agrees that "The way of Confucius and Mencius for cultivating the body, regulating the family, and governing the country is the same as our way," but he adds that it is necessary to bring out the profound differences, particularly their failure to address either the Real Lord per se or posthumous becoming.

To put Wang's response in more Islamic terms, he is saying the Muslim understanding of religion (*dīn*) includes three fundamental principles of thought, that is, *tawḥīd* (the assertion of divine unity), prophecy (*nubuwwa*), and the Return to God (*ma'ād*). Confucians ignore the first and the third, and this means that their instructions on how to achieve right thought, right speech, and right activity fail to address the fullness of the human situation, even if these instructions are congruent with Islamic ethics and morality. In chapter 1.7 Wang shows his sympathy with the Confucian teachings when he says that the reason for their inadequacy must be the burning of the books by the first emperor of the Qin dynasty (in 210 BCE), an event often recalled with sadness by Confucian scholars.

Wang implicitly acknowledges that Confucius was a prophet, that is, the highest category of human being in Islam. The fact that the Huiru adopted the word *sheng* 聖, sage, to translate the Arabic words for prophet (i.e., *nabī* and *rasūl*), suggests that they generally considered this to be the case. In fact the Huiru understanding of sagehood (which in Chinese is before all else the station of Confucius) parallels the manner in which Muslims in the central Islamic lands understood the Qur'anic teachings about prophecy: Although God sent prophets to every people, the original teachings were lost or distorted, so Muhammad was sent to restore them to their pristine and unadulterated form. For those living in the Chinese realm, it was hardly a stretch of the imagination to say that Confucius was one of the 124,000 prophets sent by God, beginning with Adam.

We should grant at the outset that Wang Daiyu is not attempting to bring out the subtleties of Chinese thought or to acknowledge that the Three Teachings do in fact address issues of *tawḥīd* and the Return in their own ways. Wang differs here from Liu Zhi, who takes a much more conciliatory position, drawing freely from the Three Teachings on issues of metaphysics, cosmology, and spiritual psychology. When we do acknowledge Wang's goal of providing an adequate picture of Islamic teachings in Chinese while discouraging Muslims from looking for guidance outside their own tradition, we can better appreciate the extent to which he has succeeded in harmonizing Islamic and Chinese thought without distorting the essential principles and teachings of Islam.

Wang Daiyu

Little is known about Wang Daiyu other than what he says about himself at the beginning of *The Real Commentary*. He mentions neither his teachers nor his students, though some details can be gleaned from the text studied by Benite in *The Dao of Muhammad*, that is, *Jinxue xi chuan pu* 經學系傳譜 (Register of the lineage and transmission of the classical learning), written by Zhao Can 趙燦 in the 1670s. According to Zhao, a school was established in Nanjing by one of the students of Hu Dengzhou, namely Feng Yangwu 馮養吾. Feng's teachings were then continued by his student Ma Zhenwu 馬眞吾, who was succeeded by Ma Junshi 馬君實, of whom Wang Daiyu was a student.[9]

The most detailed account of Wang Daiyu before modern scholarship is found in Lan Zixi's *Tianfang zhengxue* 天方正學 (The true learning of Islam) published in 1862. The author tells us that his book is a simplified version of the teachings of Wang Daiyu and Liu Zhi. The first chapter provides six diagrams outlining Islamic learning, including a depiction of the chain of prophets. Chapter 2 has six sections explaining the twenty-eight letters of the Arabic alphabet, not only in terms of script and pronunciation, but also in terms of cosmological symbolism. Chapter 3 deals with the meaning of the Shahadah or testimony of faith in twenty-nine sections. Chapter 4 clarifies nature and mandate (*xingming* 性命), that is, the spiritual and cosmological roots of the cosmos. Chapter 5 explains the invisibility and concealment of the Real One in twenty-four sections. Chapter 6 has thirty-eight sections explaining "the essential purport of *The Real Commentary*," that is, Wang Daiyu's book. Chapter 7, called "Epitaphs of the Real Humans" (*zhenren mouzhi* 眞人墓誌), describes forty-nine prophets and friends of God, beginning with Adam. Among those depicted are Qur'anic prophets, the legendary emperors Fu Xi 伏羲 and Shennong 神農, Mary, Jesus, and Muhammad's parents. After describing Muhammad himself (number 22), the text turns to his family and the rightly guided caliphs, and then mentions some of Islam's well-known saintly figures. In the fortieth section it describes Wang Daiyu as the first of ten Chinese figures. With the exception of the scholar Ma Minglong 馬明龍 (d. 1679), the remaining eight "real humans" of China have not been identified.[10] Here is Lan's description of Wang Daiyu:

> This real human's family name is Wang, his given name Dai, and his honorific Daiyu. At the time of the Ming Dynasty, he was commended as a worthy scholar of Chinling [Nanjing]. In order to take an examination for the third degree he traveled to Beijing. He spent many years accumulating the learning of the way of Islam. He wrote *The Real Commentary on the True Teaching*, *The True Answers of the Very Real*, and *The Great Learning of the Pure and Real*. His interpretations of the Western Classics are evidence that his learning is of the utmost truth and his principles of the utmost clarity. His explanations of the rich and deep content of the Western Classics are refined, extensive, and accomplished. He penetrated thoroughly everything from ancient times to the present. Those who read him will surely sigh deeply and say, "The learning of this real human is not easy to obtain!" The learning of the Western Classics is refined, extensive, and accomplished. Never has there been such a person! How rare is the learning of the real human! Not easy is it to obtain!
>
> The Western Classics have deep purport. While listening to the recitation of the texts, the quick-witted hear spiritual penetration in the sound. Their hearts become still and their intentions satisfied; they repent of previous transgressions and advance straight to the Root Origin. But if someone who is not quick-witted listens, it will be as if he has never heard it before. Those who have penetrated the books of Confucianism but have not penetrated the Western Classics do not understand the language or what the talk is all about. People know that there are sages and worthies in Confucianism, but they do not know what makes the sages and worthies of the West sages and worthies.

There are some who can recite but cannot expound, there are some who can expound but cannot penetrate to the essence, and there are many who can neither recite nor expound. There are also many who have penetrated the books of Confucianism but are not acquainted with the Western Classics. This real human penetrated the Confucian books as well as the Western Classics that are refined, extensive, and accomplished—this indeed is not easy to obtain, so people sigh deeply. This real human cultivated the real nature and principle and, with genuine nature, he went home to the Real. His tomb is in Sanlihe, outside the Fuzheng gate of Peking, where he became the centerpole of the landmarks.

How then did Wang Daiyu "penetrate the Confucian books as well as the Western Classics"? A few words of introduction about his basic teachings may help readers understand what Lan Zixi had in mind. Otherwise, readers familiar with Islamic thought but unacquainted with the Chinese worldview will find it difficult to see Wang's deep Islamic training. In any case, it will be helpful to say something about the original Arabic/Persian form of Wang's teachings.

Tawḥīd Chinese Style

At all times and places, Muslims have affirmed that their tradition is built on the notion of *tawḥīd*, literally, saying one or voicing oneness. To be a Muslim is to acknowledge the unity of God, the ultimate reality. All else follows upon this. One of *tawḥīd*'s first implications is that the universe along with everything it contains comes forth from God, is constantly sustained by God, and finally returns to God. This teaching is commonly discussed in terms of the doctrine of the Origin and the Return (*al-mabda' wa'l-ma'ād*). The overall picture is sometimes called the circle of existence (*dā'irat al-wujūd*). Liu Zhi's *Nature and Principle in Islam* is built on this circular plan, and Wang Daiyu's book refers to it repeatedly, though not with such clarity or detail.

Notice that the Return, the third principle of Islamic thought, is understood as the necessary complement of the Origin. In looking for a Chinese equivalent for these two terms, the Huiru settled on Former Heaven (*xiantian* 先天) and Latter Heaven (*houtian* 後天), a pair much discussed in Confucianism. Typically, the Former Heaven is said to be a realm of formlessness (*wuxing* 無形) before things enter into existence; the Latter Heaven is then the realm of forms (*xing* 形) in which we dwell now. The Former Heaven is thus the descending arc of existence, in which all things enter into formal existence from the Real One. The Latter Heaven is the ascending arc, in which all things travel back to the invisible and formless realm from which they arose.

Wang's basic critique of the Chinese traditions has to do with *tawḥīd*. According to his reading, the Three Teachings either miss it entirely (Daoism and Buddhism), or they offer inadequate and vague formulations (Confucianism). He typically speaks of Daoism and Buddhism together, characterizing them as teachings that focus not on the Real but rather on emptiness (*kong* 空) and nonbeing (*wu* 無). He faults Confucianism for not grasping the subservience of the Three Ultimates to the Real Lord. More generally he criticizes all Three Teachings for forgetting both the Origin and the Return. As he puts it, "If you constantly examine the classic books and the histories by the various scholars, you will hardly see and hear matters concerning the original beginning and the essential end" (130–31).

The doctrine of the Three Ultimates became a mainstay of Neo-Confucian thought with a short text called *The Explanation of the Diagram of the Great Ultimate*, by Zhou Dunyi 周敦頤 (d. 1073). The three are the Non-Ultimate (*wuji* 無極), the Great Ultimate (*taiji* 太極), and the Human Ultimate (*renji* 人極). According to an influential interpretation by the great Zhu Xi 朱熹 (d. 1200), the Non-Ultimate designates reality before the appearance of forms, and the Great Ultimate designates reality after the appearance of forms.[11] Using similar language, Wang writes, "The Non-Ultimate is the beginning of formlessness in heaven, earth, and the myriad things, and the Great Ultimate is the beginning of form in heaven, earth, and the myriad things" (53). As for the Human Ultimate, he is the person who becomes a sage, thereby integrating the whole of reality and achieving the final goal of human existence.

It is easy to find many teachings in Islamic thought that provide a depiction of the cosmic role of prophets similar to that of the Confucian sage. One of the most salient examples in the later period is the doctrine of perfect humans (*al-insān al-kāmil*), the most sophisticated version of which is found in the writings of Ibn al-'Arabī. In one of many ways of explaining the general Islamic position on the role of the perfect humans in the scheme of things, Muslim authors cite a saying of God, "But for thee [O Muhammad!], I would not have created the creation." In other words God knew Muhammad as the foremost of the perfect human beings before He created the universe, and He created it in order to actualize the fullness of Muhammad's perfection.

In this way of understanding the human role in existence, God's eternal knowledge of Muhammad—often called "the Muhammadan Reality" (*al-ḥaqīqat al-muḥammadiyya*)—is the uncreated Logos, the archetype of every possibility of creation and manifestation. The universe and all that it contains are latent in this Reality, and its human embodiment appears in the persons of the prophets generally and the historical Muhammad specifically. Thus the Muhammadan Reality is the perfect transcription of God's knowledge of both being and nonbeing. If not for its presence in the divine knowledge—that is, if not for God's foreknowledge of all things—nothing would come into existence.

According to Qur'an, "His only command, when He desires a thing, is to say to it 'Be!,' and it comes to be" (36:82). Typical interpretations of this verse explain that God can only desire and speak to something that He already knows. Since He is one and the thing that He desires does not yet exist, He must know the thing—along with all other things—within His own self. For Wang Daiyu, the Muhammadan Reality—the sum total of God's knowledge of the universe—is precisely the Human Ultimate. As he puts it, "Heaven, earth, and the myriad things have come into being because they are rooted in the Human Ultimate. Were there no Human Ultimate, none of the myriad things would have been established" (204).

In keeping with Islamic thought generally, Wang Daiyu situates the Human Ultimate at a point that is both the beginning and the end of the circle of existence. At the beginning, it is the seed of all things, and at the end, it is the fruit of all. Because of the exalted position of Muhammad, he is "the great origin of the Human Ultimate" (79). The Human Ultimate in turn has two sides to its reality, which are precisely the Non-Ultimate and the Great Ultimate. In explaining this, Wang uses the typical Confucian language of "substance" (*ti* 體) and "function" (*yong* 用). The substance of a thing is its inner reality, and the function is its outward manifestation. Wang says that the Utmost Sage is he "whose substance is the Non-Ultimate and whose function is the Great Ultimate" (79). "The Great Ultimate manifests the

Non-Ultimate, so the function of the Non-Ultimate is the substance of the Great Ultimate" (74). In other words, the substance of the Human Ultimate is the Non-Ultimate, which is the root of all formlessness, and its function is the Great Ultimate, which is the root of all forms. Wang summarizes the cosmic role of the Human Ultimate in these terms:

> Before heaven and earth, the human became the root origin of the myriad beings; as the embodiment of the Real One, he became the firm principle from antiquity until now. After heaven and earth, he will be the origin to which the myriad laws go home.
> When he goes beyond the myriad levels, he begins to go home to the Real One. Among the myriad things, he is second to the Real One, so nothing has greater honor than the human. Just as the flourishing of grass and trees and the abundance of flowers and fruits are all contained in the seed, so also the greatness of heaven and earth and the manyness of the myriad things are all included in the Human Ultimate. (117)

In discussing the concept of unity expressed by the doctrine of *tawḥīd*, Wang sometimes refers to the three Ones, a notion that Liu Zhi was to develop in more detail. According to Wang the three are the Unique One (*duyi* 獨一), the Numerical One (*shuyi* 數一), and the Practicing One (*xiyi* 習一): "The Unique One is the Real Lord, the Numerical One is the Seed, and the Practicing One is the Real Human Being" (154). In other words, the Unique One is the transcendent One of Islamic theology. The Numerical One is the Human Ultimate as embracing both the Non-Ultimate and the Great Ultimate. The Practicing One is the Perfect Human Being inasmuch as he has actualized the full human potential and returned to God by traversing the arc of ascent back to the Origin.

In terms familiar to the Islamic heartlands, we can say that the Unique One is God in His Essence, unknown to any but Himself. The Numerical One is the Muhammadan Reality, which is the uncreated prototype of all creation, embracing all that is demanded by God's names and attributes. The Practicing One is the Perfect Human Being, who achieves the goal of human existence by actualizing the whole range of divine self-manifestation in the world. In still other terms, the Unique One is God in His exclusive unity (*aḥadiyya*), which belongs to the Divine Essence alone; the Numerical One is God in His inclusive unity (*wāḥidiyya*), which embraces the principles of all multiplicity; and the Practicing One is the human being who reaches the final stage of *tawḥīd*.

Cosmic Hierarchy

In Islamic thought the cosmos or universe (*'ālam*) is often defined as everything other than God. The Huiru commonly refer to it with the Chinese phrase "heaven, earth, and the myriad things," which corresponds nicely with the Qur'anic expression, "heaven, earth, and everything between the two." Liu Zhi provides many diagrams illustrating various ways of analyzing the macrocosm (the universe as a whole) and the microcosm (the human self) in terms of both the descending and the ascending arcs of existence. Wang is by no means as systematic, but he clearly has the same sort of structure in mind.

To talk about the cosmos is to refer to everything contained by the two realms: heaven (the high realm) and earth (the low realm). Highness is defined by nearness to the Source, and lowness by distance from It. Nearness and distance are not spatial but qualitative and relative. They are determined by the relative presence or absence of the inner, invisible qualities of existence: life, awareness, desire, power, compassion, justice, and so on. These qualities are nothing but the divine attributes, for God is alive, aware, desiring, powerful, compassionate, just, and so on. Things in the cosmos are near to or distant from the Real in keeping with the intensity or weakness of these inner qualities. Beings that are relatively near can be called *shen* 神, spirits, and those relatively far can be called *xing*, forms.

Wang uses *shen* as a general designation for the interior, invisible realm of life and awareness—whether we are talking about plants, animals, or humans. Thus spirit is the formless side of things in contrast to the formal side, which is manifest or perceived. The two terms correspond almost exactly with the common Arabic pair, *meaning* (*ma'nā*) and *form* (*ṣūra*). Wang also uses spirit to refer to the two basic sorts of subtle beings, the angels and the jinn. Angels are created of light, jinn of fire, and animals of clay. Hence the jinn have an ontological status below angels and above animals. Note that *shen* is sometimes translated into English as god or God, but that translation is clearly inappropriate in the Islamic context.

Wang uses a second term, *ling* 靈, in a way that overlaps with *shen*. To keep the two distinct I translate *shen* as spirit and *ling* as spiritual. *Spirit* is used more generally, in the range of senses just mentioned. *Spiritual* tends to be used for the specific quality of human beings that sets them apart from other creatures. Most commonly Wang uses it in the expression *xingling* 性靈, "the nature of the spiritual."

It is important to understand that *xing* 性, nature, cannot be contrasted with what we would call the supernatural. *Xing* is used as a near synonym for *li* 理, principle. The two terms play such an important role in Neo-Confucian thought that the school itself is often called simply "Nature and Principle" (Wang refers to it with this expression in several passages). The title of Liu Zhi's book *Nature and Principle in Islam* can as well be translated "Islamic Neo-Confucianism." Both Liu and Wang use both nature and principle to designate the realities of things inasmuch as they dwell in the invisible, formless realm of heaven rather than the visible, formal domain of earth. For his part Liu Zhi consistently translates Arabic *rūḥ* or "spirit" as nature, and he often uses "principle" to translate *'aql*, which means intelligence or intellect. In Islamic thought, *rūḥ* and *'aql* are taken as near synonyms, though *rūḥ* connotes life wherever it may be found in the universe; and *'aql*, though it governs the universe on behalf of God, can only be fully actualized in the human state. On the higher levels of existence *rūḥ* and *'aql* become indistinguishable. Hence the Prophet is often quoted as saying that the first thing created by God was "the Intellect" or "my spirit."

Wang uses *nature* as a virtual synonym for both *shen* and *ling*, spirit and spiritual, though generally with a broader significance. As for *the nature of the spiritual*, this designates the characteristic of human beings that sets them apart from other creatures; in Arabic, this characteristic is typically called intellect (*'aql*) or rational soul (*nafs nāṭiqa*).

To a large extent Wang's description of human nature derives from similar discussions in Islamic texts, which in turn are not unrelated historically to Aristotelianism. In short, what distinguishes plants from minerals is the vegetal spirit; what distinguishes animals from plants is the additional presence of the animal spirit; and what distinguishes the human from the animal is the addition of the human spirit, also called the intellect and the rational soul. Thus

Wang writes, "The lowest level is called the nature of begetting, the middle level the nature of awareness, and the highest level the nature of the spiritual" (113).

Wang also discusses nature as tightly bound up with mandate (*ming* 命). Neo-Confucian scholars frequently discuss these two together with a view toward the first sentence of the Confucian classic, *The Doctrine of the Mean*: "What heaven mandates is nature; following nature is the way." (Wang explains why he is unhappy with Confucian interpretations of this sentence in chapter 1.11.) Along with the Huiru generally, Wang uses mandate to translate Arabic *amr*, command. On the basis of Qur'anic usage, theologians often differentiated between two divine commands, the engendering or creative command, and the prescriptive or religious command. The first is the divine word "Be!" (*kun*), through which God bestows being (*kawn*) on all things; its distinguishing feature is that it cannot be disobeyed. The second is the multifarious instructions that God has revealed by means of the prophets. These can be disobeyed, because they address human free will. As to the degree in which human beings are actually free, that is a constant discussion among theologians, Sufis, and philosophers. Typically they conclude that people are neither completely free nor completely constrained. Hence they must put what freedom they do have to the best use. Wang offers his thoughts on the issue mainly in chapter 1.3.

Each being is what it is because of the mandate of heaven, which is the divine command that gives existence to all things at the level of their own specific natures, their distinctive existential characteristics. Hence, as the *Doctrine of the Mean* says, "What heaven mandates is nature." Nature derives from the mandate of heaven, which determines the modality of a thing's being. In one passage, Wang describes the basic levels of existence in the following terms, using *mandate* to designate the divine command that bestows distinctive qualities upon things and *nature* to mean the sum total of these invisible qualities within the things:

> The mandate of begetting and growth is the nature of grass and trees, which can support the begetting and growth of grass and trees. When grass and trees wither and decay, this nature disappears and perishes.
>
> The mandate of knowledge and awareness is the nature of birds and beasts, which can adhere to the begetting and

growth of birds and beasts and allow them to see, hear, taste, know, and be aware through eyes, ears, nose, tongue, body, and heart. They are not able to deduce principles, however, and when they die, this nature also perishes.

The mandate of the spiritual and intelligence is the nature of the human. It combines the two natures of begetting and awareness, supporting people's growth and nourishment and allowing them to know and be aware and also to deduce the principles of affairs. Although the body dies, this nature exists everlastingly. (113)

Wang uses the term *mandate* to designate not only the creative command but also the religious command. For example, at the very beginning of chapter 1.1, he refers to the creative command by saying that the Real One is "the Being that does not receive the mandate," which is to say that the Real One is eternal Being, whereas everything else comes into existence by receiving the command, "Be!" As he puts it in chapter 1.10, "Before there were heaven and earth, the Real Lord turned the Non-Ultimate and opened the Gate of All Subtleties. At this very moment, each thing was granted its nature and mandate." Wang's second mention of mandate in chapter 1.1 alludes to various Qur'anic commandments that summarize the religious command, which he frequently calls the clear mandate (*mingming* 明命): "Drawing conclusions based on the teaching of the way is that one must comply with the clear mandate in all things, like recognizing the Lord and recognizing self, bearing witness to the Sage, going home to the Real, the five human relationships, and the one hundred actions."

In some passages, Wang uses the term *mandate* in a way that embraces both the creative and the religious command. For example, he sums up the circle of human existence as three stages of "real solicitude" (*zhenci* 眞賜), which is how he translates the word *īmān*, faith. The first stage is people's predetermined nature and mandate, before they enter into the world. The second stage is their individual growth and development once they dwell in the world. The third is their return to God after death. The mandate received in the Former Heaven is that of coming to be. The mandate recognized in this world is the clear mandate. The mandate actualized in the next world is the return to the creative command. Thus he writes,

> There are three meanings for real solicitude: obeying the One, recognizing the One, and becoming the One. Obeying

the One is the time of receiving the mandate while existing in the Former Heaven. It is the seed. Recognizing the One is the time of complying with the mandate while existing in this world. It is the nurturing. Becoming the One is the time of returning to the mandate while existing in the afterworld. It is the fruit. (72)

On occasion Wang differentiates between nature and mandate in terms of the Former Heaven and the Latter Heaven. In the Former Heaven, people (or the natures that will eventually be actualized as people) are in the process of coming into existence. Once they are born into the Latter Heaven, they gradually actualize their potentials, thereby acquiring the natures in stages—the vegetal, animal, and human. In a more systematic treatment of these successive natures, Liu Zhi distinguishes clearly among six levels, each of which becomes manifest on the basis of a lower nature or, in the case of the mineral nature, on the basis of the four elements. If Liu were talking about temporal succession, one might be tempted to say that he is an evolutionary thinker. But like other Muslim authors who describe the ascending levels of being (Rūmī is well known for this), he is careful to point out that the return to the Origin—the "evolution" of the being—takes place by traversing, in reverse order, the descent from the One, the being's "devolution." The ladder of increasing subtlety and spirituality that we see before our eyes is the reverse of the stairway of decreasing subtlety and increasing density that preceded our entrance into the world. Liu Zhi sums up the doctrine of the Origin and Return in these terms:

The Former Heaven undergoes transformation through the ongoing flow of the One Principle. This brings forth the nature of continuity, the nature of the spiritual, the nature of the living, the nature of growth, the nature of minerals, and the nature of the four agents. They descend in succession and stop when they reach the original vital-energy. . . .

The Latter Heaven undergoes transformation through the differentiation and revelation of the original vital-energy. This brings forth soil, water, fire, and wind; metal and stone; grass and trees; and birds and beasts. Gradually they issue forth in clarity and stop at the human. . . .

This is the meaning of "Descent is from the seed, and ascent is to the fruit." The fruit of the Latter Heaven is the seed of the Former Heaven. The coming of the microcosm is that it comes at the same time that the macrocosm descends from its ascent. Its going back is that it goes back after the macrocosm has completed its ascent from descent. To go back as the very last is to go back as the utmost essence.[12]

Liu Zhi's explanation here might be taken as an amplification of the following words of Wang Daiyu: "The Former Heaven is the mandate, and the Latter Heaven is nature. The mandate is the seed, and nature is the fruit. The mandate is not nature, yet it is not apart from nature. Nature is not the mandate, yet it is not apart from the mandate. Without the mandate, there is no nature, and without nature, [the mandate] is incomplete" (103).

Unlike Liu Zhi, Wang does not use the terms macrocosm (the universe as a whole) and microcosm (the human self), but unsurprisingly he alludes to the standard teaching about these two, which is that everything differentiated in the macrocosm is found in an undifferentiated manner in the microcosm. What is objectively present in the outside realm is subjectively present (at least potentially) in the inside realm; hence man has the capacity to know all things, for their realities are latent in human intelligence. To actualize knowledge of the outside realm is to bring about understanding of one's own self. This is what Wang has in mind when he writes, "Just as the human is not able to abide by himself without heaven and earth, so also the myriad things are not able to exist by themselves without the human. . . . The myriad things exist through the spiritual of the human, and the human is preserved by the forms of the myriad things" (118).

Moral Perfection

Like Sufi authors in general, Wang discusses divine unity, the universe, and the creation of the myriad things because he wants to bring out the perilousness of the human situation. People have no escape from their responsibilities toward God and the universe. They have appeared in the world for a purpose and will be asked to account for themselves after death. The Dao of heaven and earth, which is nothing but the way in which reality unfolds, demands human engagement. Before all else such engagement asks people to dominate over the dispersive tendencies inherent in their mineral, vegetal, and animal natures. Only then can they actualize "the nature of the spiritual" and achieve the true human state.

As a good Chinese, Wang acknowledges the importance of the five relationships that form the basis of a stable society, not least the relationship between emperor and subject. But he keeps to the mainstream of Islamic moral teachings by insisting that the key to all good lies in taking responsibility for oneself and exerting every effort to bring one's own self back to nature's original purity. During his time the idea that Islamic teachings aim to build a utopian society had not yet sprouted in the minds of Muslims, least of all in China. For example, Wang dedicates chapter 2.5 to an explanation of a saying of Muhammad. The Arabic text, found in the collection of Bukhārī, reads like this:

> Each of you is a shepherd, and each of you will be held responsible for your sheep. The commander who directs the people is a shepherd, and he will be held responsible for his sheep. The man is a shepherd over the members of his household, and he will be held responsible for them. The woman is a shepherd over the household of her husband and his children, and she will be held responsible for them. The servant is a shepherd over the property of his master, and he will be held responsible for it. Verily, each of you is a shepherd, and each of you will be held responsible for your sheep!

Wang interprets this saying as a command to establish priorities in life and activity. Before all else, each person must attend to himself. This means that the heart (the mind, the inmost center of the person) must take charge of the body and all its faculties. Here Wang alludes to another hadith transmitted by Bukhārī: "There is in the body a lump of flesh. When it is sound, the whole body is sound, and when it is corrupt, the whole body is corrupt. Indeed, it is the heart." In his words,

> The sovereign king has responsibility for all under heaven. The district magistrate has responsibility for one area. The head of a family has responsibility for one family. Someone who lives alone has responsibility for his own body.

Although all these are equal in responsibility, of most concern are the people and things of your own body, for they are the most important root. The heart is the lord-ruler of the whole body. Intention, deliberation, memory, and wakefulness are among its close attendants. Seeing, hearing, smelling, and speaking are its ministers of state. The four limbs and one hundred members are its people and things. As one body the whole of this body is one country. If the heart is unjust, then the whole body will be unjust; if the heart is true, then the whole body will be true. How can this be a small affair? (166–67)

To Wang it is eminently clear that establishing harmony in the community and the nation depends on establishing the soundness and wholesomeness of the self, and this in turn is impossible without having a clear vision of the way things actually are, a vision founded on *tawḥīd*. He summarizes the relationship between right knowledge and the goal of human existence toward the beginning of his *Great Learning*:

When the Lord and the servant are clearly separated, and the Real One and the Numerical One are established, then only can the fountainhead of clear virtue be known. When the fountainhead of clear virtue is known, the clear virtue will be clarified. When the clear virtue is clarified, there will be real knowledge. When there is real knowledge, the self will be known. When the self is known, the heart will be made true. When the heart is made true, intentions will be sincere. When intentions are sincere, words will be firm. When words are firm, the body will be cultivated. When the body is cultivated, the family will be regulated. When the family is regulated, the country will be governed.[13]

The Confucian ideal, as Tu Weiming likes to say, is to learn how to be human. In the ontological terms that Wang Daiyu often employs, learning how to be human demands rootedness in the nature of the spiritual, which is characterized by intelligence, self-awareness, and the ability to see into the principles that govern the universe. Wang takes it for granted that the process of becoming fully human actualizes the Five Constants (*wuchang* 五常), that is, the virtues of humaneness (*ren*

仁), righteousness (*yi* 義), propriety (*li* 禮), wisdom (*zhi* 智), and faithfulness (*xin* 信). Discussion of these virtues in Chinese texts runs parallel to Islamic discussions of Qur'anic virtues and character traits.

The most important of the five virtues, the one that embraces all, is *ren*, humaneness. Scholars have translated *ren* in a variety of ways, trying to catch the range of connotations in the word—benevolence, perfect virtue, human-heartedness, love, benevolent love, goodness, altruism, co-humanity, true manhood. If I had to translate it into Arabic, I would choose the word *iḥsān*, "beautiful-doing," which catches the range of meanings and plays a similar role in the Qur'an, where it designates the foundation of all human good.[14] As is often remarked and as Wang also points out (117), the character for *ren* 仁 is a compound of the characters for "human" (人) and "two" (二). Thus the word connotes a benevolent, proper, wise, and faithful relationship between two people. As for the Confucian "five relationships," they designate the archetypal two-person situations that must be governed by humaneness and its attendant virtues: ruler-subject, father-son, husband-wife, elder sibling-younger sibling, friend-friend.

This having been said, it needs to be pointed out that Wang sticks to the mainstream of Islamic moral teachings when he ascribes all of these virtues to the Real One. Ethicists such as Ghazālī often describe human perfection as "becoming characterized by the character traits of God" (*al-takhalluq bi akhlāq Allāh*). Much of the discussion of the virtues in Islamic texts designates them with words that also designate divine attributes, such as wisdom, compassion, justice, love, forgiveness, generosity, clemency, and patience. Not least among these divine attributes is my choice for translating *ren*, "beautiful-doing" (*iḥsān*). The Qur'an calls God the Beautiful-Doer (*muḥsin*) and says in five verses that God loves the beautiful-doers. Thus we should not be surprised that Wang ascribes humaneness to the Real Lord, as in the passage, "The Real Lord is the utmost humaneness who made the Classic descend and sent the sages to direct and guide the perplexed to the path" (104). If the attribution of humaneness to God sounds odd in English, this is because I am translating *ren* consistently. If I had chosen to render it as benevolence (which is a common translation of *iḥsān*), no one would blink an eye at this sentence, nor at the following statement, which sums up the common Islamic notion that no one can achieve true human status without becoming characterized by God's character traits: "Were there no complete human beings, there would be no one to embody the utmost humaneness of the Real Lord" (189).

In Islamic moral teachings, the most deeply rooted obstacle to human perfection is often called *hawā*, caprice, or self-centered desire. The Qur'an criticizes it frequently, and later literature takes it as the worst of the false gods that people worship, often citing the verse, "Who is more misguided than he who follows his own caprice without guidance from God?" (28:50). Sufi literature pays a great deal of attention to conquering caprice, though more commonly it uses the term *nafs*, which means literally self and soul. This word functions as a reflexive pronoun and as such can refer to anything. When the Qur'an refers to *al-nafs*, "the self" without qualification, translators typically render it as "the [human] soul." Sufi authors cite various Qur'anic verses to support the notion that the soul is the source of misguidance. They also cite prophetic sayings, such as "Your worst enemy is the soul between your two sides." In philosophical and medical treatises the word *nafs* is used neutrally to designate psyche, self, or soul, but in Sufi literature it typically has a strong negative connotation. At the same time, this literature also acknowledges the positive potential of the soul when it talks about three ascending levels, using Qur'anic terminology: the soul that commands to ugliness, the soul that blames (itself for its own shortcomings), and the soul at peace (with God).

For his part, Wang talks about *nafs* in the sense of caprice by using the term "self-nature" (*zixing* 自性). One of his recurrent topics is that one needs to overcome self-nature in order to achieve human status. Here his teachings are in perfect alignment with both the Qur'an and Confucius. Several times in the text he discusses "conquering the self" (*keji* 克己), the locus classicus for which is in the words of Confucius, "To conquer self and return to propriety is humaneness [*ren*]" (*Analects* 12:1). In a typical passage Wang writes, "Only by conquering self and forgiving the people will you enter into the True Way" (163). Or again: "The most important thing in which to exert effort is nothing but conquering self. Although conquering self and having self are the same in form and appearance, they are distant from each other in right and wrong. One is good and the other evil. How is it possible for you not to discriminate between the two?" (187).

Conquering self leads to the state of not having self. For Wang the goal of the Confucian activity known as "cultivating the body" (*xiushen* 修身) is to achieve "no-self" (*wuzi* 無己), a common Buddhist expression. Here he is reiterating one of the major themes of Sufi literature, a theme summed up in a hemistich of Arabic poetry sometimes attributed to the great teacher Junayd of Baghdad (d. 910): "Your existence is a sin to which no other sin can compare." Concerning the central importance of overcoming self, Wang writes, "Although there are many sorts of good and evil, each has one root. The root of good is born from knowing self, and the root of evil emerges from not knowing self. Knowing self is to become no-self, and becoming no-self is to demean self and be modest. Not knowing self is to have self, and having self is to honor self and be arrogant" (190).

Here Wang interprets no-self in moral and ethical terms. In other passages he uses a language that recalls Sufi discussions of the Perfect Human Being, Neo-Confucian depictions of the sage, and Buddhist and Daoist descriptions of buddhas and immortals (for a parallel explanation by Liu Zhi of the same mysterious realm, see the last diagram of *Sage Learning*). A good example is provided by the following passage drawn from chapter 1.19. Wang calls the chapter Huihui 回回, which I translate as "The Returning Returners," in keeping with the explanation that Wang provides in the chapter. The word *huihui* (or simply *hui*) is commonly used as a designation for Muslims. The main point of the chapter seems to be that Muslims are completely out of touch with their own tradition. As he says toward the end of it, "Most people today falsely take on the name *huihui* and do not devote their attention to the reality. When asked about the principles, they know nothing at all. Are they not ashamed before *huihui*'s meaning?"

What then does the word *huihui* mean? Why are Muslims called by this strange expression, which might be translated literally as "return-return." According to Wang, the word indicates that the goal of human life is to return to the Unique One by way of the Numerical One and to achieve the original state of humanity, the Human Ultimate. People must actualize their true heart (*zhengxin* 正心; Persian *dil-i ḥaqīqī*), an organ which, in Islamic terms, embraces God. As a famous divine saying puts it, "Neither My heavens nor My earth embraces Me, but the heart of my faithful servant does embrace Me." Or, as Wang translates this saying, "Heaven and earth are not able to receive and carry the Real Lord—only the heart of a true person" (108).

If the Chinese word for heart, *xin* 心, is commonly translated as "mind," this is not least because of the emotive connotations of *heart* in English and the exalted nature of the heart in Chinese thought. Mencius points to the heart's role in achieving human perfection when he writes, "He who fully realizes his heart knows his nature. He who knows his nature knows Heaven" (7.A.1.1). Wang often talks about the heart's primary importance, but in discussing the status of the true *huihui* he refers to a still higher stage of realization—probably inspired by Buddhist language—that of "no-heart" (*wuxin* 無心). If we want an Islamic equivalent, perhaps the closest is Ibn al-'Arabī's "no station" (*lā maqām*), a term he uses to designate the exalted rank of the Perfect Human Being in union with God.[15]

Here then is Wang's description of the true *huihui*, those Muslims who achieve full conformity with the One. Notice that he describes two stages of ascent to God, the first of which is shared by the Three Teachings, and the second of which can be achieved only by followers of the Utmost Sage.

> When they think again about the Origin, they will quickly search for the path to go home. They will mold feelings and desires so as to act in keeping with the principles of heaven. They will transform the myriad images so as to take them back to emptiness and nonbeing. This is the return of the true heart. This is the very moment of seeing Thusness, perfecting the Great Ultimate, opening the Gate of All Subtleties, and attaining the way of being and nonbeing. This is what is meant by saying that no one can advance beyond the True Real, above which is nothing.
>
> If you want to advance one step further, you must tear away the curtain of Thusness, pierce and crush the circle of the Great Ultimate, and break and smash the Gate of All Subtleties. Then you will go beyond the way of the Three Teachings. Outside this way is a house that people do not discern, for they are searching leisurely for the nest inside the way. If you can once again obtain the nest and arrive at this house, you will certainly return to the no-heart. When you return to the no-heart, the fountainhead of the mandate will become manifest and you will attain the Non-Ultimate. When you embody the Non-Ultimate and recognize the Real Lord, that is the utmost return. (140–41)

Observing Propriety

A calligraphic motif often seen in Chinese mosques consists of the three characters *li* 禮, *dao* 道, and *zhen* 眞—propriety, way, and real.

Such did the Chinese Muslims translate a well-known triad in Islamic texts: Shariah (*sharī'a*), Tariqah (*ṭarīqa*), and Haqiqah (*ḥaqīqa*), that is, the revealed law, the path to God, and the Reality. At least from the eleventh century, many Sufi teachers, among them Rāzī at the beginning of *Mirṣād al-'ibād*, took these three as the fundamental components of the religion. For them the Shariah designated the Qur'an and Sunnah generally and the practical instructions of the texts specifically. The Tariqah designated the stages on the journey to God, the archetype of which was established by the Prophet's *mi'rāj*, the ladder that he ascended on his "night journey" (*isrā'*). These stages were described as inner qualities of the soul, classified under headings like character traits (*akhlāq*), virtues (*faḍā'il*), stations (*maqāmāt*), and states (*aḥwāl*). The Haqiqah was then understood to designate God in Himself, the Real (*ḥaqq*), who determines both the Shariah and the Tariqah and who is their ultimate goal; or God inasmuch as He is realized by those who achieve perfection.

Wang Daiyu frequently employs the terms *li*, *dao*, and *zhen*, but he does not explicitly describe them as three parts of a whole. Liu Zhi in contrast often talks of the three and dedicates diagram 4.6 to their explication. There he describes them in terms of their correspondence with three levels of the human macrocosm: body, heart, and nature (spirit):

> Propriety is the rules of behavior for daily interaction; this is the true practice of the body. The Way is the tendency to resist things and to circle back to the Real; this is the true practice of the heart. The Real is deep unification with the Root Suchness, which becomes the reality-moment of Propriety and the Way; this is the true practice of nature.

As already noted, propriety is one of the Five Constants in Confucian thought. It also plays a special role inasmuch as it designates the sum total of appropriate human activity in keeping with humaneness, the fundamental virtue. This can be seen in the already quoted passage in which Confucius defines humaneness as conquering self and returning to propriety. His disciple asks, "May I ask further how this is to be brought about?" Confucius replies, "Look not at what is contrary to propriety, listen not to what is contrary to propriety, speak not of what is contrary to propriety, and act not in what is contrary to propriety" (*Analects* 12.1). Wang refers to this passage twice, and much of the *True Commentary* can be understood as his attempt to explain exactly how one can follow this directive. As he makes clear repeatedly, however, he understands propriety as the Sunnah set down by the Prophet and transmitted by the great Muslim teachers. In the second of his two references to the practice of humaneness (chapter 2.12), he offers three levels and ten regulations that seekers must follow in order to walk in the path of the Prophet. Describing the path to God in terms of a set number of stages is commonplace in the Persian and Arabic literature. Rāzī for one speaks of twenty steps in *Mirṣād al-'ibād* (*Path* 260–66), some of which clearly overlap with Wang's regulations.

The Contemporary Relevance

I offer this work as a contribution to the scholarship on the history of Islam in China, but I do not want to pretend that I have no ulterior motives. If it were not for a meeting of a few scholars at Harvard called by Tu Weiming and Seyyed Hossein Nasr in 1994, I would never have learned about the rich tradition of Chinese-language Islamic thought. Their purpose was to initiate a dialogue between scholars of Islam and Confucianism in the wake of Samuel Huntington's famous essay on the clash of civilizations (Huntington had passed a copy of the original essay to his colleague Tu before its publication). That meeting set a number of events in motion, not least a conference on Confucian-Islamic dialogue in Kuala Lumpur in 1995 at which Professor Lee Cheuk Yin of the National University of Singapore delivered a paper on Wang Daiyu's *Real Commentary on the True Teaching*, the first I had ever heard of such a work. Over the next fifteen years several similar conferences were held in China, and in the spring of 2012 William Chittick and I shared a position as the Ken'an Rifai Visiting Professor of Islamic Studies at Beijing University. During that semester we met frequently with scholars of Chinese Islam.

Putting aside the fact that Wang Daiyu represents an important resource for understanding the relationship between two great civilizations, he also offers a clear point of reference for reflecting on the contemporary situation of Muslims in China. It is well to remember that events of the twentieth century were catastrophic for Muslims, even more so than for Confucians, Daoists, and Buddhists. Especially after the communist revolution of 1949, all forms of religion and tradition were treated as the enemy, in practice if not in theory. Islam was singled out for special persecution, not least because non-Muslim Chinese had always perceived the religion as a foreign import. As a result the Muslim community lost two generations of scholars along with the intellectual link with the past.

When China opened up again to the outside world, students were able to leave the country with the aim of regaining Islamic learning. Most of them returned to China as a new type of scholar, having received their education in places like Saudi Arabia and Pakistan at institutions founded with a view toward spreading ideological readings of Islamic history and society. They came back with some knowledge of Qur'an, Hadith, and Shariah, but complete ignorance of the Islamic intellectual tradition as represented by fields like Sufism, philosophy, and Kalam. In my several trips to China I did meet a few scholars who were aware of this situation and trying to buck the trend, but they were rare exceptions. And even in their case, they were usually unable to see the close connection between the classical Islamic sources and the specifically Chinese forms of Islam that had been flourishing down into the twentieth century. It seems to me that unless Chinese Muslims reestablish the links with their own Islamic past by way of figures like Wang Daiyu and Liu Zhi, they will find no remedies against the corrosive influence of ideology, consumerism, and politicized Islam.

Perhaps the best way for a visitor to China to grasp the difference between the Islam that is being propagated by the new generation of Chinese ulama and the Islam of their great-grandparents is to observe the difference between traditional Chinese mosques and the new mosques that are sprouting up like factories in Muslim communities. The few mosques that were not destroyed during the Cultural Revolution are barely distinguishable from the remaining Confucian, Daoist, and Buddhist temples. They are beautiful buildings, seamlessly integrated with their natural and social surroundings. They illustrate in marvelous fashion the Far Eastern ideal of harmony and balance—an ideal that appears in traditional mosques throughout the Islamic world. They can be recognized as mosques only from up close, when suddenly much of the apparently Chinese calligraphy turns out to be Arabic. Inside they are unquestionably Muslim places of worship, with a mihrab and carpets, even though the general ambience is fully harmonious with Chinese forms. As for the brand-new mosques, they are intrusive, concrete facades, starkly out of place in villages and towns, much like the skyscrapers that have destroyed the ambience of old Beijing.

In short, the forms of pre-twentieth-century Chinese Islam—whether in the minds of Muslims or in their architecture, calligraphy, and other arts—were harmonious with Chinese civilization, whereas the new style has nothing in common with traditional China.

If we ask how it came about that Chinese Muslim scholars were able to express Islamic teachings in a language that has nothing in common with the other languages of Islamic civilization, the simplest answer is that they were able to see the truth and beauty of traditional Chinese forms because they themselves were rooted in the inner dimension of Islam—what I am calling "Sufism" for want of a better term. This allowed them to see the message revealed to all 124,000 prophets resonating within Chinese civilization, so they felt at home in both the social and intellectual environment.

In order to understand the significance of the Muslim-Confucian synthesis developed by Wang Daiyu and others, we need to keep in mind the manner in which Islamic thought developed over history, especially in the Persianate lands of Islam, where Islamic learning came mainly through the writings of Persian-speakers, even if many of them wrote mostly in Arabic. Among the greatest of these scholars was Ghazālī, who is universally recognized as a great synthesizer of the various branches of Islamic thought. But Ghazālī's influence on the development of Islamic civilization came to be overshadowed by later figures. We should not forget that the five hundred years between Ghazālī and Wang Daiyu was one of the most creative and productive periods in Islamic intellectual history. Even though some historians have been inclined to see Ghazālī as the culmination of Islamic scholarship, a more careful look at the centuries after him shows that he worked at the outset of a great flowering of activity, much of it aiming to synthesize and harmonize the diverse directions in which Islamic scholarship had developed.

Despite Ghazālī's prominence in the secondary literature, not even his Persian books were read in lands like China where Persian was the predominant language of instruction. This is because later authors wrote books addressed to a wider audience, and these played a greater role in propagating the mature Islamic worldview. Some of the best examples are provided by Persian poets like 'Aṭṭār, Rūmī, and Ḥāfiẓ, whose work is permeated with explanations of the key themes of Islamic thought as developed by Muslim theologians and philosophers in a language readily accessible to any Persian speaker. Throughout a good portion of the Persianate lands, Rūmī was a far more influential teacher than Ghazālī, even if we have not yet found much evidence that Persian poets were widely read in China.

Another author who gained tremendous influence throughout the Islamic countries was Ibn al-'Arabī, not least because of the work of his numerous Persian commentators. He can be considered the greatest philosopher-theologian of the Islamic tradition, even if historians commonly label him a "Sufi" and forget about his enormously diverse scholarship. He offered a vision of God, the cosmos, the human soul, and the realm of law and ethics that was far more comprehensive than that offered by any other Muslim thinker before or after. The major characteristic of this worldview, the broad outlines of which were shared by most Muslim scholars after him, can be called "anthropocosmism." Tu Weiming uses this word to describe the Far Eastern worldview as developed by the great Neo-Confucian thinkers. An anthropocosmic vision is one that looks on the universe and human beings as two sides of the same organismic reality.

In the Islamic version of this vision, God, who is the Absolute Reality, reveals Himself in two basic forms. One form is the universe in its entirety, which is the infinite deployment of the divine attributes in an external manner. The other is the human being, who is the concentrated gathering of all the divine qualities in an internal manner. Everything dispersed in the outside world is potentially present within human awareness. The goal of human life is to actualize self-knowledge, which must develop hand-in-hand with knowledge of the universe that informs the self; this self-knowledge alone allows one to know and recognize God. As the constantly quoted saying of 'Alī puts it, "He who recognizes himself recognizes his Lord"—a major theme in the *Real Commentary*. The key to the actualization of this knowledge is found in the teachings of the prophets, who were given the role of guiding people to true knowledge of the self, the world, and God and to the practice that is appropriate to this global knowledge.

In this vision of things, human beings fall into misery because of their failure to understand their own selves and their relationship with God and the universe. They become forgetful and ignorant, and as a result they upset the balance between the microcosm and the macrocosm. Without the harmony that can be established only by human wholeness, the world becomes ever more chaotic and disordered.

The Neo-Confucian version of the anthropocosmic vision dominated over East Asian civilization until recent times, and the Muslim version permeated the writings of the Islamic scholars who were the main sources of the Huiru. This confluence of visions helps explain how Liu Zhi could write his brilliant synthesis of Islamic and Confucian metaphysics, cosmology, and psychology. The Muslim Confucians saw the worldview of their Muslim forefathers as congenial with that of their native land and easily translatable into Confucian terminology and concepts. If they based their major teachings on certain specific Islamic texts, it is precisely because these texts provided clear and systematic examples of the anthropocosmic vision.

If one asks Muslims today which Arabic texts should be translated into other languages, most would respond with Qur'an, Hadith, and works on jurisprudence, perhaps some Kalam, and maybe Ghazālī. The Huiru, however, did not bother to translate Arabic works. They knew Arabic, of course, because they were trained in the Islamic sciences. But the issue was not what one needed to know to be a scholar of Islam. The issue was what the Muslim community needed to understand in order to accept the Islamic worldview and to live their lives accordingly. It is well and good to teach people how to say their prayers, perform the other rituals, recite the Qur'an, and observe Islamic law. But how does one explain to them, in their own language, the necessity of doing these things? In other words, people cannot simply be told that they must do x, y, and z because God says so—even if many, if not most, ulama do in fact say precisely this. In order for people to conform willingly to certain guidelines, they need to know why they should do so. Given that these guidelines touch upon every dimension of human life, the rationale needs to be stronger than the rationale for anything else. This was the quandary faced by the Confucian Muslims: how to explain convincingly in the Chinese language the worldview that lies behind Islamic social and ritual teachings.

The Huiru solved their quandary by writing and translating books that explained the meaning of existence, the role of human beings in the cosmos, the consequences of human action, and the necessity of prophetic guidance. In order to do so they had to master Chinese thought, and that meant being thoroughly familiar not only with Neo-Confucianism, but also with Daoism and Buddhism. When Wang Daiyu wrote *The Real Commentary*, he met a good of criticism, because many of the Chinese ulama wanted to stick with Persian and Arabic—even though most people in their communities could not read these languages. He replied,

> There is nothing lacking in the classical canon of Islam, but there is no one outside the teaching who knows about this. This is because our languages are different. I wrote and discussed using their expressions precisely to make our teachings comprehensive. I used all these borrowed expressions because of my concern to show how the principles work.

The "principles" are the spiritual and intellectual realities that lie behind the outward forms. Wang Daiyu is reminding his readers that Muslims cannot be expected to follow the instructions of their teachers if they do not understand the fundamental realities that determine their own selves and their situation in the universe.

There is no question that Ghazālī represents a milestone in Islamic learning and that Muslims are right in wanting to "bring back to life" (*iḥyā'*) his great book, the *Iḥyā'*. That would be a powerful antidote against the ideologies that are so often offered as Islamic teachings today. But there are other ways of reconnecting with the living spirit of the past, and Chinese Muslims are fortunate to have the Huiru teachers as doorways into a more recent tradition of the central Islamic lands, one in which practically all of the great philosophers, theologians, Sufis, and poets saw reality in terms of an anthropocosmic vision. Without knowledge of the manner in which Muslim sages and thinkers expressed this unitary vision and how they understood it to be the very vision of the Qur'an, it is impossible to understand that the line of transmission of Islamic thought from Ghazālī down to Wang Daiyu and Liu Zhi is in fact unbroken. If Chinese Muslims today cannot grasp that the principles and most of the details of their ancestors' thought are drawn directly from sophisticated expositions of the Islamic vision written by great Muslim scholars, they will imagine that they must reject their own intellectual heritage in order to regain an imagined pristine Islam of the first period. They will be faced with the task of reinventing the Islamic worldview in the Chinese language on the basis of information imported from the West and the various politicized forms of Islam that dominate discourse in the contemporary Middle East.

The Text and Translation

The Real Commentary was printed at least eight times before the twentieth century.[16] I relied on the 1657 edition, collated with the editions of 1642, 1873, 1904, and 1922. I could find no more than a handful of minor differences among these texts, and those that seem to be anything more than typographical errors or alternative characters with the same meaning are mentioned in the footnotes. I also compared these editions with the modern edition by Yang Huaizhong 楊懷中 and Yu Zhengui 余振貴, which adds a few more textual variants.

The copies I had at my disposal are as follows. The first four are wood-block prints, the remaining three modern type.

- 1642, from the rare book collection at the Harvard Yenching Institute. The edition has these parts: 1. Preface by Liang Yijun 梁以浚, dated 1642. 2. Instruction by Ding Yan 丁彥, the editor of Wang's work *Addendum* (*Shengyu* 剩語); undated. 3. Table of Contents. 4. Self-Narrative. 5. Record of Questions and Answers. 6. List of Chinese books used. 7. The text in two volumes of twenty chapters each. At the beginning of both volumes there are the words "written by 'the old man of the real Hui' (*zhenhui laoren* 眞回老人); examined by 'the fugitive of heaven and earth' (*tianrang bumin* 天壤逋民)." The former is the pen name of Wang, the latter the pen name of Liang Yijun. 8. Postscript by Zheng Yingsu 鄭應騳; undated. This copy has a few defects in volume 1: One folio is missing between the second and third folios of Liang's preface. Folio 18 and 19 are reversed. Folio 35 is wrongly bound (chapter 1.5). Folio 41 is handwritten (at the beginning chapter 1.7). Some pages are repeated.

- 1657, from Toyo Bunka Kenkyusho of Tokyo University. Dated by the new preface of He Hanjing 何漢敬. Except for the preface, the text is identical with the 1642 edition, including the repetition of pages. There are no binding mistakes, but folios 95 and 96 (from chapter 1.16) are each missing one page.

- 1873, from Toyo Bunko. This appears to be the same as an edition that was reprinted in Ningxia in the 1990s. It includes imperial edicts starting in 1729 and a preface for a re-carving dated 1801, in addition to the prefaces by Liang and He. It does not include Ding's Instructions.

- 1904, available at Harvard-Yenching and Toyo Bunka Kenkyusho. The edition has the same content as the 1873 edition, except that in place of Zheng's postscript, there is one by Rong Jing 鎔敬 dated 1904. This seems to be the worst edition, with many obvious errors.

- 1922, based on the 1904 edition, but Rong's postscript is placed between the first and second books.

- 1987, edited by Yang Huaizhong and Yu Zhengui. It contains the prefaces of Liang and He, the instructions by Ding, the postscript by Zheng, and the preface from 1801.

- 1999. Reprint of the 1987 edition along with a translation into modern Chinese.

I have attempted to translate the text as literally and consistently as possible. I have provided explanatory footnotes in many passages, but a full-blown commentary on the text would have easily doubled the size of the book. I have noted wherever the modern edition by Yang and Yu (hereafter Yang-Yu) differs from the text I follow (except in a few instances where the different reading has no effect on the meaning). The index functions as a glossary of important Chinese terminology.

Notes

1. See the collections *Qinzhen dadian* 清真大典, 25 vols. (Beijing 2005) and *Huizu diancang quanshu* 回族典藏全書, 235 vols. (Gansu/Ningxia 2008). For a brief review of the two, see Kristian Petersen, "Understanding the Sources of the Sino-Islamic Intellectual Tradition," *Philosophy East & West* 61 (2011) 546–59.

2. The word Han Kitab was first used by Lan Zixi 籃子羲 in *Tianfang zhengxue* 天方正學 (The true learning of Islam), published in 1862, though the author's preface is dated 1852. In the book's "self-narrative" (p. 9), he writes, "I wrote this book, *Tianfang zhenxue*, as a *han qituobu* 漢启佗補. Although I dwell in the eastern lands, my expounding on the classics and discussion of the Dao are based only on the western classic, the Qur'an. This classic, the

Qur'an, is called *qituobu*; but since I have explained it in Chinese characters, I call it *han qituobu*."

3. The expression *huiru* seems to have been first used by Ma Chengyin 馬承蔭 in 1681, in an introduction to *Qinzhen zhinan* 清眞指南 (Guide to Islam) by Ma Zhu 馬注. He wrote that Wang Daiyu "was a *huiru* with extensive learning and erudite writing" and went on to say that he had a thorough understanding of Buddhism and Daoism and that his *Real Commentary* was read all over China (Jin Yijiu 金宜久, *Wang Daiyu* 87; Benite, *Dao of Muhammad* 143–44). Most Chinese scholars have read this sentence to mean that Wang Daiyu "had extensive learning in Islam and Confucianism" and have held that *huiru* in the sense of "Confucian Muslim" was coined in 1925 by Kuwata Rokuro (in his article "Minmatsu"); I take a minority position with Professors Jin and Benite.

4. Benite sums up Wang's context, works, and importance in *Dao*, pp. 134–37. See also Murata, *Chinese Gleams*, pp. 19–24; Tazaka, *Chūgoku* 1353–431; Jin Yijiu, *Wang Daiyu*; Horiike, *Chūgoku Isurāmu*.

5. On the problematic nature of the term (and the even more problematic nature of terms like "esoterism" and "mysticism"), see Chittick, *Sufism*; Carl Ernst, *The Shambhala Guide to Sufism*.

6. See Jaschok and Shui, *History of Women's Mosques*, pp. 21–22.

7. See the provisional list compiled by Leslie et al., *Islam in Traditional China*, pp. 73–75. Most of these texts have not been identified, not even to the extent of whether they were written in Arabic or Persian.

8. See also Murata and Chittick, "The Implicit Dialogue of Confucian Muslims."

9. Tazaka (*Chūgoku* 1425) says that Ma Junshi was Wang's student, not his teacher, based on Ma Junshi's preface, dated 1658, to Wang Daiyu's *True Answers of the Very Real* (*Xizhen zhengda* 希眞正答).

10. For more on the book, see Murata, "Lan Zixi's 'Epitaphs of the Real Humans.'"

11. Wing-tsit Chan, *Source Book* 464–65.

12. Murata et al., *Sage Learning* 430.

13. Murata, *Chinese Gleams* 85.

14. For its role in Islamic thought, see Murata and Chittick, *Vision*, Part III.

15. See Chittick, *Sufi Path of Knowledge*, Chapter 20.

16. Donald Daniel Leslie, *Islamic Literature in Chinese*, p. 22.

The Real Commentary on the True Teaching

Self-Narrative

My ancestor was a native of Tianfang.¹ For various reasons he came to China as a tribute for Emperor Gao.² He edited fine and delicate affairs of astronomy and corrected mistakes and errors in the calculation of the calendar. He fathomed the height of the nine heavens and plumbed the depths of the nine seas. He surpassed the ancients, making not the slightest mistake. The Emperor's heart rejoiced and thought that if my ancestor had not received a real transmission of a true learning, he could not have reached this level. He finally conferred on him the official duty of the board of astronomy, solicited for him a dwelling place here [Nanjing], and granted him a remit for his labor in government service. So it remained throughout the dynasty. For three hundred years my ancestors became habituated to the customs of this land. I trace back the roots and investigate the origins so that I will not venture to forget about them.

I did not study the Confucian learning at a young age. By the time I became an adult, I could read the language only roughly, no more than for purposes of social intercourse and letter writing. When

---

1. Tianfang 天房 means literally "heavenly house." Like the more common expression Tianfang 天方, "heavenly direction," it was used to designate the Kaabah specifically and the Islamic realm generally.
2. Gao 高 or Zhu Yuanzhang 朱元璋 is the Hongwu Emperor 洪武帝 (1328–98), founder of the Ming dynasty. Muslim astronomy certainly played a role in his reign, but whether Wang Daiyu's remarks here represent anything more than a family legend is impossible to determine. See Benite, "The Marrano Emperor."

I reached the prime of life I was ashamed of my simple and rustic knowledge. I began to read the books on Nature and Principle and the histories, reading widely in the writings of the scholars of the various schools. When I penetrated a little into the general meaning of those books, I became aware that their arguments are strange and their ways different and mutually contradictory. If I measure them in terms of Islam,[3] the differences and distinctions are like those between heaven and earth. Regardless of my own ability, I dared use my words to clarify the utmost principle.

Sometimes I met with scholars face to face, and many discussions sprouted from that. They usually did not compete with me in my reasoning. The gentlemen who were gladly convinced all regretted that they had no ability to read the books of the true teaching.

Sometimes I was moved in the midst of the discussion and, on returning home, would select and record some of the discussions. Further, when I had spare time I wrote randomly. I gathered it all together over several years, and as a result consumed a great deal of paper and ink. After preserving the essentials and weeding out the vague, I was left with forty chapters. Within them the principles of the way are totally rooted in the Honorable Classic. I consulted with the canon and did not venture to follow my own feelings or to add or subtract even a little.

When I was among the various scholars, I was sometimes too extreme, but this is only because I also am human. I do not want to be seen as a bellicose man. What I mean is that belittling the illness of a sick person is not the same as giving medicine and applying acupuncture. But my conscience is unhappy, for compared to the classical canon of the midmost country Tianfang, what I have had access to in this country is only one ten-thousandth, or one one-hundred-thousandth. And what I have studied cannot be more than one one-hundredth or one one-thousandth of what I had access to. As for this book, it cannot be more than one tenth or one hundredth of what I have learned.

If I have put myself among the class of authors despite lacking qualifications, this is like a person who passes through the vast ocean, bringing back a single drop and considering it as the ocean. Will I not become the laughingstock of discerning men? But those among

---

3. Throughout the text "Islam" translates *qingzhen* 清眞, "pure and real."

my relatives and friends who are fond of me have forgotten that I am just a pebble. Actually they said that I am an unpolished, rare gem, and they conferred on me a wood engraving. I could not keep on refusing, so finally I placed myself among the class of authors. Alas!

Even though these arguments and writings are strictly matters of my own private person, the principles are the public affairs under heaven. If I were vainly to praise others in order to express my modesty, it would ruin the public principles under heaven and not allow them to be transmitted. Truly that is not my first intention.

Someone also said that the books of Islam are seldom seen by Confucians. My book is incomplete, so perhaps later scholars of noble aspiration will add to it, expanding on the teachings and going further. So I will probably be the opener of the field. Just as my ancestor gained the pleasure of the sage ruler by editing and correcting astronomy, perhaps I, though I lack in eloquence, may be able to open up and put forth the Ultimate Way. This may lead true and profound persons under heaven to neglect my scattered expressions and fully grasp the principles of the true teaching. Then I will not have betrayed my ancestor's purpose in coming from the West, nor will I have betrayed the continuation of the True Learning's virtues received from my grandfathers in successive generations, and thereby I will imitate my ancestors.

Thus have I stated at the beginning of this account the circumstances of my writing the book.

An old man of the Real Hui.
Thoughtfully recorded by himself.

Record of Questions and Answers

Once I had completed this book, a reader said: Your book will clarify the way. To talk about the way of Islam, however, is to make known clearly what is true and what is false. People can discriminate by themselves. What need is there to quote from other scholars and to argue with them? Is this not to make many enemies? If so, in the end no one will bear in mind your painstaking effort.

You should know that the teachings and the way of Islam serve to point the deluded back to the truth, to encourage people to do good, and to stop people from doing wrong. This is what the human way should be. Without these actions, the human way will be defective. I have already acquired the real knowledge of the true learning, but if I do not talk about it, that will be concealing the way. Hence I wrote the book and talked about the learning. If I could not be completely sincere and earnest in doing so, I would not talk about anything.

In a similar manner, if a physician prescribes medicine without clearly informing the patient about the cause of the sickness and the location of the distress and suffering, the patient will certainly have doubts about the physician, thinking that he does not grasp the sickness and is giving medicine blindly. Even if he gives him cinnabar, he will dismiss it as trash. So also, when you see people sharing a house and fighting, unless you are simply wood and stone or a wicked and obstinate man, you will urgently wish to separate them.[1] Though I am a worthless man, how could I not wish that?

Someone else said: If we leave the schools of Buddhism and Daoism aside, the way of Confucianism is extensively broad and deeply subtle. The worthies of the Song Dynasty offered refined and purified views about Nature and Principle. You have quoted only superficial and extraneous arguments. You have certainly not sought deeply after their subtlety.

I answered: Even though affairs under heaven are not alike, there are not two principles. I do not take other scholars into account. I discuss only sameness and difference. A country has a ruler, a prefecture has a prefect, a state has a magistrate, a household has an elder, and the world has a Lord. The way is one. One after another the Confucian scholars have focused entirely on two issues: principle and vital-energy. On their account, countries and families could be governed without rulers and elders.

I discuss only what is different from our way. I have no leisure time to take into account shallowness and depth. If there is a difference on the shallow level, then the deeper one goes, the more will be the difference. The way of Confucius and Mencius for cultivating the body, regulating the family, and governing the country is the same as our way, so why would I presumptuously venture to discuss where it is right and wrong?

Someone else said: You have discussed the two doctrines [Buddhism and Daoism] deeply, and you have quoted many sayings from

---

1. The sentence refers to Mencius 4.2.29.6.

them in your book. You have almost entered the school and the mystery. Why?

I said: There is nothing lacking in the classical canon of Islam, but there is no one outside the teaching who knows this. This is because our languages are different. I wrote and discussed using their expressions precisely to make our teachings comprehensive. All the borrowed expressions I used were because of my concern to show how the principles work. The expressions do not carry the same meaning, but if I had not borrowed them, how could I make clear that these two doctrines are different from ours?

Nonetheless, I am deeply ashamed that my learning is shallow and superficial, my words and expressions rustic and unpolished, and my chapters not in order. I tried as best I could, but I was not able to do any better. I could not reject arguing about the gist of the matter because I am afraid that the way has not been clarified. Hence I wanted to exhaust my heart in doing so. Can I not hope that people will have full faith and follow it?

Moreover, even Confucius talked about "making men know me and making men condemn me."[2] Who am I? I do not presume to know their knowing and condemning. Even if I have some knowledge of it, it is impossible to examine it fully.

Thus I recorded the questions and answers so that those in this society who look kindly at my book will be informed about them.

Also thoughtfully recorded by Wang Daiyu.

---

2. The quote is from Mencius (3.2.9.8), who says that after Confucius composed the *Spring and Autumn Annals* (*chunqiu* 春秋), he said, "Yes, it is the Spring and Autumn [Annals] that will make men know me, and it is the Spring and Autumn that will make men condemn me."

Book One

1.1. The Real One

The Real Lord is the Only One, and nothing can be compared to Him. He is the Original Being without beginning, the Being that does not receive the mandate. No matter how hard you try, it is impossible to attain the details of the Real One's original Being with the words of those who have come into being. Why? Because the Root Suchness of the Real One never begets, nor was it ever begotten. Nothing whatsoever is similar to it. It has no going or coming, no beginning or end. It has no place of abiding or time, no rising or falling, no opening or closing. It relies and depends on nothing. It has no vital-energy and stuff.[1] Nothing encloses it and nothing is together with it. Neither the wakeful awareness of wisdom and intelligence nor deliberation on the basis of sounds and colors[2] is able to act in its regard.

Know that the Real One is the Self-Single One, not the Numerical One. The Numerical One is not the Unique One. When it is said, "The Great Ultimate begets the two wings, the two wings beget the four images" [*Yijing*], this is the Numerical One. When it is said, "one root with a myriad variations" or "the myriad dharmas going home to the one" [Buddhism], this also is the Numerical One. When it is said, "The nameless is the beginning of heaven and earth; the named is the mother of the myriad things" [*Laozi* 1], this also is the Numerical One. From this standpoint, each of these so-called ones is the one seed of heaven,

---

1. Vital-energy (*qi* 氣) and stuff (*zhi* 質) are near synonyms designating things that have fixed form. When the two are differentiated, vital-energy is relatively subtle and stuff relatively dense. See, for example, Liu Zhi's "Diagram of the Sequence of the Transformation of Forms in the Latter Heaven" (*Sage Learning* 163).

2. By "sounds and colors" (*shengse* 聲色) Wang means what is heard by the ears and seen by the eyes, that is, the realm of sense perception.

earth, and the myriad things. Each is the Numerical One. The Real One is the lord of the Numerical One. Only the Real is the Unique One.

The way accords with the Real, so it cannot alter or change. Its principle is one from beginning to end. If the Real One is not attained, then the root will not be deep. If the root is not deep, the way will not be firm. If the way is not firm, faith will not be authentic. Not one, not deep, not authentic—how can such a way be eternal?

Thus the true teaching honors only the Real One, and the Real One is together with the Numerical One.

The Numerical One is together with the myriad beings. If it did not exist along with the myriad beings, the myriad beings would be destroyed. If it were together with the myriad beings, it would be enclosed by all of the myriad. Here, however, being together means that it is both together and not together; it both is and is not. This is not like the things that are together with I's.[3]

Were the Real One together with the myriad things, then the Original Being and the newly born would not be distinct. For example, the nature of the spiritual in the head and the nature of awareness in the heart come together in one body.[4] If someone encounters calamity and harm and the nature of the spiritual in the head is unsettled, the nature of awareness in the heart will also be disordered, for the one cannot be governed when the other is disordered. Man's perplexity and

---

3. Wang's basic point is that God is both transcendent and immanent, a teaching apparent in the Qur'an, which speaks of God in terms that make Him both far and near, both absent and present. Theologians commonly use paradoxical expressions in an attempt to describe this situation. For example, the mainstream Ash'arite theologians employ what is known as the Kullabite formula to assert the status of the divine attributes: "They are neither He nor other than He" (*lā hiya huwa wa lā hiya ghayruhu*). Sufi authors are especially fond of paradoxical sayings, such as Ibn al-'Arabī's reduction of this formula to its bare essentials: "He/not He" (*huwa lā huwa*). By this he means that things, or attributes, or creatures are both He, inasmuch as they derive their existence and reality from God, and not He, inasmuch as they are themselves. See Chittick, *Sufi Path of Knowledge*, passim.

4. The word for body here is *ti* 體, which I translate as "substance" when it is used as the complement of *yong* 用, "function." *Ti* is used to designate everything from physical bodies to the Real One, and in many passages neither body nor substance seems quite appropriate, since "body" is too concrete and "substance" too abstract; when in doubt I opt for body. Another word for body, *shen* 身, is used specifically for the corporeal substance. The combination of the two characters as *shenti* 身體 means the body before the eyes; I translate this as "corporeal body." As noted in the introduction, "the nature of awareness" (*xingjue* 性覺) corresponds to the animal spirit and "the nature of the spiritual" (*xingling* 性靈) to the human spirit. For Liu Zhi's explanation of these terms, see *Sage Learning* 167, 430.

disorder, however, can have no part in the peaceful settledness of the Real Lord. The Real Lord's purity and cleanness will never be tainted by the darkness and obscurity of the human heart. This is enough to see that in itself the Real One has nothing to do with the myriad kinds.

The nature of awareness in the heart is rooted in the bodily form and completed at its boundary. The nature of the spiritual in the head begins in the Former Heaven and later comes down to the bodily ground; after the Creative and the Receptive[5] are established in succession, it gradually becomes manifest. It waits for the time to issue forth, like flowers and fruit. It is completed when a man reaches the age of twenty-eight. It matures as he reaches the perfection of old age.

At root people nowadays are deceived and mistaken only because they are unable to discriminate why things are so. Inwardly things are so because of yin and yang and the four agents. Outwardly things are so because of the making of the Master Workman.

The ways in which things are together are of more than one kind. Sometimes a thing is inside something else, like a person inside a room. Sometimes a thing is in a body, like the four limbs of the body. Sometimes that which is reliant is together with that which stands by itself, like the spots of a leopard or salt in water. Sometimes one thing and another thing have the same reason for why they are so, like the sun's light interwoven with the brightness of a moon or a lamp, which are undifferentiated and appear as one body. If you differentiate them, their principles are different, but they do not hinder or obstruct each other. The root bodies and root natures of these things do not blend together or taint each other, for each of them has its own place. Thus water moves bamboo's shadow, but these two bodies have nothing to do with each other. Wind plays with the flowers' fragrance—they are together but do not share.

When the togetherness of these principles is examined, there are differentiations of pure and turbid, inside and outside, as well as discriminations of far and near, large and small. The turbid is near and small; it combines the outside with the inside. The pure is far and large; it does not have an outward and inward. Thus water is purer than soil, wind is purer than water, light is purer than wind. Those who travel on land travel a hundred *li*,[6] and those on water travel

---

5. Creative (*qian* 乾) and Receptive (*kun* 坤) are the names of first two hexagrams of the *Yijing*. The characters are often used interchangeably with those for heaven (*tian* 天) and earth (*di* 地), or yang 陽 and yin 陰.

6. One *li* is equivalent to about one-third of a mile.

a thousand *li*. The wind travels a thousand thousand *li*, and light travels beyond measure. Water enwraps soil, wind enwraps water, fire enwraps air—all because of the self-so of the principles.

Although sun and moon are bright and illuminate every place, they cannot penetrate a dark room. The light of a candle fills the room, but it cannot advance outside to heaven and earth. Hence far and near, inside and outside, all belong to place. They pertain to the existence of the newly born, not togetherness with the Original Being. For if the Original Being were together with them, there would be nothing of the pure and turbid, the inside and outside, which bring about stagnation and obstacles. If we talk about it as together with them, that has nothing to do with the myriad things. If it is together, it cannot be together everlastingly. If we say that it is not together, how will it encompass and penetrate the myriad things? Even if it is not together, it cannot be not together everlastingly.

Know that before there were heaven and earth, and after heaven and earth came to be, the Original Being, the Self-Single One, was and is uniform. If you want to determine how things are together with the Most Great by depicting various levels, how can you treat it in a manner similar to one ten-thousandth of it? Even in the case of tiny things, like crickets and ants, man cannot entirely know their natures—how much more so in the case of the most honored and most mysterious Real Lord! Only the principles that are of the utmost refinement are clear in themselves. The man of knowledge will transmit the way, but if there is no such person, the way will not reach anyone.

The principles, however, are mysterious and hard to clarify; the meanings are deep and difficult to realize. When you know them, it is difficult to speak; surely you must know this. All who examine them have clear evidence in their own bodies. The Classic says, "When someone attains recognition of his own self, only then will he attain recognition of the Real Lord who created and transformed the self."[7]

Certainly those who can thoroughly penetrate this principle will be superior to the most talented people under heaven, far beyond ignorant and stupid men. Hence the Sage said that when someone attains recognition of his own Real Lord, as a matter of course he will

---

7. Translation of the famous saying of 'Alī (usually attributed to the Prophet), "He who recognizes himself recognizes his Lord."

speak. But, he also said that when someone attains recognition of his own Real Lord, as a matter of course he will not speak.[8]

"He will not speak" means that he cannot speak about the subtlety of the Root Suchness, because it is pure and clean, without taint. It is the ultimately honored and the ultimately noble, the utmost subtle and the utmost mysterious. It does not fall into sounds and colors, so no one can deliberate upon it or consider it. The heart cannot think of it, the eyes cannot see it, the ears cannot hear it, and the mouth cannot speak of it.

"He will speak" means that he will be able to speak about the secret of movement and stillness as well as the subtlety of drawing conclusions.

You should know that movement and stillness in relation to the Root Suchness are like heat and cold in relation to summer and winter. Cold and heat should not be taken as winter and summer, but without winter and summer there would be neither cold nor heat.

That which has not yet issued forth is called "stillness," and that which has already issued forth is called "movement." Stillness is the Root Substance, and movement is the work and function.[9]

The moment between that which has issued forth and that which has not yet issued forth is called "movement-stillness." Even if we talk

---

8. The two sayings, not usually attributed to the Prophet, are well known and often juxtaposed: "When someone recognizes God, his tongue will flag [*kalla lisānuh*]." "When someone recognizes God, his tongue will wag [*ṭāla lisānuh*]." Wang's explanation follows the typical interpretation offered in the original texts. For example, Tahāwanī, an eighteenth-century author of a well-known book on technical terms, says that the sayings mean that those who recognize God in His Essence become speechless and those who recognize Him in His attributes become long-winded. *Kashshāf iṣṭilāḥāt al-funūn* (under *ma'rifa*).

9. Here Wang turns to a discussion of the relationship between the divine Essence and the divine names (or attributes) employing two standard pairings in Chinese thought, substance and function, and movement (*dong* 動) and stillness (*jing* 靜). He uses the compound word *movement-stillness* (*dongjing*) to express the manner in which each name designates the Essence along with a distinct quality of manifestation. Each name, to use the Kullabite formula, is neither identical with the Essence (because it designates a specific attribute other than the Essence) nor different from the Essence (because the Essence is the only reality that is truly present in the attribute). For example, "God is powerful over all things," as the Qur'an says in several verses. The Powerful is neither God (because God embraces all attributes, but this is simply one attribute), nor is the Powerful other than God, because none truly has power but God.

about stillness, the secret has already been disclosed. Even if we talk about movement, the trace has not yet been seen. Only when these two are designated as substance and function will the principles be proper. As soon as movement-stillness becomes manifest, the honorable names are displayed. Then the Lord's honorable designations issue forth in words.

Movement and stillness are included in the meanings of the principles. If we talk about the two as united, they are varied; if we talk about them as differentiated, they are not different. You must know this.

As a whole, movement-stillness is of two types, but there are three levels of drawing conclusions about it.

The two types are the movement-stillness of the Root Suchness and the movement-stillness of sustaining.[10] The movement-stillness of the Root Suchness is like the original knowledge and the original life, the root looking and the root listening, and the various kinds of self-power and self-standing. You should know that the Real Lord's original knowledge is that He knows without the heart, so all of Him knows and there is nothing that He does not know. His original life is that He lives without life, so all of Him is alive and there is nothing in which He does not live. His root looking is that He looks without eyes, so all of Him looks and there is nothing at which He does not look. His root hearing is that He hears without ears, so all of Him hears and there is nothing that He does not hear. His self-power is without hands, so all of Him is powerful and there is nothing over which He is not powerful. His self-standing is without feet, so all of Him is standing and there is nothing on which He does not stand. By itself this movement-stillness has nothing to do with the myriad kinds and is unlike that of man and spirits, which relies on the assistance of eyes, ears, nose, tongue, body, and heart.

As for the movement-stillness of sustaining, it has the power, for example, to cause man's birth and death, his nobility and mean-

---

10. As becomes clear in the next two paragraphs, Wang has in mind the distinction commonly drawn between attributes of the Essence (ṣifāt dhātiyya) and attributes of the acts (ṣifāt fiʿliyya). Attributes of the Essence—such as life, knowledge, desire, power, speech—belong to God whether or not creation is taken into account, but their opposites do not belong to Him (death, ignorance, etc.). Attributes of the acts—such as exalting and abasing, life-giving and death-giving—take into account the differing relationships of the One to the many; even when such attributes are opposed to each other, both belong to God.

ness, his seeing and hearing, his knowledge and awareness, and the creative transformation[11] of heaven and earth.

If the movement-stillness of the Root Suchness is taken as the movement-stillness of sustaining, or if the movement-stillness of sustaining is acknowledged as the movement-stillness of the Root Suchness, this is all outside the way. Why? Because the movement-stillness of the Root Suchness in itself is a firm stillness, so it does not shift; it remains the same in both being and nonbeing. The movement-stillness of sustaining is on account of the things; it becomes manifest when functioning and stays hidden when not functioning. Since these two are different and distinct, how can they be talked about as the same?

The three levels of drawing conclusions are drawing conclusions based on the myriad things, based on our own body, and based on the teaching of the way.[12]

Drawing conclusions based on the myriad things is like the height of heaven and the solidity of earth, the heat of fire and the cold of water, the movement of wind and the firmness of soil, the ascending and descending of sun and moon, the darkness and brightness of day and night, the going and coming of cold and heat, the waxing and waning of the four seasons, the highness and lowness of flyers and divers, the prosperity and decay of grass and trees, and the alteration and transformation of metal and stone. Were it not for the Real Lord's creative transformation, how could anything have these powers? Were any of these lacking, there would be no world. Anything that rebels against His creative transformation will surely never be at ease or settled.

Drawing conclusions based on our own body is like the four limbs and the hundred bodily members, the five viscera and the six entrails; seeing, hearing, smelling, and speaking; knowledge and awareness, the spiritual and the living, the hand's grasping and the foot's walking. The principle [of the body] is united with heaven and earth, surpasses the myriad levels, and goes through and penetrates being and nonbeing. Were it not for the Real Lord's great power, how could anything come to be like this? Were any of these lacking, there

---

11. "Creative transformation" (*zaohua* 造化) is the typical translation of the Arabic word *khalq*, creation.

12. These are the three basic sources of knowledge of the Real: the cosmos, the self, and scripture. In chapter 1.4, Wang explains them as "the three great classical learnings."

would be no corporeal body. Anyone who rebels against His great power can surely not be looked upon.

Drawing conclusions based on the teaching of the way is that one must comply with the clear mandate in all things, like recognizing the Lord and recognizing self, bearing witness to the Sage, going home to the Real,[13] the five human relationships, and the one hundred actions. Were this not so, how could one cultivate the body, conduct oneself in society, regulate the family, and govern the country? Were it not for the Real Lord's mysterious pointing, how could anyone be like this? Were any of these lacking, there would be no teaching of the way. Anyone who rebels against His pointing and showing will surely be perplexed and disordered.

This explanation of the Root Suchness of the Real Lord and His movement-stillness, however, is only a bit of help, for it is sketched roughly, like dust motes gathered in the great earth, or like drops of water following the vast ocean.

It may be that a wise and profound person will attempt to seek out the utmost way. He will seem to be on the true path, but he does not know the great learning of going home to the Real. He is like a blind person who chooses a road and is annoyed at where it goes. His great pains over his lifetime will certainly turn out to be absurd.

Furthermore, our fathers and mothers bestowed on us corporeal body and hair and skin, so we should show filial piety and respect. The ruler confers on us fields, villages, and enjoyable tasks, so we should be fully loyal. Much more so is this the case for the Real Lord of all fathers and rulers, who creates and transforms heaven, earth, and the myriad things, mandates man's birth and death, causes his nobility and meanness, and confers on him clothing and wages. How can it be possible not to recognize Him and instead to pay attention to specters and heretics? A poet said,

> The Non-Ultimate and the Great Ultimate
> are the root of heaven and earth, being and nonbeing.
> They are suited to be the seed of the myriad things,
> but not of this Human who planted the root.

---

13. "Going home to the Real" translates *guizhen* 歸眞, which is used in Buddhism to mean both death (especially in the case of a high monk) and entrance into nirvana. Wang Daiyu often uses it to mean death, like the similar expression, "returning to the mandate" (*fuming* 復命), and in some places (e.g., chapter 1.18), he uses it to signify the "great learning," which is true recognition of God.

You cannot but know this.

Someone said: When we rely on the principles and deduce the details, the Non-Ultimate is the Great Ultimate, which is the Lord of yin and yang, the five agents,[14] and the myriad things.

I said: The utmost principle of Islam is not apart from our own body. If we speak about the principle as apart from our own body, that would be absurd and without evidence. Why? Because the root human nature has the pattern of the Non-Ultimate, and the root stuff of this body is the clear evidence of the Great Ultimate. The head is round in the image of heaven, and that which is light and pure ascends above and belongs to yang. The foot is square in the image of earth, and that which is heavy and turbid descends down and belongs to yin. The five viscera correspond to the five agents, and the whole body is like the myriad things.

Acting and stopping as well as knowing and awareness depend on the spiritual nature of the Non-Ultimate, but the one hundred members certainly emerge from the root stuff of the Great Ultimate. Nonetheless, life and death, success and failure, peace and danger, gain and loss, are not within the ability of the root nature and root body. Thus we come to know that the Non-Ultimate receives the Real Lord's mandate to act as His representative in the Creative and the Receptive and in the myriad things, but the authority to decide life and death, nobility and meanness, certainly does not rely on the independent ability of the Non-Ultimate and the Great Ultimate. This is the utmost great affair amidst heaven and earth. How can the foundation of the True Way let people conjecture without restraint?

1.2. The Original Beginning

The people of the world do not comprehend the original beginning of the creative transformation. Some confusedly argue about principle and vital-energy and some discuss empty nonbeing and silent perishing, but all are guesses and suppositions in the dark, without any real evidence.[15] The true teaching, having obtained the clear mandate of the Real Lord and the real transmission of the Utmost

---

14. That is, the five elements: soil, water, fire, metal, and wood.

15. By the first group Wang means Neo-Confucians and by the second Daoists and Buddhists.

Sage, understood it fully without any double-mindedness. I wish to clarify this according to what has been transmitted by the classics and the histories, but there are meanings that cannot be conveyed in today's language or described with similes and comparisons. It is difficult to speak of this, but I will do my best.

The Classic says that when the Real Lord first began to create and transform, the subtle clarity of the human had utmost perfection and complete uprightness. Later He made it descend to the lowest of the low.[16] This indicates that the human is the ultimate level, the highest and the lowest, totally enwrapping the myriad images. It means that the Real Lord is the Original Being with no beginning, and the Human Ultimate is the original ancestor with a beginning.

Only the Lord is without beginning and end, self-single and uniquely one. He is honorable and great, pure and clean, equipped with all in Himself, borrowing nothing from outside. If there were no heaven, earth, and the myriad things, He would not decrease, and even though heaven, earth, and the myriad things are there, He has not increased.

As for humans, spirits, and heavenly immortals,[17] all have beginnings, but they do not have the power to create their beginnings by themselves. Only the Real Lord has the power to create them, and His power is complete power. Hence He is all-powerful, and everything made is based totally on His power. His power brings all things into being, no matter how large or tiny, how many or few. He has no need for creative activity, He does not wait for time, and He does not differentiate between difficult and easy. When He wishes being, there it is. When He wishes nonbeing, there is nothing.[18]

Before the appearance of things, the Real Lord wished to create heavenly immortals, spirits and demons, the Creative and the Receptive, and the myriad things. From the surplus light of the Only One,

---

16. Reference to Qur'an 95:4–5: "We indeed created man in the most beautiful stature, then We sent him down to the lowest of the low."

17. Spirits and heavenly immortals are jinn and angels (see chapter 1.16).

18. The typical Qur'anic reference for this discussion is "His only command, when He desires a thing, is to say to it 'Be!,' and it comes to be" (36:82). This is one of several verses that mention the creative command (as contrasted with the religious command).

He made manifest the original chief of the myriad sages, Muhammad, who is the root origin of the Non-Ultimate and the beginning of all the subtle clarities.

The meaning of the surplus light is connected to the Real Lord's Being, which has the two levels of Original Being and Powerful Being. The Original Being has nothing to do with the myriad things, but the Powerful Being protects and nourishes the myriad things; this is the meaning of the surplus light.

For example, holding and grasping or taking and granting belong to the Original Being, but good writing and good drawing belong to the Powerful Being. If someone is good at taking and granting but has no ability to write and draw, this does not harm the root substance of taking and granting. Without the root power of taking and granting, however, there is certainly no power to practice writing and drawing. If you were to say that holding and grasping are writing and drawing, you would fail to differentiate between the root and the practice. Even if you say that writing and drawing are not holding and grasping, writing and drawing cannot by themselves come to be without holding and grasping. But this example can barely illustrate one of the myriad similarities between the two levels.

Then the Real Lord illuminated the root origin of the Utmost Sage with His original good pleasure. At this very moment, a fountainhead of shame issued forth, like the moment when one faces the emperor and sweat runs down the back. It issued forth from a place not reached by awareness. This was the first beginning of spiritual awareness. From the subtlety of this fountainhead of the mandate, He then made fully manifest the surplus light of spiritual awareness and completed the creative transformation of the ordinary sages' origin. From the ordinary sages' origin, He completed the creative transformation of the worthies' origin. From the worthies' origin He completed the creative transformation of the good people's origin. From the good people's origin He completed the creative transformation of the common people's origin. From the common people's origin He completed the creative transformation of the perplexed people's origin. From the origins of the various kinds of people He completed the creative transformation of the origin of all the heavenly immortals. From the origin of the various heavenly immortals He completed the creative transformation of the spirits' and demons' origin. From the surplus of all the various things He completed the creative transformation of the origin of all things in water and land, all who fly and walk.[19]

The differences in kind among the various levels are like the many kinds and degrees of sugar created from the white center of sugar cane. That which floats up at first becomes crystal-sugar, followed by rock-sugar, then white sugar, then yellow sugar, then red sugar. What is left after this is the dregs of the juice. Although there are several kinds of sugar, both the high and low grades come to be by themselves, without anyone's deliberate intention to make them into former and latter, better and worse. In the end, however, nothing emerges without the prearrangement of the Master.

Someone said: In the midst of the Only One's light, something like various levels of good and evil, high and low, are originally either nonbeing or being. If we say they are being, then the light of the Only One might not be perfect. If we say they are nonbeing, whence does the origin of the Utmost Sage come to be?

I said: Since the origin of the Utmost Sage has a beginning, it receives the movement and stillness of the newly born, but in the midst of the Only One's light, it is originally nonbeing. Here there are two reasons: The first is that anything with an arising and a beginning will certainly have the blackness and darkness of birth in the midst of its being. That which does not have an arising and a beginning is the light and clarity of the Original Being in the state of its undifferentiated suchness.

The second reason is that the Real Lord has the movement-stillness of both mercy and severity, and these two are not the same. The light and clarity in the midst of human spiritual awareness is the surplus light of the movement-stillness of the Real Lord's mercy and compassion. The blackness and darkness in their spiritual awareness is the surplus light of the movement-stillness of severity and majesty. Then from the principle of the fountainhead of wisdom, He made fully manifest the surplus light of nature and principle. He completed creating and transforming the origin of all those without spiritual awareness, that is, the various heavenly worlds, the sun,

---

19. This and the following four paragraphs are based on a passage in Rāzī's *Mirṣād al-'ibād* (*Path* 60ff.). Liu Zhi bases much of his cosmological scheme on the same passage. See *Sage Learning*, diagrams 1.6 and 2.1.

the moon, and the stars; soil, water, fire, and wind; grass and wood, metal and stone.[20]

The origins of the myriad things and the various levels of subtle clarity were all completed in less than an instant. The saying that creative activity has no time, nor anything difficult or easy, points precisely to this. The act of the Great Ultimate was to preserve turbidity in the midst of the pure. On the basis of the illumination and shining of the Real Lord's humaneness and compassion as well as His severity and majesty, water and fire were transformed, and dust came to be stored in water and air in fire. When these encroached upon each other, fire surpassed water, and foam issued forth from inside water. The lightweight and pure ascended upwards and were transformed into the bodily form of heaven. The heavy and turbid descended downwards and were transformed into the bodily form of earth.[21]

Thus the Non-Ultimate is the beginning of formlessness in heaven, earth, and the myriad things, and the Great Ultimate is the beginning of form in heaven, earth, and the myriad things.[22] If we talk about them as differentiated, they are being and nonbeing; if we talk about them as united, they are not two substances. When you observe the concealed and refined details, how is it possible not to distinguish between the two levels of origin and power? Without the real transmission of the true teaching, how could you know for sure even one affair of the utmost principle of the Former Heaven and the great origin of the creative transformation? Man is not able to suppose and guess the sequential order of man and things from the time of the opening up and cleaving [of heaven and earth]. You must base yourself on the proclamations of the Real Lord as recorded in the classics and the histories so as not to make the smallest mistake.

---

20. Notice the distinction between two sorts of beings: those dominated by nature (*xing*) have spiritual awareness (*lingjue* 靈覺), and those dominated by principle (*li*) lack spiritual awareness. Liu Zhi bases a good deal of his cosmology on this distinction, which he often calls the difference between "things" (*wu* 物) and "I's" (*wo* 我). For his depiction of the full range of the two sorts, see *Sage Learning*, diagram 2.5.

21. For Liu Zhi's explanation of this process, see *Sage Learning*, diagrams 1.9 and 1.10.

22. In other words, the spiritual awareness of the formless I's makes manifest the Non-Ultimate, and the lack of such awareness in the forms of things makes manifest the Great Ultimate.

Let me provide a rough example of the sequential order of man and things after the first differentiation of the chaos. On the Days of the Portent, first heaven and earth were created and transformed. These Days of the Portent existed between color and subtlety, attached to neither position, so they were not ordinary days.[23]

Heaven is the largest of the things having no spiritual awareness. Its form is perfectly spherical, its body solid, clear, and transparent. It is not similar to other things, which can be altered and spoiled. Altogether it is one heaven, but it has seven layers that are able to rotate and revolve. Above the seven layers are two more layers of ultimate clarity and ultimate greatness that never turn and move. These are called "the heavens of stillness."[24] In their midst are all the great sages and great worthies, while the heavenly immortals serve nearby. Beyond these two layers there is no place to go, for that does not belong to the creative transformation. They are enduring, secluded, clear, and silent, without scent or sound. No one can go beyond their limit, though not because the place is prohibited. Rather, this is like the things on land that cannot walk in water, or the things in water that cannot travel on land—all are so by the self-so. Only the Utmost Sage can go there.

Earth is a name for the unification of water and soil. Although its form is round, its principle is square. This means that it has come to a stop and does not travel. The body of earth is heavy and turbid and goes down to the ultimate lowness. When it takes up a dwelling in the midst of heaven, it settles down and becomes secure and does not go farther down.

Earth is like one spot in the midst of heaven, so it does not have much body, though it is deep. At the outset of its creation, water covered the soil completely. After it was created, the Real Lord issued the mandate for the water to retreat so as to make the oceans, without

---

23. By the Days of the Portent (*zhenri* 朕日) Wang means the six days of creation (mentioned in four Qur'anic verses), which Muslim scholars rarely took as ordinary days, but rather as something like the 1,000- or 50,000-year days mentioned in Qur'an 32:5 and 70:4. Because these days are situated between the divine creativity and the world, Wang places them between color (*se* 色) and subtlety (*miao* 妙), which typically designate form and formlessness, that is, visibility and invisibility, or body and spirit.

24. For Liu Zhi's depiction of the nine layers of the Latter Heaven, see diagram 2.3.

allowing it to go beyond its root boundaries. Then the earth began to appear and became uncovered so it could carry things.

Except for the two uppermost levels, all else was perfected during the Days of the Portent. On the first day the mountains and rivers were created and transformed, on the second day grass and trees, and on the third day hatred and dislike, which became darkness, fogginess, obscurity, and disturbance in heaven and earth, and calamity, misfortune, and sickness in man and things. On the fourth day, the sun, moon, and stars were created and transformed; on the fifth day the things that fly and walk. There is nothing of this that was not provided for the sake of human use. This principle is in reality not apart from our own body.

On the sixth day, at the time of the monkey,[25] the Real Lord first issued the mandate to the heavenly immortals to bring soil from the five directions. He created the bodily form of Adam, the human ancestor, who is the ancestor of the bodily form that people have had from ancient times until now. His body was perfected in forty days and nights. Hence it took forty-six days from the creation of heaven, earth, and the myriad things. This is the time scale of the everlasting world, where every day lasts one thousand years of our time.[26]

Someone may say that the whole is one world. Why should there be different measures of long and short like this?

I would reply as follows: This is similar to the stories people tell, like the prince who sought to become an immortal or Ling Wei, who was transformed into a crane. Their time periods are very different. This is also like a crane, which lives a thousand years but is not itself aware of the length. In the same way a mayfly, which is

---

25. The time of the monkey (*shen* 申), 3 to 5 p.m., is the ninth of the twelve two-hour periods of the day. Instead of *shen*, the Yang-Yu edition has *jia* 甲, clearly a typographical error.

26. The description of the six days seems to be based on Rāzī, *Mirṣād* (*Path* 87), who is explaining a sound hadith that he quotes (*Path* 80): "God created soil on Saturday, He created the mountains therein on Sunday, He created the trees on Monday, He created the disliked on Tuesday, He created light on Wednesday, He scattered the beasts therein on Thursday, and He created Adam in the afternoon of Friday, at the end of the last hour between afternoon and night." Given that in Islamic time reckoning the day begins at sundown, this means that Adam was created at the very last moment of the six days.

born in the morning and dies in the evening, does not itself know the shortness. So also, the sea is salty and the river fresh, though they may penetrate each other. The things in salt water are not aware of the saltiness, and the things in fresh water are not aware of the freshness. If you are able to go beyond salt and fresh, long and short, you will not be bound by the restraining conditions before the eyes.

At the moment the human ancestor's corporeal body was perfectly completed, the Real Lord also sent his original, real nature to travel through the two fountainheads of mandate and wisdom until they combined inside his body. After that, the four limbs and the one hundred members, the eyes, ears, nose, and tongue, all turned and moved with spiritual clarity.[27]

Once again, with caps, robes, and clothing, the Lord showed solicitude to the ancestor and made him ascend the throne. He issued the mandate to all the heavenly immortals to prostrate themselves before him, and He made them rise up carrying him and traveling around the various heavenly spheres. All complied with the mandate. The Real Lord also showed solicitude to the human ancestor with great wisdom and real knowledge, so he penetrated thoroughly into the principle of heaven and earth and into the nature of all of the myriad things and was allowed to establish the name of every kind of thing. Although the human ancestor often remembered that his origin is pure and clean, when he reflected further on the fact that his body belongs originally to muddy dirt, he kept on hoping to be modest, so pride was not born in him.

When the human ancestor was sleeping deeply, the Real Lord created and transformed his wife from his left rib and named her Eve. Husband and wife are intimate because they are originally one body, so they love and respect each other. The wife emerged from the husband, and the husband is the origin of the wife, so she should comply with his mandate.

Thus you should know that the one body of the human ancestor was transformed into man and woman. You will then come to know

---

27. Spiritual clarity (*lingming* 靈明) designates the awareness that governs the human being once the "bodily apertures" (*tiqiao* 體竅), that is, the bodily parts and organs, become established. Liu Zhi describes the apertures and spiritual clarity in diagram 3.5.

the yin and yang of the Great Ultimate, the mandate and wisdom of the Non-Ultimate, the mercy and severity of the Real Lord, the highest and lowest, and the subtlety of the Original Beginning without end, all of which are endowed upon the human and contained within him. If someone fails to grasp this principle, his whole life will be a drunken dream. That would be a great pity!

Then the Real Lord gave the mandate to these two so that they would live in the Heavenly Country forever and have the success of complete bliss everlastingly. But there was a wheat tree that had reached maturity, another name for which was "the tree of causes and conditions." The Lord forbade them to take from this tree. Unexpectedly, the chief devil ascended stealthily to the Heavenly Country in order to seduce them to eat from the tree, for he thought they were of the same kind as he. At this time they happened to become confused for a moment and were seduced by the devil and disobeyed the contract with the Lord. Although it was like this in name, in reality they could not avoid hitting the target. At root the devil wanted to harm them, but that turned into an advantage for them. The secret in this was such that the devil was not able to know it.

At this time the couple's caps and robes fell off and they became naked, so they covered their bodies with the leaves of the fig tree of the upper world. They did not look at each other, and they fell to the earthly world.

Someone may say that the human is the most spiritual and the most noble of the myriad things. Why should he fall into trouble like this at the very beginning?

I would reply that there are two reasons here: At the very moment of the creation of man, the heavenly immortals and the various spirits did not know why he was created. Because of this, the Real Lord issued a proclamation, saying, "Truly I want to create man to represent Me in the world." The heavenly immortals protested and said, "His body is made of the four contraries—earth, water, fire, and air—which were gathered together to become the body. They will conflict with each other and perhaps make him do something unworthy in the future." The chief spirit also said, "Man has desires, and seducing him will be very easy." Thus they all looked at man with disdain. Then the Real Lord issued another proclamation and said, "Indeed, there are affairs I know that you certainly do not know."[28]

---

28. This dialogue between God and the angels is based on Qur'an 2:30.

The first reason for the descent of the human ancestors was that the Heavenly Country would become the place of ultimate happiness and complete bliss for good people. From ancient times to the present, myriads of people can be traced back to the one body of the human ancestor, and they are of two kinds—good and evil. If the ancestors had not descended and were still living there, good and evil would not have been differentiated. Hence moving to the earthly world is for the sake of living in the midst of good and evil. Afterwards, people will follow their own kind. Good people will go up in ascent, but evil people will descend further.

The second reason was so that the Real Lord could reject the protest of the heavenly immortals and shame the empty effort of the devils. At root the Real Lord wanted people to be noble, but first He made them suffer. Reaching this situation, human ancestors actually came to know the humaneness and compassion of the Real Lord. They began to wake up to their own disobedience and to become more modest and humble.

The ancestors eagerly took the heavenly immortals' protest to heart and guarded themselves against the devil's deception. They complied with the clear mandate and conquered the selfishness of their selves. They left aside their bodies and lives for the sake of loyalty to the Real Lord. From the lowest they ascended again to the highest, so the protest of the immortals and the deception of the devil died down and dissipated as a matter of course. The Real Lord's mysterious secret was bright and uniquely brilliant. From this standpoint, although the name is "falling into trouble," in reality this was an increase in the level of their completion.

For three hundred years after descending, heaven was dark and earth obscure. The two of them lamented and wailed all day and repented of their former mistakes. The Real Lord acknowledged their real sincerity and forgave their unintentional sins. Heaven and earth opened up with brightness, the sun and the moon had great clarity, and the husband and wife met repeatedly and began to comply with the clear mandate, to establish the teaching, and to govern the world.

When you reflect on this situation, you will know that the Non-Ultimate is the seed, the Great Ultimate the tree, and the Human Ultimate the fruit. The seed is the fruit, the tree is concealed in the fruit, and the fruit is concealed in the tree, enwrapping and thoroughly penetrating and equipped with everything. Thus the Classic says, "When people are attached to words and talk about principles apart from their own body, this is only because their selfishness has not been purified, the eyes of their hearts have not been opened, and their breasts are filled with dregs. How can they grasp the original beginning of the great transformation?!"

This explanation has probably reached no more than skin and hair, for the refined subtlety and utmost principle can never be exhausted by pen and ink in a short time.

1.3. Predetermination

The Real Lord completed the creative transformation of man and spirits as well as that of the affairs and things used by man in order to try him with good and evil.[29] Good and evil are established by predetermination, but using good and evil depends on free will.[30] Were there no predetermination, there would be no free will; and were there no free will, predetermination would not become manifest. Free will, however, does not become an obstacle to predetermination, nor does predetermination become an obstacle to free will. These two seem to stand together while not standing together.

The Classic says, "Predetermination is a great ocean. If anyone searches for it, he will certainly drown therein."[31] It is not only that the secret of transformation cannot be fathomed, but also that the principles of things cannot be fathomed. Why? Fish, for example, hear without ears, and cicadas chirp without mouths. On the basis of human calculation, it is surely impossible to fathom this. This is enough to see clearly that the secret of transformation surpasses human knowledge and seeing.

---

29. Wang has in mind several Qur'anic verses that talk about God's testing and trying human beings, such as "We try you with evil and good, as a testing" (21:35).

30. Here Wang has in view a standard list of the objects of faith: God, the angels, the scriptures, the prophets, the Last Day, and "the measuring out, the good of it and the evil of it" (*al-qadar khayruhu wa sharruhu*). "Measuring out" is frequently translated as predetermination or predestination. The word translated as free will, *ziyou* 自由, can also be translated as self-reliance; Wang clearly means the freedom to make choices without constraint. For Liu Zhi's discussion of *ziyou*, see diagram 4.7.

31. This may be a reference to this saying of 'Alī: "Predetermination [*taqdīr*] is God's secret, so we do not unveil it. It is a tremendous ocean, so we do not importune it."

Predetermination is a differentiated branch of the Former Heaven that is issued and disclosed in the Latter Heaven. This is the meaning of the saying, "If you want to discern the real seeds of the Former Heaven, look at each of the roots and sprouts issuing forth before your eyes." Although there is no alteration and change in seeds, increase and decrease are certainly found in flowers and fruit.

Someone said: The Real Lord is the most merciful. Why does He test people with the difficulties of life and death?[32]

I said: Take for example literary contests in the hall of the imperial examinations. In repeated examinations, [you will ask yourself], "Will it be difficult, will it be easy, will there be suffering, will there be happiness?"

This is like the case of Emperor Yao, who knew for a long time that Shun was worthy.[33] Everyone spoke to Yao. He said, "I will test him." Yao gave Shun his two daughters as wives so that his virtue would become manifest. He let him face fierce winds, loud thunder, and heavy rains in the mountain, forest, river, and marsh [for thirteen years], but he was never deluded. It was at this time that Yao first announced to the people that all of Shun's actions were those of a worthy man. If Yao had not put Shun into danger intentionally, the people under heaven would never have known his worthiness. The people of the world knew only that Yao was causing difficulties for Shun, but they were completely ignorant that this was in order to display Shun's brilliance.

Someone said: The Real Lord has the utmost justice, but people's wealth and poverty, nobility and meanness, beauty and ugliness, longevity and early death, are not the same. Why is this?

I said: Wealth and nobility in a dream are at root empty nonbeing. Poverty and meanness before the eyes are not real being. When you go beyond the crossroads of life and death, you will begin to attain constant existence per se. This world is like an illusory image of flowers in the sky. At root it is a place of lodging at a long distance [from the next world]. How can you consider this real evidence?

Were there no this and that and no high and low, this world would certainly not come to be. Things are high to accord with this

---

32. Cf. Qur'an 67:2: "He created life and death to try you, which of you is most beautiful in works."

33. Yao 堯 and Shun 舜 are two of the legendary Five Emperors.

world's highness and things are low to accord with its lowness. The profound person employs the actions of a profound person, and the small person employs the actions of a small person, thus allowing each of the myriad things to attain its own place. This is the meaning of utmost justice.[34]

In ancient times the sage Moses was walking in the wasteland when someone suddenly called his name. He looked back and saw a man standing in a kiln, his upper body naked and his lower body concealed by a broken wall. The sage asked him, "What do you want?"

He replied, "My body does not have a single thread and my house does not have a single grain. I dare ask you, my sage, to pray to the Real Lord for my sake so that I may be satisfied with a small amount of clothing and food." The sage fulfilled his request.

A long time later, when the sage was traveling around the town markets, he saw the same poor man, his body wearing a cangue and lock. He asked the reason, and the people said that he was violent and cruel and committed murder. The sage immediately woke up: "This person's calamity was caused by my own foolish prayer!" As the poet said,

> If the clever, nimble, thieving cat had wings,
> it would have stolen the magpie's eggs from its nest.

The clearly allotted predetermination makes no mistakes or errors. Foolishly he asked for a prayer and his time caught up with him.

Thus poverty is granted to the man who ought to be poor, and wealth is granted to the man who ought to be wealthy, and these are acts of utmost justice and utmost compassion. If their positions were to turn and shift, both would be injured.

Given that Guangcheng lived happily and Yi and Qi died happily, their happiness was equal.[35] Given that Xiahui hated evil and Dao

---

34. A standard definition of *'adl*, justice, is "putting a thing in its own place" (*waḍ' al-shay' fī mawḍi'ihi*).

35. Guangcheng 廣成 was an ancient Daoist teacher said to have achieved immortality. Bo Yi 伯夷 and Shu Qi 叔齊 were two brothers at the time of transition between the Shang and Zhou dynasties (11th c. BCE). Their death by starvation is remembered because it was for the sake of moral convictions.

Zhi hated good, their hatred was equal.[36] Suppose that Guangcheng was deprived of his life and it was granted to Yi and Qi, and Yi and Qi were deprived of their deaths and it was granted to Guangcheng; or Xiahui's good was given to Dao Zhi, and Dao Zhi's evil was turned over to Xiahui. None of this would accord with their will.

The utmost justice and the utmost completeness are lodged properly among differences. Were this not so, the utmost justice and utmost completeness would have nothing to bestow and arrange. Why? Without differences, the myriad completions would not become manifest, and without crookedness and oppression, the utmost justice would not become manifest.

In the midst of heaven and earth, the noblest is the human; inside the human body, the noblest is the heart. If in the midst of heaven and earth there were only the human without the myriad things and if inside the human body there were only the heart without the various apertures and the one hundred bones, how could you call this the utmost justice and completion? When there are the myriad things, there must also be high and low; when there are one hundred bones, there must also be variations and differences.

Based on the human view, the years should have only spring and summer, the time should always be broad daylight, human life should be everlasting, and all affairs should come with wealth and nobility. Really, why have you not woken up to the fact that spring and summer come to be from autumn and winter, that broad daylight emerges from black night, that wealth and nobility are hidden in poverty and meanness, and that everlasting life is lodged in death? Only then will you know that disadvantage is advantage, and advantage disadvantage, and you will nearly be at the way. Ah! The myriad things are parts of the way, one thing is a part of the myriad, and the people of the world are parts and things. Regarding oneself as a knower of the way is ignorance.

So from the viewpoint of the Lord, nothing at all is unjust and nothing at all incomplete. From the viewpoint of man, nothing at all is just and nothing at all complete. A green tree with a withered branch, one kind with five colors—all have their own cause and effect. It is not that the great transformation is unjust.

---

36. The two were brothers, the first a virtuous governor, the second a thief. Xiahui 下惠 is mentioned in *Analects* 18.2, and both play a role in chapter 29 of the *Zhuangzi*, a passage in which Confucius tries to bring Dao Zhi 盗跖 back to righteousness.

Also, flowers without fruit are certainly brought about by themselves. Why? At root the color of spring does not differentiate between high and low, but flower branches have short and long. When people drink pure wine at a banquet, the red or yellow of everyone's face is different. The shortness and longness and the colors of the faces do not belong to spring and wine. This is the meaning of the great transformation.

Someone said: Whence is good begotten and from whom does evil come forth?

I said: Good comes from the root origin, but evil is a new being. However, there are two principles. One is the principle of the self-so, the other the alteration of human feeling. Flowing water does not alter over a thousand ages, but stagnant water becomes different after several mornings. The roll of thunder gives birth to mushrooms; things emerge when air rises as steam; all are so by the self-so.

At the time of remote antiquity, people stored excess food at the head of the footpath between rice fields, and they put infants in nests in the trees, where wild beasts could follow them and huge snakes could crawl. People today are greedy and cruel, never satisfied, taking advantage of others to profit themselves. Heaven and earth are influenced by this and produce various evil things that correspond to it. Does this not come forth from human feelings?[37]

Someone said: How can we discriminate between predetermination and free will?

I said: There is no free will outside predetermination. The "will" in free will is encompassed by predetermination. For example, fish travel in water and there are no fish outside water. The secret of predetermination is vast, deep, and unfathomable. Talking about it is like blowing at shadows, and thinking about it like engraving on dust. Although the One Thread is penetrating, it is clear only in itself.[38] All this discussion and talk belong to forced explanation. How can I give a good description of even one of a myriad?

---

37. Wang may have in mind the verse, "Corruption has appeared in land and sea because of what people's hands have earned" (Qur'an 30:41).

38. "One Thread," an expression drawn from the *Analects* (4.15, 15.2), is typically understood to designate an underlying unity of all things. In the first section of *Nature and Principle*, Liu Zhi uses the term like this: "Observe the forms and discriminate the meanings, look at the images and awaken to the principles—The Former Heaven and the Latter Heaven are on one thread, nothing more" (*Sage Learning* 120).

1.4. Universal Compassion

The Real Lord is universally compassionate in this world and uniquely compassionate in the afterworld.[39] He is able to satisfy all the needs of the myriad things, without any lacks. His mercy and kindness are broad and great without obstruction and blockage, most fair without selfishness, reaching everything in the various heavens and worlds, benefiting even the tiniest shellfish and the smallest worms.

Someone said: Among the people of the world the disparity of nobility and meanness, poverty and wealth, peace and danger, is no less than that of heaven and earth. Why do you call this "universal compassion"? You say that the afterworld lasts forever and that this world is nothing but a lodging place. Some who occupy this lodging place, however, are at peace. Why are they happy? Others who occupy it are sick, afflicted, and lonely. Why are they unhappy? Moreover, there is a class of people who do not know the True Way and live in this world with ultimate suffering and ultimate meanness; some become beggars, some slaves, some prisoners, some prostitutes, and some suffer from disease, hunger, and cold. They toss about in dejection until they die. If they are receiving the results of their own actions, then it is possible to talk about them like this. But if they are not receiving the results of their own actions, should they not be pitied? And they will have no way to escape when they reach the afterworld. Do they not receive defects in both worlds? How can such people submit their hearts?

Moreover, in the various teachings, there are great men who have humaneness, clarity, truthfulness, honesty, loyalty, filial piety, uprightness, and chastity. If we suppose that they are granted the True Way, they may be able to comply with it and practice it, though we do not know that. If there is nothing to show them the details of the classical canon or any true learning to point it out to them, this will prevent good and virtuous people from seizing true awareness and going home to the Real. How can this not result in even more pain and sorrow?

---

39. It is common for theologians to say that the names *raḥmān* and *raḥīm*, found in the formula "In the name of God, the All-Merciful, the Ever-Merciful," both designate God's mercy or compassion, but the first connotes God's universal mercy in this world, and the second His particular mercy in the next world. See, for example, Nasr, *Study Quran* 6–7.

I said: Among the people of the world are obedient and disobedient, noble and mean, poor and wealthy, at peace and in danger, high and low, large and small. Each of the myriad affairs and the myriad things is at ease in its own position. This is the meaning of universal compassion, not that everyone should be equal and even. If everyone were of the same rank, there would be no high and low, noble and mean, lord and subject, father and son, husband and wife, honorable and lowly. How would the world come to be? If there were no differentiation between this and that, there would be nothing to talk about. There are yin and yang in heaven, and noble and mean among human beings. Without yin, yang cannot come to be, and without the small person, the profound person will not become manifest. Stone can be used to polish jade and lead to purify gold—all by the principle of the self-so.

For example, heaven is yang, dwells above, and moves; and earth is yin, dwells below, and is still. Suppose that heaven turned completely into earth. Then sun, moon, stars, and constellations would have nothing to be connected to and no place to be carried. Rain, dew, frost, and snow would have no place from which to fall. The myriad things would be dry and withered, and man's world would have everlasting night. Or suppose that earth turned completely into heaven. The myriad things would have no place in which to be received and carried, grass and trees would have no place to take root and stand, and the world would belong entirely to the empty void.

From this standpoint yin and yang must exist, heaven and earth must be different, noble and mean must not be the same, and profound and small people must both be there. Those who are high go high, and those who are low go low, for all have their own talents and functions with which to attain what is suitable. If this is not universal compassion, then what is?

You must know that the variations of the diverse levels have been created and transformed at root, but they also have the self-so.

What is regarded as human honor and disgrace is of two kinds. One is real honor and real disgrace, and the other is worldly honor and worldly disgrace. Real honor and disgrace are rooted in the creative transformation, but they also belong to man's account, like right and wrong, life and death, longevity and untimely death, clothing and food. Worldly honor and disgrace begin with vital-energy and stuff, but they meet with occasions such as poverty and wealth, nobility and meanness, peace and danger, gain and loss.

Those who have the True Way have real honor without real disgrace. Sometimes they may have real disgrace for a limited time, and they may also have both worldly honor and worldly disgrace. Heretics have real disgrace without real honor, but they may have both worldly honor and worldly disgrace.

Real honor and disgrace do not alter and change, lasting forever in the afterworld. Worldly honor and disgrace alter and shift, floating in the void of this world. When a man of the True Way practices good, he increases in real honor and decreases in real disgrace. Perhaps he will increase in worldly honor and decrease in worldly disgrace. When a heretic practices good, he will only lessen real disgrace, but he cannot be without real disgrace. Perhaps he will increase in worldly honor and decrease in worldly disgrace. The one who practices evil is the contrary of all this.

I wish that the people of the world would observe and reflect upon right and wrong, real and false, and I sincerely hope that they will sort them out and choose before it is too late.

It may happen that some people are touched by ultimate suffering and ultimate meanness, but at such times sages and worthies do not resist the moment, nor do they resent heaven or blame others. For people like that, this is good: Although it does not increase them in worldly honor or decrease them in worldly disgrace, it certainly lessens greatly their real disgrace.

You must know that increasing worldly honor and decreasing worldly disgrace are nothing. They will never be like lessening real disgrace, which, in reality, is a great affair. How lamentable! If the people of the world do not know that wealth and nobility, poverty and meanness, are empty anxiety, has not all their life been a sleeping dream? They know only that nobility belongs to an emperor or a king who has made all under heaven his own wealth. They do not know that although his name is different from that of the people, his reality is the same. Once the body perishes, he will not have any possessions of his own. How could this be real wealth and nobility?

As for real attainment, that is the good and evil that accompany you in both life and death from beginning to end without any gaps. If you can bring to light the important crossroads between the real and the false, then wealth and nobility before the eyes will not be worth mentioning.

As for what was asked, "If they are not receiving the results of their own actions, [should they not be pitied?]," other people do not see it like this. Those who see it like this see only forms and colors, sounds and scents. How can they have real knowledge of the hearts and intentions of others? At the time when the Duke of Zhou was fearful and full of dread at the rumors, he filled his breast with loyalty and righteousness.[40] When Wang Mang was modest and respectful toward the lower ranking scholars, he wrapped and concealed his malicious heart.[41] If they had died earlier in their situations, only the Lord would have real knowledge of the distinction between the two. Ah, a summer insect knows nothing of ice and snow, and small knowledge does not reach great knowledge! The Real Lord alone judges and regulates with utmost justice and according to His own heart and intention. How can human knowledge and eyesight glimpse His concealed secret?

There are people belonging to the various teachings who have humaneness, clarity, truthfulness, honesty, loyalty, filial piety, purity, and chastity. Among them are those who are intelligent but suffer a great deal of loss, and their knowledge and discernment are such that the common people cannot reach it. Certainly they practice virtue all their lives, in contrast to those who are obsequious, obstinate, rebellious, greedy, and licentious, and they firmly increase worldly honor and lessen real disgrace. They will not be wronged in the slightest. If they do not attain the True Way, this is not outside the principle of predetermination and free will. Otherwise, there would be talk of the so-called equality and evenness of everything. Thus the reward and punishment of the Real Lord will not wrong the human body and heart.

Were there no clear evidence, certainly none of this would be given to the people. Why? There are four great sages in the afterworld, three great classical learnings in this world, and six fountainheads of comprehensive guidance in our own body. All these are firm evidence against man.

On the day of the equitable judgment in the afterworld, the sage Solomon, who had the utmost wealth and nobility without disobedience and transgression, will provide clear evidence against the

---

40. The Duke of Zhou 周公 (ca. 1000 BCE), who is said to have written the judgments on the 64 hexagrams of the *Yijing*, played a major role in the Zhou dynasty.

41. Wang Mang 王莽 unsuccessfully emulated the Duke of Zhou and ruled over the short-lived Xin 新 Dynasty (9–23 CE).

wealthy and noble. The sage Jesus, who had the utmost poverty and affliction without thought of resentment, will provide clear evidence against the poor and afflicted. The sage Job, who had much sickness and suffering without becoming idle, will provide clear evidence against the sick and the suffering. The sage Abraham, who was meager in knowledge without being deluded and perplexed, will provide clear evidence against those meager in knowledge.[42]

In Abraham's time everyone throughout the country, including his father and mother, venerated according to the Way of the Buddha, and there were no people of the truth. When the sage was four years old, he looked up at heaven and looked down at the earth, considering and observing the root substance. Having awakened by himself, he said, "There must be a Real Lord, one and utmost honorable, the manager and controller of the myriad things. Why are people so dark in their hearts like this?" Hence he detested the error and falsehood of heretics.

He asked his mother "Who is your lord?" She answered, "Your father." He asked, "Who is my father's lord?" She answered, "The king of the country." Then he asked, "Who is the lord of this country's king?" She answered, "Buddha." Again he asked, "Who is the lord of Buddha?" She answered, "I don't know." When he repeated the question to his father, he said that the Buddha can give birth to heaven and earth; he is the utmost honorable above whom there is no one and that there is no other lord.

Afterwards, when he was not yet twenty, he seized the opportunity to take an axe and secretly enter into the pavilion of the Buddha. He chose the greatest Buddha and split its head into fragments, putting the ax at the nape of its neck, and then he came out. At the time of the ritual reverence by the multitudes, they saw that the Buddha's head was broken into pieces. Finally they asked the sage, "Who did this?"

The sage said, "If he cannot protect his own body, how can he bless and shelter the people of the world? You say that the Buddha is the chief ruler of the myriad things. Why do you not ask him about

---

42. Wang has in mind a saying of the Prophet according to which anyone on the Day of Judgment who offers the excuse of being distracted by wealth from obedience to God will be presented with Solomon as proof against him. So also the sick will be shown Job, slaves will be shown Joseph, and the poor will be shown Jesus. Abū Nu'aym, *Ḥilyat al-awliyā'* 3:288.

it in person?" His father was ashamed and enraged because he could not answer.[43]

Ah! Throughout the country, everyone was deluded, and only this sage was awake. There was no one to receive guidance.

The three great classical learnings mean the great learning of the Great Classic, the root learning of the Root Classic, and the classical learning of the true teaching. Although these three are clearly manifest and plainly displayed, the people of the world do not take part in examining them carefully.[44]

Covering and carrying by heaven and earth,[45] the ascending and descending of sun and moon, the rolling and unrolling of day and night, the transitions of the four seasons, the waning and waxing of the myriad things—from ancient times until now, things like this have been much alike and always the same. All these are proof of the Unique One. Is not the clear differentiation of the principles of recognizing the Lord the great learning of the Great Classic?

The corporeal body of man comes into being from parents, but not from the parents' own power. Life and death, benefit and damage, stopping and going through, gain and loss—as far as we are concerned, nothing can be fathomed. Drinking blood in the womb, sucking milk after birth—does this sort of settling and arranging with utmost subtlety belong to your parents or to yourself? When prosperity and deficiency are weighed, who makes them rotate and revolve? When the tiny turns into the strong, who is it that can stop this shift? All these are principles of the Unique One. Is not the clear

---

43. For the story of Abraham and the idols, see Qur'an 21:51ff.; Nasr, *Study Quran* 367ff.

44. As becomes clear in what follows, the three classics are the macrocosm, the microcosm, and the Qur'an, a correspondence often discussed in Islamic texts. The Qur'an uses the word *āyāt*, "signs," to designate both its verses and the phenomena that appear in the outside and inside worlds, that is, the macrocosm and the microcosm. For example, "We shall show them Our signs on the horizons and in their souls" (41:53). In *Insān-i kāmil* ("The perfect man"), Nasafī speaks about the macrocosm and microcosm as two books written by God: "Whatever was in the large book He wrote in the small book, without increase or decrease, so that whosoever reads the small book will have read the large book." Murata, *Tao of Islam* 46.

45. The common idea that the attribute of heaven is to cover (*fu* 覆) and that of earth is to carry (*zai* 載) is found already in the *Yijing*.

differentiation of the secrets of recognizing the Lord the root learning of the Root Classic?

When sages and worthies receive the mandate, they cultivate the way, establish the teaching, and sweep away and destroy the varieties of harmfulness, serving the Real Lord alone. There has been no change under heaven in the ritual prayers from daybreak until night from ancient times until now. All these are instructions of the Unique One. Is not the clear differentiation of the proofs of recognizing the Lord the classical learning of the true teaching?

The Real Lord, who has the utmost compassion and utmost justice, granted everyone the six fountainheads, which are eyes, ears, nose, tongue, body, and heart. People also have the evidence of the four [sages] and the proofs of the three [learnings]. These illustrate clear awakening from drunken dreams for those born over the thousand ages.

The eyes look at the color of the myriad things, the ears hear the sounds of the myriad things, the nose smells the scents of the myriad variations, the body embraces the principles of heaven and earth, the heart penetrates the secrets of the creative transformation, and the tongue transmits the subtleties gained by the heart.

Given that the four sages, the three learnings, and the six fountainheads of comprehensive guidance are completely embedded, even if people do not discern the Real Lord of heaven, earth, and the myriad things as explained here, they will still have no excuse to flee from the public way. When there are proofs for punishing them, why should we have pity?

1.5. The Real Solicitude

The real solicitude is called *yimana* [Arabic *īmān*]. (The three syllables *yimana* are the root sound of the Western regions; they translate as "the fountainhead of clear virtue").[46] It is the Real Lord's movement and stillness showing solicitude to man; only by this solicitude can the Real Lord be recognized and attained correctly and properly. Hence it is called the real solicitude; it is not a created thing.

The signs of the real solicitude are three—fear and dread, looking forward and hoping, and real happiness. If you have fear and dread,

---

46. This and the sentence explaining *dunya* are interlinear notes in the Chinese text.

you will not disobey; if you do not disobey, you will escape the Earthly Dungeon and stay far from it. If you look forward and have hope, your deeds will be compliant; if your deeds are compliant, you will ascend to the Heavenly Country. If you have real happiness, you will know only that there is the Lord and you will forget altogether the myriad things.

Those who attain these signs see gold and jade as mud and sand. They look at wealth and nobility as possessions in a dream. They see life and death as no different. They are not alarmed by gain or loss. They surely have the comfort of the heavenly suchness, which is not comparable with the small happiness of name and gain. This is what is called seeing the large and forgetting the small.

Heaven, earth, and the myriad things, wealth and nobility, merit and name—all are made for the sake of the human. Together they are called the merciful solicitude. However, they change and alter unexpectedly and become a dream in the twinkling of an eye. How could this be the real solicitude? The Classic says, "Indeed the life of *dunya* is one act of a drama."[47] (The two syllables *dunya* are the root sound in the Western region. They translate as "the world of dust.") This is the meaning.

When you reflect carefully on all the details, only one affair—*yimana*—always is and will exist eternally, neither decreasing nor increasing. It is the midmost, utmost truth. It surpasses the myriad beings and transforms and subjugates all evil. Indeed, it is the real solicitude.

The real solicitude is prior to heaven and earth and is the honored teacher of the Human Ultimate. It is the rule of conducting oneself in the world and the axis of the True Way. Thus, when there is the real solicitude, there is real knowledge. When there is real knowledge, there is the firm principle.

From ancient times to the present the firm principle is not two; in both distant and near it is one. But this is not what is now called the way. Why? Because people have different endowments, and their levels are as numerous as the hairs of a cow, their natures not the same. Therefore Confucius spoke of the scholars, Laozi spoke of the Way, and the Buddha spoke of release. Each claimed that what he thought was right. The variations in the way are not less than a myriad fragments, because each of them depended on willful nature.

---

47. Reference to 6:32: "The life of this world is naught but play and diversion" (also 47:36 and 57:20).

In the same way the masters have consistently offered teachings in keeping with their own natures. They have kept up a jumbled dispute about right and wrong, and they are stiff and obstinate toward each other. The ordinary people are mostly in confusion and perplexity, so they do not know what to follow. How can they stay firm in the One?

If heaven is not firm, the sun and the moon will move in disorder. If the earth is not firm, rivers and streams will overflow. If people are not firm, right and wrong will be upside-down. From this standpoint, the situation is like someone who is crossing a vast ocean. If he does not have a compass, he cannot possibly escape bewilderment.

There are three meanings for real solicitude: obeying the One, recognizing the One, and becoming the One. Obeying the One is the time of receiving the mandate while existing in the Former Heaven. It is the seed. Recognizing the One is the time of complying with the mandate while existing in this world. It is the nurturing. Becoming the One is the time of returning to the mandate while existing in the afterworld. It is the fruit.

Thus has it been said, "If you want to discern the real seeds of the Former Heaven, look at each of the roots and sprouts issuing forth before your eyes." If there were no seed, how could life issue forth? If you do not attend to the nurturing, how can the fruit be perfected? This is simply the self-so of the principles.

You should know that heaven, earth, and the myriad things along with sun, moon, and stars were all founded at root for the sake of planting the one seed of the real solicitude. Whoever does not have this real solicitude is like a mirror without light. If a mirror does not have light, how can it be a mirror? If heaven and earth did not have people, that would be a mirror-stand without a mirror. If a mirror-stand did not have a mirror, what would we get from it? This is enough to see that the creative transformation of heaven, earth, and the myriad things was all for the sake of the human.[48]

At root the creative transformation of man and spirits is for the sake of receiving this utmost treasure of the real solicitude. If people clearly understand the honor and nobility of their own body

---

48. For Liu Zhi's discussion of the human being as the goal of the cosmos, see under diagram 1.12.

and fully attain the utmost treasure of their own substance, at that point they will know that this body revolves everywhere in heaven and earth, subtly uniting being and nonbeing, without any excess or lack whatsoever. People in the world, however, abandon and put aside the utmost treasure of their own bodies without knowing how to benefit from them. Instead they toil laboriously toward flowers in the sky outside the body. Truly this is a life of drunkenness and a death in dreaming. The Classic says, "People in the world are deep in sleep, and after death they become aware."[49] However, when they reach this stage their regret will have no effect.

Whoever talks about his dreams is certainly awake. If he knows his own mistakes, he will surely reform and do good.

There are proofs for the manifestation of *yimana* as such. This solicitude is called real, and the other is borrowed. Whoever attains real solicitude will be as if guarding a piece of precious jade while walking, stopping, sitting, and lying down; it will be as if he is afraid to lose it while facing a great enemy. Whoever gains the borrowed will be like someone who borrows something from someone else. Although he might make an error and lose it, he has no worry or fear.

Whenever someone rises up without thought of the root, he will be depending on willful nature, or seeking name, taking profit, fearing people's admonitions, or wanting to take assistance from them. He will be like someone walking along in the dark night with someone carrying a torch. When the two arrive at a divide in the path, the one without the torch will be left in darkness. How can he walk any farther?

Whenever someone knows that the real solicitude is the utmost treasure, he will surely take cleanliness[50] of the heart as root and sincerity of intention as foremost; he will always protect and sustain [the solicitude] and will take a stand with virtuous deeds in gravity and seriousness. An unclean heart has no place to receive and contain it. An insincere intention has no place to nourish and beget it. If there is no protecting and sustaining, it will not attain completion. If there are no virtuous deeds, how can there be any proof or evidence? You must follow this sequence to comply with it and guard it, and then it may be that you will not lose it.

---

49. Often cited as saying of the Prophet, this is more likely a saying of 'Alī.
50. The Yang-Yu edition has "stillness" (*jing* 靜) in place of "cleanliness" (*jing* 淨).

1.6. The Real Sage

The Classic says, "Before heaven, earth, and the myriad things came to be, first the origin of the Utmost Sage was created and transformed."[51] This is what is called the Non-Ultimate. The Great Ultimate manifests the Non-Ultimate, so the function of the Non-Ultimate is the substance of the Great Ultimate.[52] The Real Lord turned the Non-Ultimate and opened the Gate of All Subtleties[53] in order to transform and beget heaven, earth, and the myriad things. All these are the surplus light of the Non-Ultimate, the root substance of which has no deficiency or lack.

Higher things are able to bring together lower things.[54] Here there are certainly three levels: First is the body that penetrates and encompasses lower things. Such is the body of the human, which embraces all four agents—soil, water, fire, and air. Second is the nature that penetrates and embraces lower things. Such is the nature of the human, which contains without differentiation the knowledge and

---

51. This probably refers to the prophetic sayings, "The first thing God created was my spirit" or "my light," both of which are mentioned by Rāzī in *Mirṣād al-'ibād* (*Path* 60). Several of Liu Zhi's diagrams explain the creative role played by this spirit, especially 1.6 and 2.1–2.6.

52. Liu Zhi does not use the expression Great Ultimate, but he does refer to the Non-Ultimate in a sentence that clearly accords with what Wang Daiyu says here: "The Complete Substance of the sage is the Non-Ultimate and the utmost purity" (*Sage Learning* 543).

53. The Gate of All Subtleties, mentioned as the very last words of the first chapter of the *Daodejing*, has been translated and interpreted in numerous ways. In *Great Learning*, Wang identifies it with the Utmost Sage, who is like an ocean: "Receiving all the rivers, it never overflows, and pouring into all the rivers, it never becomes exhausted" (*Chinese Gleams* 93). As for the "turning" of the Non-Ultimate, perhaps Wang means that in order for creation to occur, the Real had to turn the attention of the Muhammadan Spirit away from Himself and toward the cosmos, which is everything other than God. By doing so, He opened the gate that separates the realm of eternal omniscience from the realm in which the things come to exist at their appropriate times. This interpretation is supported by the fact that in *Great Learning* Wang also identifies the Utmost Sage with the Supreme Pen; according to a famous hadith, God commanded the Pen to write out His knowledge of creation until the resurrection.

54. This simple sentence summarizes Islamic metaphysics and can be called the organizing principle of Liu Zhi's *Nature and Principle*.

awareness of animals and beasts as well as the nature of animals and beasts, which in turn contains without differentiation the begetting and growth of grass and trees.[55] Third is the principle, which in its purity embraces the lower things. Such is the origin of the Real Sage, who brings together the natures of the myriad things, assisting them in their beginning and being begotten.[56] He should not be compared, however, with the Real Lord, the Self-Single One, who in Himself has nothing to do with the myriad things.

Thus the Utmost Sage is prior to heaven and earth. He is the fountainhead of the myriad beings. Heaven and earth are like the trunk of one great tree on which the flowers and leaves of the myriad images are all complete. Its outcome is bearing fruit at the tips of the branches. Trees are begotten for the sake of the fruit and seeds. Without the fruit, why would a tree exist? Heaven, earth, and the myriad things are all for the sake of the human. Man and spirits are like luxuriantly growing flowers and leaves.

When the Utmost Sage became manifest in body, he was the perfect fruit. When the moment was right, the affair was right. When the affair was right, the moment was itself right. He who could bring forth the affair in proper response to the moment was the Utmost Sage. If there had been the proper moment but not the person, then the moment could not have responded. If there had been the proper person but not the moment, then the affair could not by itself have come forth. At this time the midmost harmony had been achieved, heaven and earth were positioned, and the myriad things were nourished. Guidance for the deluded opened up so that they could go home to the Real, recognize the Lord, and honor and venerate the clear mandate. Then the teaching spread.

---

55. Remember that "nature" is a translation of Arabic *rūḥ*, spirit. Wang has in mind the same classification of spirits that Liu Zhi follows in *Sage Learning*, derived from the writings of 'Azīz Nasafī: human spirit, beneath which are psychical spirit, animal spirit, and vegetal spirit (see *Sage Learning* 373, note 1).

56. Several of Liu Zhi's diagrams illustrate this emanation of all lower natures from "the nature of the utmost sage," which he identifies with the principle of Aershi (Arabic *'arsh*), that is, the Throne of God. In diagram 1.6 he shows how all reality, whether external and "objective" or internal and "subjective," goes back to the single principle of Aershi, which is none but the single nature of Muhammad, God's first creation.

The true teaching of Islam has three essentials: First is the mandate of heaven, second the principle of heaven, and third the governance of the Sage. These three affairs are the roots of the myriad deeds.

The mandate of heaven cannot be reached by human strength. Such are the mysterious secret of recognizing the Lord, the concealed subtlety of one's own body, the root origin of heaven and earth, and the cause of the myriad things. Were there no real transmission of the clear mandate, how could anyone reach these? The meaning of the mandate of heaven is the Real Lord's imperial mandate to the heavenly immortals, who descended and then transmitted it to the Utmost Sage. Since it came down from heaven, it is called the mandate of heaven, not because it was heaven that made the mandate descend.

The mandate of heaven has three levels called the mandate of clarity, the mandate of signs, and the mandate of awareness.

The mandate of clarity has the clear evidence, the mysterious decree, and the laws and regulations, but not the signs and the awareness. This means that at the time of our Sage, the clear mandate descended with 6,666 verses and was transmitted to him; then the whole of the Heavenly Classic was complete. The subtlety of this Classic penetrates the secret of the myriad things, going beyond and outside of being and nonbeing. Before heaven and earth, there was real attainment. After heaven and earth, there was the real mandate. This is the utmost teaching of the True Way.[57]

The mandate of signs is the mandate received during dreams, like the promotion of Fenghou and Limu by Huangdi, or the promotion of Fuyue by Wu Ding, or the promotion of Ziya by King Wen.[58]

---

57. Wang is saying that the invisible reality of the Qur'an, God's Word, pervades all of reality. In the Former Heaven, before the existence of forms, it is the "real attainment" (zhende 眞得), meaning what was actually present in the formless realm of nature and principle. In this world it is the "real mandate" (zhenming 眞命), or the command of the Real. In other words, the Qur'an in its invisible reality coincides with the creative command and in its visible reality with the religious command.

58. Huangdi 黃帝, the Yellow Emperor, was the mythic founder of Chinese civilization, and Fenghou 風後 and Limu 力牧 were two wise ministers whom he appointed. Wu Ding 武丁 (13th c. BCE), the ruler of the Shang 商 Dynasty, dreamed about the common laborer Fuyue 傅說 and raised him up to be a minister. Ziya 子牙 (also known as Lu Shang 呂尚) was the disciple of a Daoist immortal who left his master at the age of 72 and eventually helped King Wen 文王 establish the Zhou 周 Dynasty (11th c. BCE).

The mandate of awareness is the awakening of the heart, like the station of Confucius when he had knowledge of the mandate of heaven at the age of fifty and like Mencius's mandate without specific injunctions.[59]

Someone asked why the sages of China speak only of awareness and signs, not the mandate of clarity.

I said: The people of the world, for example, have never seen a phoenix, even if the phoenix originally existed. Because you have never seen one, can you say that there have never actually been any phoenixes?

The three levels of heaven's mandate are complete only in the true teaching. With the other teachings, there are only awareness and signs. The mandates of awareness and signs are such that, when someone attains them, he governs the country while keeping people at ease, and he cultivates his body while practicing the good. These also are affairs of a sage. But how can he be compared to him who recognized the Lord and knew both the original beginning of man in the Former Heaven and the dwelling place to which he will go home in the Latter Heaven?

The second [essential of the true teaching] is the principle of heaven, which is what ought to be. Since it is not connected to the mandate of heaven, it is not a deed of the Sage. It is the sincerity of the heavenly suchness that emerges from the root heart, which is so in the self-so. For example: having pity on orphans and children, sympathizing with the poor and distressed, relieving the hungry and cold, assisting in the grief of death, inquiring after the sick, solving litigations and ending fights, caring for and loving relatives, bringing harmony and friendship to neighbors, sacrificing during the Small Festival, and doing the ritual of the midnight prayer. These affairs do not wait for teaching and proclamation, but they simply should be so. This is the original virtue.[60]

---

59. Confucius's famous description of the stages of his life and his coming to know heaven's mandate at age fifty is found in *Analects* 2.4. Wang has this passage of Mencius in mind: "'Did Heaven confer its mandate on [Emperor Shun] with specific injunctions?' Mencius replied, 'Heaven does not speak. It simply showed its will by his deeds and affairs'" (5.1.4–5).

60. The notion that ethics and morality accord with the nature of things (and do not need prophetic guidance to be understood) permeates Islamic teachings and is discussed especially by the Muslim philosophers. It accords with the view of Mencius that nature is good (to which reference is made in chapter 1.11).

The third [essential] is the governing of the Sage, which emerges from the deeds of the Sage. It is two: the governing of the Sage's person and the governing of the Sage's laws. The governing of the Sage's person concerns himself, and the governing of the Sage's laws concerns the people. Thus the Sage said, "The utmost way is my moments, the midmost way is my deeds, and the constant way is my words."[61]

His words are the laws. They pertain to seeing, hearing, smelling, speaking, walking and stopping, sitting and lying down, drinking and eating, sprinkling and sweeping, and responding to affairs in the midst of stillness. All these have principles and then become habitual virtues.

He who complied with the clear mandate of the Real Lord was completely equipped with all three essentials and sufficiently embedded with the myriad deeds. His spirit was transformed as the Non-Ultimate, upon which the universe relies, and he has proclaimed the truth from antiquity until now. He indeed is the one who is said to embrace heaven and earth and to regulate the myriad things. He is the Utmost Sage of the true teaching.

Someone asked about the firm evidence that he is the original chief of the myriad sages.

I said: For Islam, giving evidence of the Sage is a true affair of the utmost importance. If someone does not give evidence, he has no *yimana*. It is not only that the heavenly immortals received the mandate from the utmost sage Muhammad, but also that the spirits and demons hide from him in awe, and he influences and responds to the myriad affairs.

From the time of the first division of the opening and cleaving [of heaven and earth], there was the clear mandate of the Real Lord, which began to be recorded and arranged in the classics and was transmitted from sage to sage. Already it set down the year and month of the dynasty, and the signs and good omens of the time of his emergence. Then, at that time, all the people longed for his birth, and certainly he was brought forth at the turn of good fortune. This and everything recorded in the classics and handed down by transmission

---

61. This is probably a reference to the purported saying of the Prophet, "The Shariah is my words, the Tariqah is my acts, and the Haqiqah is my [inner] states," though Wang has reversed the first and last clauses. Nasafī cites this saying in *Maqsad-i aqsā*.

fit together like the two halves of a tally. This is known by everything in the universe, and there is no place whatsoever for guessing.

There are people who emulate the sages and emulate the spirits, those who vainly boast of having fortunate and good omens, and those who falsely manifest spiritual penetration, but they gaze on themselves with their own human I's. How can they be compared with the Sage?

1.7. Similarity to the Real

Similarity to the Real means being similar to Islam. The root of Islam is complying with the clear mandate, recognizing the Real Lord who transforms and begets, and knowing that the Utmost Sage is the great origin of the Human Ultimate. Furthermore, one needs to be able to know oneself.

As for the Real Lord who transforms and begets, He is the Original Being without beginning who lasts forever without end. He does not fall into being or nonbeing, nor is He grasped by deliberation and consideration. Only by going forth in the real transmission and attaining true awareness can you begin to awaken to the self-single Unique One, who is of the utmost subtlety and utmost mystery.

Someone said: If something is not, it is nonbeing. If it is not nonbeing, it is being. How can you say that He does not fall into being or nonbeing?

I said: The meaning of being and nonbeing does not go beyond the circumstances of the creative transformation. When something has a beginning, it comes to be, and when something has an end, it ceases to be. When something has no beginning, then it has never been without being. How could it have been nonbeing before that? It can be said that everything that has a beginning was formerly nonbeing and later made into being, but this cannot be declared about that which has no beginning.

Knowing the Utmost Sage is to know him whose substance is the Non-Ultimate and whose function is the Great Ultimate. The two wings [yin and yang] are his differentiated display, the four seasons his alteration and transformation, heaven and earth his covering and carrying, and the myriad things are put in good order by him.

Knowing self is to awaken to how mandate and nature came to be, what kind of thing is bodily form, where you began, when you came to be, which affairs you must practice having reached here, and where you will dwell after returning to the mandate and going home to the Real.

If you cannot recognize self, then you cannot investigate things. If you cannot investigate things, you cannot thoroughly investigate the principles. If you cannot thoroughly investigate the principles, you cannot purify your nature and clarify your heart. If you cannot purify your nature and clarify your heart, you cannot discern your origin. If you cannot discern your origin, you cannot know the Utmost Sage. If you cannot know the Utmost Sage, you cannot respectfully serve the Real Lord. Thus, when you examine this with care, once you obtain the first thing, you will obtain everything. How straightforward this is! The various ideas of scholars—such as destroying the root, stopping up the fountainhead, empty nonbeing, and silent perishing—cannot be compared with this.

As for sayings in the books like "respecting and surrendering to the vast heaven"[62] and "brilliantly serving the Supreme Ruler,"[63] if you ask whence the vast heaven emerges and whence comes the Supreme Ruler, no firm arguments have been given until now. Ever since [the first emperor] of the Qin dynasty buried the Confucian scholars alive and burned the books, the classical texts have been deficient. Although the Confucian scholars of the Song dynasty took great pains to collect the ruined texts, they were not able to avoid deletions and additions. They probably could not obtain the complete collections of Yao, Shun, the Duke of Zhou, and Confucius.

Moreover, in China the *Yijing* is taken as the ancestor of literature. When we look at the people who discuss the *Yijing*, we see that there are no firm principles. Scholars of the same class constantly express different opinions. For instance take the sayings, "How great is the sublimity of the Creative . . . which governs heaven"[64] as monarchs and fathers [govern]; and "The Emperor emerged in the sign of the Arousing."[65] Master Ziyang[66] explained this as meaning,

---

62. Classic of History (*Shujing* 書經), *Yao Dian* 堯典 2 (Legge 3:18).

63. Classic of Poetry (*Shijing* 詩經), Decade of Wan Wang, *Da Ming* 大明 3 (Legge 4:433).

64. *Yijing*, Confucius's commentary on the first hexagram.

65. *Yijing*, commentary on the trigrams (Shuo Gua 說卦 5).

66. Master Ziyang 紫陽 is better known as Zhu Xi 朱熹 (d. 1200).

"The Emperor is regarded as the chief ruler of heaven and earth." On points of utmost importance like this, there are never uniform opinions. There cannot be two right principles, so one of them must be wrong. If we suppose that both are right, there will be two chief rulers. To which do we go back?

If it has already been said that the Supreme Ruler is begotten from the Great Ultimate, then the Great Ultimate dwells above the Supreme Ruler. Why then is the Great Ultimate not served instead of the Supreme Ruler? If it is said that the Supreme Ruler is the Great Ultimate, from which classic does this opinion come? Why did ancient people hide this and not transmit it?

Also, everyone takes the Great Ultimate as the principle. A commentary on the *Diagram of the Great Ultimate* says, "The principle is not a thing. Were there no principle, there would be no things." Thus Master Zhou had confidence that the principle is the origin of things.[67] Although the principle emerges prior to affairs, it cannot stand by itself; it certainly needs a place on which to lean. This is like the principle in literature before it falls from the tip of the brush to the paper. The heart should already be equipped with the principle and the meaning. And certainly there must be a scholar who brings forth the principle and perfects literature. Thus the Great Ultimate—the principle of heaven, earth, and the myriad things—is established by the Real Lord. After that, the forms of heaven, earth, and the myriad things come to be. No one who grasps this principle will regard the original seed of heaven, earth, and the myriad things to be the Original Lord of heaven, earth, and the myriad things.

It is also the case that from ancient times until now, whenever the world has encountered disorder and divisive wars among groups of strong men while the real ruler has not yet been decided, loyal and righteous men have probably looked deeply for a rightful ruler to whom to give their lives without hesitation. When a state must have a lord, is it possible for heaven and earth not to have a lord? When a country only becomes firmly established with one lord, is it possible for heaven and earth to have two? So much more so in the case of the self-single Unique One, the Real Lord of the creative transformation of heaven, earth, and the myriad things. How can it

---

67. For a translation of this highly influential diagram by Zhou Dunyi 周敦頤 (d. 1073), see Chan, *Source Book* 463–65.

be possible that true people do not recognize Him and fail to think deeply about Him?

The *Tongjian* is the essential record from ancient times until now.[68] In the opening chapter it says, "Pangu was born in the great wilderness, but no one knew in which place he began."[69] Hah! When people cannot examine the details of the Latter Heaven with form and color, how then can they penetrate into the mysterious signs of things in the Former Heaven without sound and scent? All their explanations are derived from their own willful natures and conjectures, not from the clear mandate and the real transmission. Why? Every tiny thing that exists has a lord—how much more so in the case of huge things like heaven and earth! Heaven and earth are like a mansion in the midst of which things have an orderly arrangement, namely the myriad things. But a mansion surely has a master who has established it. If you know who the master is, then you must know that the mansion is after all a mansion, and the master is after all the master. The mansion can never be called the master. Thus the Lord Ruler is Lord Ruler by himself, and heaven is heaven by itself. Nowadays people call heaven Lord Ruler. Worshiping heaven, serving heaven, listening to heaven, and sacrificing to heaven—all are of this kind.

Also, if the myriad things have names, the principle is that before heaven and earth the Lord Ruler does not Himself have a designation. Who, after all, established that "heaven" is the name of the Lord Ruler? If we say that He Himself established it and that we will not venture to violate the designation of the ruler, how could the Lord of heaven and earth establish His honorable designation as the same as that of something that He created and transformed? When designations are confused and not differentiated, how can the Lord be distinguished from the servant?

If we say that the people established it, this would be like saying that the servant named the master, or that the children and grandchildren named the parents and grandparents. Given that He is already

---

68. *Zizhi Tongjian* 資治通鑒 is a comprehensive history of China completed in the year 1084 in 294 volumes.

69. Pangu 盤古 is said to have emerged from the original balance of yin and yang and to have created the universe over a period of 18,000 years, first by splitting heaven from earth with his axe.

the Lord of heaven and earth and has the power to create the myriad things and to establish the myriad names, why should his honorable designations have to wait for the servants in order to be established for the first time? Careful examination shows that there can never be this kind of principle.

Only in the true teaching of Islam does each detail of the explanation have the Original Root. If one character or one sentence[70] were not from the clear mandate, the real transmission, and the actual impartation of the Sage, it would never have been lightly written into the text of the classic. This is why it is praised by all of the universe and will never change for a myriad ages.

1.8. Changing the Real

What is called "changing the Real" is like scattering chaff so that the people's eyes will not see clearly. They will not be able to differentiate black from white, above from below, or the four directions, so all of these will naturally change their positions. This is done by the heretics of our way. Outwardly they carry the name of the true teaching, but inwardly they act according to the principle of emptiness and mystery. They alter the truth with falsehood and do not differentiate between for and against, uniting the same and the different in accordance with people's desires. They gather all the principles together and make all the teachings into one school.

Those who have clear vision and real knowledge are few, and those who take as seen what they have only heard are many. When outsiders look at the teachings, they become more tainted as they go deeper. Their delusion becomes such that it cannot be cured. This is indeed lamentable.

There are those with crude knowledge of the Chinese classics who have learned something of the purport of the [Islamic] classics and on occasion published commentaries on them. They offer nothing but superficial discourse and shallow advice, going no further than cultivation of the body. Others have penetrated neither the Chinese classics nor the Islamic classics and talk only about what they have heard in the street. They foolishly collect their own material and then

---

70. The Yang-Yu edition has "name" (*ming* 名) in place of "sentence" (*ju* 句).

compile it as a book. *Avoiding Perplexity about the Real Origin*[71] is of this sort. When you look at it, you will secretly laugh at the author. He knows nothing of shame. Has he not disgraced the utmost way of Islam?

Those who are shallow are not harmed by such shallowness. As for those who attain the truth, how can such foolishness hinder them? These authors can easily be known with one glance and are not worth discussing. They are like a cloud that covers the sun's light and will soon scatter by itself. How is the sun's clarity harmed?

I worry about those who write in a polished style but have little knowledge of the meaning of the classics. Their nature has a clear and intelligent disposition, but unfortunately they did not receive the right direction and in the end they distorted Islam with heretical learning. They appear to be right but are wrong. Their cleverness and attractiveness can snatch away the will of people's hearts. This is most detested by Islam and completely avoided by true people. *The Silent Exposition of Witnessing the Lord* is of this sort.[72] Let me try to offer a few examples as evidence of its falsehood.

Its first argument is the idea that the myriad variations come from one root and that there is no differentiation between this and that; not only the human species, but also the various kinds of birds and beasts, insects and worms, are all of one body with the Creator, without any distinction whatsoever.[73] Who would dare say

---

71. *Avoiding Perplexity about the Real Origin* (*Xingmi zhenyuan* 省迷眞原) was printed in 1914, though its author and original date of publication are unknown. Written in plain language and consisting of 33 chapters in 34 pages, it often uses Buddhist and Daoist expressions but shows no trace of philosophical or theological thought. It was reprinted in *Qinzhen dadian*, vol. 18.

72. According to Yang Xiaochun 楊晓春 (*Zaoqi hanwen* 早期汉文 11–22), this text, *Zhengzhu mojie* 證主默解, is by Zhang Zhong 張中 (ca. 1584–1661) and is also known as *Kelimo Jie* 克理默解, an Arabic-Chinese hybrid meaning "Explication of the *kalima*." The *kalima* or "word" is Islam's foundational sentence: "I bear witness that there is no god but God, and I bear witness that Muhammad is God's messenger." This four-page treatise was published in 1631. Professor Yang's argument that the two works are the same, however, is not completely convincing, partly because some of the passages that Wang quotes are not found in *Kalimo jie*. Perhaps they are taken from one or more of Zhang's other works, two of which are mentioned by Benite (*Dao* 127–29). See also *Ji* 季, *Yiru* 伊儒 48–59.

73. The expression "one body" or "one substance" (*yiti* 一體) goes back to the *Yijing* and is much discussed in Chinese thought. Confucians hold that the sage achieves

something like this other than someone of the utmost delusion and confusion?

The author says that the myriad affairs and myriad things are like containers created of metal. At root, the [one] body's stuff is metal, but the names and guises are not the same and sometimes they become ruined and corrupted. When ice reaches the time of melting and the dispersing of bubbles, it becomes water based on its origin, for there is no opposition between ice and water.

If you rely on this, then everything will be equal, without high and low. All will go home to the great void as undifferentiated sameness. When good people listen to this, they cease being good. When bad people listen to this, they become worse.

The Classic came down and the Sage was sent. When the time arrives for the great meeting of the ancient and the now at the equitable judgment, the good will be rewarded and the evil punished, each having its own place of return. There will be only the Real Lord, the most just and the most unselfish. But [according to those views] all of this would be false.

Those who are drunk and dreaming are happy to have no restraints and to be wildly dispersed by their willful intentions. Moreover, they ridicule the true person for not having grasped the utmost principle. When a man of wisdom carefully examines this, is it not empty nonbeing and silent perishing?

Know that if things have an antecedent, then in the end they will have a place to go home. If there is a floating life, then in the end there will be an everlasting abode. Thus the Classic says that the myriad things all undergo decay and ruin. Only seven affairs do not

---

"one body with heaven, earth, and the myriad things," a notion of which Liu Zhi approves in *Sage Learning* (see pp. 76ff.). Wang clearly does not like the expression if it is taken to imply that there are no distinctions to be drawn between the Real Lord and the myriad things (a position he ascribes later to Buddhism). If Wang's criticism of *Zhengzhu mojie* is correct, the book supports the doctrine attacked by Shaykh Aḥmad Sirhindī (d. 1624) and others as *waḥdat al-wujūd*, "the oneness of being." The argument over this famous expression goes back to the fourteenth century, when it was attributed to Ibn al-'Arabī by Ibn Taymiyya (d. 1328), who claimed that those who believed in it made no distinction between God and the world. Although this is an utter distortion of Ibn al-'Arabī's position, it does seem to have been espoused by some Indian Sufis. Perhaps Zhang Zhong learned about this doctrine from the Indian teacher Ashike 阿世喀, with whom, he tells us, he studied for three years in Nanjing. See Benite, *Dao* 127–28.

perish and are preserved everlastingly: the Honorable Threshold, the Precious Seat, the Huge Pen, the Tablet of Recording, the Heavenly Country, the Earthly Dungeon, and nature and mandate.[74]

Someone said: At root the Real Lord does not have similarity or guise, and at origin there is no place for Him to have gone away. How can there be an Honorable Threshold and a Precious Seat?

I said: He established these two sorts, but He never dwelled or settled down there. The Real Lord Himself made these manifest specifically as the clear evidence of His utmost honor so that none of the human beings and spirits would fall into [the theories of] emptiness and nonbeing.

This fellow was foolish and self-determining, disavowing this clear statement. Not only did he disavow the various ways of having forms and colors, he also disavowed nature and mandate.

Evidence can be given from a Buddhist classic. It says that the eyes cannot look and the ears cannot listen; the ability to look and the ability to listen are only the subtle nature of the Real Emptiness. [This fellow] also says that the eyes and the ears belong to the "I," but the looking and listening belong to the Lord. His saying and the Buddhist classic are not different here. The difference lies only in the names Lord and Emptiness.

Spreading corrupt practices like this, which are related to both the heart and the mandate, will be left behind as a burden for a myriad generations. This is indeed lamentable and pitiful! In no way did he know that the seeing, hearing, smelling, and speaking of man and spirits all pertain to the spiritual of nature and mandate, the evidence for which are the eyes, ears, nose, and tongue. Only the Real Lord lives without nature and mandate, listens without the ears' hearing, and looks without the eyes' seeing; He embraces heaven and earth without far and near, hindrance and obstruction, hiddenness and manifestation, directions, large and small, interval and cutting off. Not even the speech of an ant, the sound of falling dust, or the obscurity of a dark chamber or hidden room can escape from His hearing and looking. But when man looks with the eyes and listens with the ears, there are far and near, directions and positions, hindrance and

---

74. Wang may have in mind the verse, "Everything is perishing except His face" (28:88). As for the seven things, he apparently means the Throne, the Footstool, the Pen, the Tablet, paradise, hell, and the divine command, all of which are mentioned in the Qur'an and much discussed in Islamic thought.

separation, dark and clear, cutting off and continuity, flourishing and decline, large and small. The Lord is utterly different from this and has no similarity with it. Why does [that heretic] foolishly say that the looking and listening of man is the looking and listening of the Lord? Careful examination shows that his dark heart is bold and excessive!

Only the true learning of Islam talks about the differentiation of the Unique One and the Numerical One and that of Lord and servant. The Unique One has nothing to do with the myriad things, but the Numerical One brings about the beginning of the myriad things. How is it possible for these two to be confused and not differentiated? How is it possible to talk only about the root origin of the myriad things and not to discern the Real Lord of the myriad things?

The Non-Ultimate and the Great Ultimate, the Real Emptiness and the Subtle Nature, the Nameless and the Named—all these are the Numerical One, the ancestor of the myriad beings. On no account can the grandfather of heaven, earth, and the myriad things be the Real Lord of heaven, earth, and the myriad things.

He is constantly telling his intimate friends that our Utmost Sage is the Lord Ruler's manifestation and transformation in order to open the way, to show it to deluded people, and to relieve all generations. Thus he says that only when the "I" has name and guise are Lord and servant different. This is what I mean.

Hah! He is thinking that when a ruler comes to the throne, everything under heaven is governed by him, but when the Lord Ruler governs the world, He descends in order to be born. Will this not mean that the Lord Ruler is not as good as a man? How is this different from the ideas of the two masters [Buddha and Laozi]? [Buddhists] say that the three positions [past, present, and future] are one body and [Daoists say] that the Three Purities are one spot.[75] This is the same as becoming manifest in the body in order to explain dharma and to save all sentient beings. Attacking heresy with this kind of idea is no different from a sick person trying to cure his own sickness. Is it possible for him to be healed?

---

75. The Three Purities (*sanqing* 三清) are given various interpretations in philosophical and religious Daoism. Generally they are considered the first manifestation of the Dao and the origin of all things. In religious Daoism they are depicted as the three highest gods or the three highest heavens. The *Daodejing* (chapter 43) speaks of "three" as the intermediate source of all creation: "The Dao begets one, the one begets two, the two beget three, and the three beget the myriad things."

He also said that the Lord Ruler has the nature of all of the myriad things. He is the original root of the myriad things and the grandfather of the myriad things, so without the Lord Ruler, there can be no myriad things. The things are begotten by the Lord Ruler, but the Lord Ruler does not emerge from the myriad things.

The utmost way of Islam, however, talks only about the creative transformation of the myriad things and the power to give the mandate of life and death to the myriad things. It does not talk about begetting the myriad things, nor about bestowing the one seed and the one root on the myriad things. Hence, it designates Him alone as the Real Lord.

Why does it never talk about the original root? Flowers, fruits, branches, and leaves emerge from the original root and one seed, but the root and seed cannot command the flowers and fruits to be born by themselves. The sons and grandsons of the myriad hundreds of millions surely emerged from the one person of the original father. But the original father cannot give the mandate of life and death to his children and grandchildren. The father of all fathers and the root of the myriad beings is the level of the Utmost Sage. This is why Islam talks only about the Real Lord and not about the original father.

Regarding mankind as the Lord Ruler and taking the meanest as the most honorable are extreme delusion. You must know that the human is the spiritual of the myriad things. What makes the human different from the birds and beasts is that he has clear wisdom, enabling him to discriminate between right and wrong, real and false. Therefore [Mencius] said that anyone who does not have the heart of right and wrong is not human. The Classic says that followers of heresy are like a camel with a skin disease that you keep far away to protect yourself. If you keep it near, you will be harmed.

If you encounter such [teachings] but you cannot distinguish them, or perhaps you know them but do not speak of them, then your stupidity is much more than that of birds and beasts.

1.9. Darkening the Real

The Classic says, "Do you not see the people who take their own nature as their lord?"[76] The fact is that at root the human body and

---

76. Reference to the verse, "Have you seen him who takes his caprice as his god?" (25:43).

mandate are created and transformed by the Real Lord. The foreign teachings foolishly say that everything comes to be through self-nature and that the root and fruit come to be formed by themselves, so there is no need to talk about branches and leaves.

If what they say is true, then every monk will surely become a buddha, every Daoist will surely become an immortal, all scholars will come to manifest prosperity, and every merchant will become wealthy. A monk, however, will not necessarily become a buddha, a Daoist will not necessarily become immortal, scholars will not necessarily become prosperous, and merchants will not necessarily become wealthy.

When there is no power over affairs and tasks, how can body and mandate come to be by themselves? If we investigate functions, we will naturally come to grasp the substance. On the basis of principles, we can know their foolishness. Foolishness, however, has roots and branches, and delusions have deep and shallow.

For example [the Daoists say], "The way is nameless at root, but we are forced to name it way."[77] Who advocates this? Who set down this law? It is as if there is and as if there is not. This is utterly vague and boundless. No one knows who is acting. This is all the blur and indistinctness of delusion.

Having supposed that his own heart is broad and great and not knowing that there is a Lord, [the Buddha] said, "Above heaven and below earth, I alone am uniquely honored."[78] His foolishness was that he saw himself as great and did not know his own smallness.

[The Confucian scholars] say that this body, heaven and earth, and the myriad things are all contained in this heart. No distance is beyond the reach of this heart, no height not ascended, no broadness not enclosed, no minuteness not entered, no hardness not penetrated. All who possess knowledge and discernment surely awaken to the fact that the Lord Ruler of the myriad things lodges in the midst of this square inch. Otherwise, how could it obtain this kind of power?[79]

How sad this is! When someone is unable to know himself, how can he know the Creator? His small, subtle body receives the mandate[80]

---

77. Apparently from a Daoist commentary on the first chapter of the *Daodejing*.
78. Words of the Buddha when he emerged from the womb.
79. Liu Zhi adopts the Confucian language in talking about "this heart" located in "this square inch" and offers more subtle explanations; see, for example, diagram 4.1.

from the Real Lord. By chance he obtains one power or one action. This is like a pond that obtains the moon, but you wrongly recognize the pond itself as having brightness. They compare themselves to the Creator's honor, saying, "I and the Creator have the same body." When sages have never considered themselves sages, how can the people of this world make themselves the lord ruler of the myriad things?

As for the things that are regulated and protected throughout the universe, these have been created by the Real Lord, so the sages and worthies always use them according to the material. Things that are originally nonbeing can never come to be by themselves. This is like making utensils. Some are made with jade and gold, some with wood and bamboo. The material, whether gold and jade or wood and bamboo, is already provided within them. Only the creative transformation of the Real Lord can give body to things that have no body. One mandate brings the myriad images into being immediately, so it is called "the measureless, great power." This cannot be compared to man, who makes things with things that already exist.

Moreover the Real Lord's creating things is like the imprint of a precious seal on paper or silk. The imprint on paper or silk is the trace of the precious seal. Wishing to transfer the imprint's trace to other things is perplexity. If the heart of the wise man contains heaven and earth and is embedded with the myriad things, this is not because it has the bodies of heaven, earth, and the myriad things, but because when he looks up and down and examines, he can grasp the principles of things from their forms.

A child born after his father's death does not think about his father, for he does not have the father's kindness in his heart, nor does he see his image in a dream, for he does not have his form in his eyes. The heart cannot obtain the forms of things that the eyes have not yet seen. This is like a clear mirror or still water reflecting the myriad things. Someone may say that in reality heaven, earth, and the myriad things are in the midst of the water or the mirror, so it can create heaven, earth, and the myriad things. Is this possible?

Speech should be united with action. Only then can it be trusted. Certainly, if man were of the same body as the Real Lord, he would

---

80. Instead of mandate (*ming* 命), the editions of 1873, 1904, and 1924 have clarity (*ming* 明).

be able to create and transform heaven, earth, and the myriad things. But has anyone ever created a person or a thing in this world?

Someone said that before there were things, all belonged to the root suchness of the pure and clean. Heaven, earth, and the myriad things came into being because of one folly, so they were corrupted by the four greats [the elements]. The feelings accompanied things in their turning, and day-by-day the nature of the real became darker, and this caused our Lord Ruler to become dark and gloomy. This is like a pearl that shines at night. If it is covered with dirt, its light decreases. Only when it is rid of dust and taint can it shine again.

Hah! This is the utmost absurdity. Moreover they take spirit as the function of form and feeling as the foundation of nature. Those who know substance and function understand [the absurdity of] this as a matter of course, without any need to discriminate.

What thing and what power can exceed the power of the Creator? When something is enclosed in the midst of the four elements, how can it be regarded as the Lord of the myriad things? If the human body were in the grasp of the Lord Ruler, no one under heaven would do evil. Why then are there so many evil people?

Again, the Lord Ruler is pure and clean, without taint, so He is the fountainhead of the myriad good things. Since He is already the Lord of the human body, why should He still be clouded by selfish desire and harmful action? At the very beginning of the creative transformation of the Creative and the Receptive, He had the power to do great things, so why should He now be unable to control something as small as this body? Having been the root of various precautions, how is it that now He cannot safeguard those precautions? Is this possible in the principles?

Someone said that the myriad things are like bodily shells whose use is caused by the Lord Ruler. If a man uses a thing, the Lord is never that thing. Since he said that if a man uses a utensil, the Lord Ruler is not that thing, the explanation that the myriad things are one body does not tally. If that were so, kites would not fly, fish would not jump, horses would not go into battle, cows would not cultivate fields, fire would not burn, water would not flow, and wind would blow on things without having anything to do with them. If an evil person's evil is not his sin because the Lord Ruler causes him to do it, why would he be punished? If a good person's good is not his endeavor, why would he be rewarded?

A thing whose nature is good and whose principle is refined can be said to be the trace of the Lord Ruler, but it is wrong to talk about it as the Lord Ruler himself. Normally those who look at a refined and subtle painting say in admiration that this is the handiwork of a master. They never take the painting as the painter.

How sad it is! They depended on a true explanation, but they concealed the Root Lord because they could not discriminate why things are so. The existence of the Real Lord in things is like the three lights [sun, moon, and stars] shining forth together. The lights are both together and not together, both existing together and not existing together. If the myriad things were not like this, they would have no way to show forth their abilities. Light provides assistance so that things may be used, but light is not the things. Rather, each thing has its own body, root nature, and root level, without mixture with others. Each thing has an existence as if existing together with others; thus perhaps its situation can be depicted.

Someone said that at root the Buddha became manifest in his body in order to explain dharma and save all sentient beings. He passed through life and death, but he was never born and never died. Who was it then who received life and death?

The ancients subdued the enemy with feasts and firmed up the country with one word. Why did the king of emptiness, beyond whom is nothing, enter into the difficulties of life and death when he wished to save sentient beings? Why did he experience the suffering of meanness and lowliness? Is it not that the uniquely honorable Buddha is on the contrary inferior to a petty human being?

From ancient times the human heart was wholly simple, thereby displaying loyalty and filial piety. Then this dharma came to be, tracing out the hidden and doing uncanny things, so the human heart became deceitful and villainous. It overturned the constant human bonds and threw countries one after another into disorder and destruction. Its good fortune and happiness did not last long. How can this be called "saving all"? And based on their classical teachings, all human beings are buddhas, and so also all things. Why then is it necessary to talk about saving?

Someone also said that the beginningless ignorance of sentient beings all arises in the wake of the pure and clean root suchness, which is the real heart of the perfect awareness of the Tathagata. All things are like flowers in the sky, their guise relying on the sky. When flowers in the sky perish, the root substance of the empty sky does not move. When ignorance and illusion perish, the pure and clean heart of awareness does not move.

In this one statement, there are four mistakes. First, if the Tathagata's real heart of perfect awareness were indeed real awareness, it would certainly not allow ignorance and folly to arise. This would mean that once the sage's heart moves, it preserves true thoughts and overcomes unjust thoughts. If not, why should he be considered a sage? If the real heart of perfect awareness allows ignorance and folly to arise, why is it called the real heart of true awareness?

Second, if he knows that it is folly but intentionally allows it to arise, how is this different from setting a fire by himself and later extinguishing it by himself? Certainly he can extinguish it by himself, but if he cannot extinguish it, will he not bring harm on himself?

Third, if he knows that folly is arising but he cannot make it perish immediately, then in the end it will be impossible for him to make it perish. Why? If it is possible to make it perish in the end, then at the very beginning he can himself prevent it from arising. Preventing it from arising at the very beginning is easy, but making it perish at the end is difficult. It has never been the case that someone is able to do the difficult but not the easy.

Fourth, if he does not know that ignorance arises in the state when the eyes are closed, this is like going mad in drunkenness or in a dream. It also cannot be called the real heart of perfect awareness. When you examine this with care, is it not the obstinate emptiness of ignorance without awareness?

They also say that the clean nature of perfect awareness appears in all bodies and hearts following what is suitable for each kind. These stupid people are saying that in reality the real nature of the pure, clean, and perfect awareness exists in this body and heart, like a pure, clean, precious jewel shining within the five colors and making each of them manifest according to the directions. Does it in fact have five colors?

Hah! In this way only the various sorts of things that do not have knowledge can be illustrated, not the real heart of perfect awareness. Why? If a true man comes upon the loyal and the deceitful, the true and the depraved, the real and the false, the good and the evil, he will follow the loyal, the true, the real, and the good and will not be tainted by the depraved, the deceitful, the false, and the evil. Not only will he not be tainted by any evil, but also he will wish to overcome every sort of non-good. How much more so if someone has the real heart of the pure, clean, and perfect awareness!

If this heart flows and turns by following the various kinds, it will increase the non-good and will be much inferior to that of the true person. Thus their explanations of the clean heart of perfect awareness and the real nature of subtle clarity are certainly foolish.

When they are asked: If sentient beings are buddhas at origin, why are they ignorant? If they have been ignorant at root from time without beginning, what is the cause from which [the heart] comes to be? They answer that body, heart, speech, and words will all be cut off and perish in the realm of hearing sounds.[81] But if they have not yet reached the personal evidence of the appearance of nirvana at the end, how can hearts with thought and action fathom the root suchness of the perfect awareness of the Tathagatha?

For all the questions they are asked, they have answers, but not for this one question, which inquires after the root and thoroughly investigates the fountainhead. Responding to it is truly difficult. Their answer is elaborate, but in fact it is a forced explanation, not letting people ask again.

Hah! The question concerns the root beginning of ignorance, and they offer excuses with evasion and deception. [They say that] the Buddha emerged and appeared for the sake of one great affair, yet he could not appear for the sake of this question. The twelve volumes of the *Tripitaka* want to comment on the complete meaning of that affair, but they cannot comment on the fact that he became manifest in his body to explain the Dharma. So all these books were written in vain.

They also say that neither sound nor hearing has any location. For example, if a drum is beaten in the east and a bell is rung in the west, then, if someone goes east to listen to the drum, he will not be able to hear the bell in the west. And if someone goes west to listen to the bell, he will not be able to hear the drum in the east. Also, if the sound leaves and goes west, there will be no echo on the eastern side, and if the sound leaves and goes east, there will be no echo

---

81. "Hearing sounds" translates *shengwen* 聲聞, a translation of Sanskrit *śravaka*, "hearer," used generally to mean a disciple of the Buddha and sometimes to designate distinguished teachers. In other words, when someone reaches the realm of *śravaka*, the limitations of the senses and language will vanish. Wang's point seems to be that they are trying to pull themselves up by their own bootstraps.

on the western side. But, if there are echoes and hearing in all four directions, how can it be that sound and hearing have no location?

Hah! If we suppose that sound has no location, following the wind and going against the wind will be the same. If hearing had no location, then a huge sound and a tiny sound will have the same grade. But if a sound is following the wind, it will go far, and if it is against the wind, it will not arrive. If a sound is loud, it can be heard, and if it is low, it cannot be heard. How can they say that sound and hearing have no location?

If you do not have a clear eye and real knowledge, you will not escape from delusion. Anyone who has the heart of the True Way and is really concerned with life and death should think carefully. All arguments will emerge from the root heart without any feeling of hatred, for the various teachings are all based on the Real Lord's creative transformation, so all are together with one root like siblings. When one of the siblings becomes ill with madness, will the other siblings sympathize with him or hate him?

Only in the true teaching of Islam is the explanation of nature and mandate rooted in the clear mandate of the Real Lord while also explaining affairs and tasks in terms of man's free will.

If you say that everything is based on the creative transformation, then reward and punishment would not be just. The Real Lord has created and transformed water and fire, so they can damage and profit the myriad things. But these are outside reward and punishment, for their root nature is to be like that, and nothing of it belongs to themselves. This should not be compared with man, who has the ability to act according to his willful intentions. And if you say that everything emerges entirely from free will, this will be similar to [the theory of] emptiness and mystery and will betray the Root.

What is based on self-determination will sometimes be straight and sometimes crooked. This proves [the necessity of] reward and punishment without defect or resentment. Lord and servant are then clearly differentiated, so there is not the slightest blur or indistinctness. How could we betray the Root and forget the Fountainhead by speaking of "empty nonbeing" and "silent perishing" without any evidence?

1.10. The Outstanding Differences

The outstanding differences between the true teaching of Islam and other teachings can be divided into seven main divisions.

The true teaching honors the self-single Unique One, but the other teachings honor the Numerical One. The Unique One has nothing to do with the myriad things, but the Numerical One is the root beginning of the myriad things.

Know that the Numerical One enwraps the myriad images without differentiation, like the ocean from which all streams emerge. The color and taste of each stream come to be in keeping with its place, but the magnanimity of the ocean's water never decreases or increases. Thus the vast ocean can make rivers and lakes, but rivers and lakes certainly cannot beget the vast ocean. The sages and the wise can appear like worldly and ignorant people, but worldly and ignorant people can never be similar to the sages and the wise. This is a principle that you must know, and it is the first difference.

The true teaching recognizes the Original Being and the newly born, and its propriety differentiates between Lord and servant. The Original Being has the ability to create the myriad things, and the newly born is created and comes to be. The other teachings say that the myriad things are of one body at origin but have names and guises that are different, as when ice melts and bubbles disperse in keeping with their origin, which is water. This is the second difference.

The true teaching knows that heaven and earth are for the sake of human dwelling and resting and the myriad kinds are for the sake of human use. This is why the human is regarded as honored among the myriad things. The other teachings make heaven and earth the great father and mother. Man is regarded as mean in himself, so they must worship the two and bow to them. This is the third difference.

The true teaching cultivates the way by complying with the clear mandate of the Real Lord so as to establish the teaching, which has not changed from ancient times until now, remaining the same in the world. The other teachings cultivate the way by following self-nature so as to establish the teachings, about which the authorities all differ and the people of the towns are all diverse. This is the fourth difference.

The true teaching is loyal to the Real,[82] who is not two; it honors only the One Lord. The other teachings worship various buddhas and pray to various spirits, which are confused and not one, so they do not know which one to follow. Is it possible to say that all of them are loyal to the Real? When we carefully examine principles, we will

---

82. Instead of "Real" (*zhen* 眞) the Yang-Yu edition has "Upright" (*zhen* 貞).

say that only this Unique One, the Real Lord, transforms and begets heaven, earth, and the myriad things and preserves and nourishes people. Every single thing in the universe was established for the sake of the human. We should be grateful for His magnanimous mercy and we must honor and worship Him with sincere hearts. How can you put aside the Real Lord, who is the Great Origin and the Great Root, and serve others instead? This is the fifth difference.

The true teaching has both predetermination and free will, but the other teachings talk about the principle of the self-so. The predeterminer is the Lord, and the one who has free will is man. Before there were heaven and earth, the Real Lord turned the Non-Ultimate and opened the Gate of All Subtleties. At that very moment, each thing was granted its nature and mandate, for the Gate of All Subtleties was itself predetermined. The causes of good and evil were already embedded and the levels of high and low were already arranged. Thus ocean water is salty and river water fresh; rivers are turbid and lakes pure. If you differentiate among them, they will not come apart, and if you unite them, they will not stick together. Each thing was granted its nature and mandate and each follows its own will. For example, a fire is burning down a large house. A rescuer enters the house, and a thief also enters. Entering the house is the same, but the reasons for entering are different. Taking and putting aside, right and wrong—each has its own benefit. From this we know that in the midst of principle and nature, there are variations and differences in themselves. Afterwards vital-energy comes to be for the first time. It is not that principle develops from vital-energy.

The other authorities all say that principle is the same and vital-energy different. In Nature and Principle, some say that there is only this principle, which accompanies vital-energy in the midst of its stuff and is itself one with nature. Those endowed with pure vital-energy become sages and worthies, like precious pearls that exist in pure water. Those endowed with turbid vital-energy become depraved, like precious pearls that exist in the midst of turbid water. What is called "clarifying the clear virtue" is wiping the pearl clean while existing in the midst of turbid water.

If the clear virtue is already tainted, who will clarify the clear virtue? If you say that what clarifies the clarity is not clear virtue, but clear virtue is the root of the myriad good things, what then can exceed clear virtue? If what clarifies clear virtue is clear virtue itself—that is, clear virtue is capable of clarifying itself—then in itself it is capable of not being tainted at the very beginning. Why is it necessary for it to become tainted in itself and later to clarify itself?

If you say that those who were aware earlier brought about the awareness of those who became aware later, then why did the emperor Yao not make Dan Zhu aware, Shun not make Shang Jun aware, Yi Yin not make King Jie of the Xia Dynasty aware, King Wen not make Zhou of Yin aware, Confucius not make Yang Huo aware, and Xiahui not make Dao Zhi aware?[83]

Moreover, the will of those who are pure and modest while living in a vile place is not disturbed even if they face death. But when those who are greedy and vile dwell in a clean land, they may be outwardly clean, but they will be inwardly vile. The worthies are worthy in themselves, and the ignorant are ignorant in themselves. How can calamities and hardships be what make them take the route of keeping company with the depraved?

If it is said that pure vital-energy makes someone take the route of becoming a sage and turbid vital-energy makes someone into an ordinary person, then Yao and Shun became Yao and Shun by chance, and Jie and Zhou became Jie and Zhou by chance. If the cause of encountering the appropriate moment relies entirely on vital-energy, then their good is not enough to be regarded as good, nor is their evil enough to be regarded as evil. Why? Because at origin these are not the root nature.

Hah! The nature of principle is the root, and the nature of vital-energy is the function. What you have seen above is that substance and function have been reversed, so neither the perfecting of man nor the perfecting of things emerges from nature; rather, all emerge from the act of vital-energy. But this principle is wrong.

Nature and Principle also says that heaven has the utmost purity and earth the utmost refinement. People who obtain these become

---

83. The emperor Yao 堯 passed over his son Dan Zhu 丹朱 for the succession because of his unworthiness, and a similar thing happened with the emperor Shun 舜 and his son Shang Jun 商均. Yi Yin 伊尹 was an official of the Shang Dynasty who counseled the king to overthrow King Jie 桀 of the Xia 夏 Dynasty. King Wen 文王 (1152–1056 BCE) was the founder of the Zhou dynasty, which overthrew the Shang Dynasty, whose last king, Zhou of Yin 趙殷 (d. ca. 1046 BCE), is remembered as utterly corrupt, an inversion of Confucian virtue. According to *Analects* 17.1, the ambitious official Yang Huo 陽貨 tried unsuccessfully to gain the support of Confucius. On Xiahui and Dao Zhi, see Book 1, note 36.

sages and worthies, birds that obtain them become fabulous phoenixes, beasts that obtain them become unicorns, shelled things that obtain them become flood dragons, grass that obtains them becomes *lingzhi* mushrooms, trees that obtain them become pine and cypress, and stones that obtain them become beautiful jade.

This explanation is very different from the former. Why? The former says that the principle is the same but the vital-energy different. This explanation says that at first there were the myriad kinds of different principles and later they obtained the vital-energy of heaven and earth, which is essentially one. Then the forms of the myriad things came to be perfected. According to this explanation, the vital-energy is the same but the principles are different. Such sameness and difference are as far apart as heaven and earth. All of this comes from the arguments of famous scholars. But which teaching should be adopted by the later scholars under heaven? This is the sixth difference.

The true teaching has going home to return, but the other teachings have only the turning of the wheel. Going home to return means to comply with the clear mandate, to embody the sages and worthies, and to advance straight to the Root Origin. Those who are high through wisdom will have high levels and enduring bliss. Those who are low through ignorance will fall into hellfire in low positions and everlasting punishment. The Real Lord will judge and call to account with the utmost properness, bringing people's hearts into the harmony of submission. This means that when you do good, you will not have to look back, and when you do evil, you will have no lucky escape.

This is not like the shaky situations of the other authorities. Why? When Buddhists become buddhas, they go home to empty nonbeing; if someone falls back, the wheel does not cease its turning. When Daoists attain the way, they are transformed and become immortals, everlasting like heaven and long-lasting like earth. If they do not attain the way, the coming and going will also have no end.

When someone becomes a buddha, he goes home to emptiness, so it is difficult to avoid the return of falsehood in the future. When someone becomes an immortal, he does not die, so he cannot avoid the ruin of the Creative and the Receptive. If we look carefully, this means that at root the immortals and buddhas do not escape or remain apart from life and death. Defect emerges originally from the self-so. Is it not that when stillness reaches its ultimate, it moves, and when movement reaches its ultimate, it becomes still?

In Nature and Principle someone said, "The Great Void must have vital-energy, vital-energy must collect to become the myriad things, the myriad things must scatter to become vital-energy, and vital-energy must transform to become the Great Void. All leaving and entering must undergo this cycle."[84] Hah! The heavenly mandate cannot come to be by itself, and the Great Void cannot be collected and scattered by itself.

The meaning of these two explanations is like the acts and affairs of people in the world, who are incoherent and reckless, not having taken the measure of their own strength. When affairs reach the end, they want to finish but are not able to finish.

Know that human beings are like the scaled and shelled tribes in the midst of water, which themselves surely emerge from the midst of the water, but certainly will never again become the body of water. It will never happen that the class of cruel, violent, and crooked rulers, the various sorts of rebellious ministers and wicked youngsters—all those who rely on the strong and oppress the weak—will one morning go home to the Great Void without the determination of good and evil. Otherwise, would that not mean that evil people are let loose and good people betrayed?

The king's law for the five punishments has three thousand regulations, each of which has codes for what should be correctly done. So much more so in the case of the Real Lord, who has the utmost justice and who created and transformed heaven, earth, and the myriad things!

A humane human is able to love people and dislike people. If the Lord of heaven and earth has nothing to do with the ascent of good people to the Heavenly Country, how can He be considered to love people? If He has nothing to do with the descent of evil people to the Earthly Dungeon, how can He be considered to dislike people?

In this world, reward and punishment may not be in conformity with one's heart. One must wait for the afterworld with its Heavenly Palace and Earthly Dungeon as the recompense suitable for intentions and thoughts, without any crookedness or injustice whatsoever. Although there have been tens of millions of generations beforehand

---

84. The quote is from Zhang Zai 張載, *Zheng Meng* 正蒙. In *Source Book* 501, Chan translates the passage like this: "The Great Vacuity of necessity consists of material force. Material force of necessity integrates to become the myriad things. Things of necessity disintegrate and return to the Great Vacuity. Appearance and disappearance following this cycle are a matter of necessity."

and there will be tens of millions of generations afterwards, the myriad things and the myriad affairs are all clear for the Real Lord, as if He sees them before His eyes.

If your faith does not reach here, how can you consider yourself to have faith in the Lord of heaven and earth, who has the utmost humaneness and the utmost justice? This is the seventh difference.

1.11. Nature and Mandate

The Sage said, "When someone attains recognition of the Real Lord, who transformed and begot his body, he attains recognition of himself for the first time." He also said, "If you see your nature completely, you can see the Lord."[85] To know this body is to know the Real Lord's creative transformation. To see this nature is to see the Real Lord's mysterious secret.

The beginning was not an undifferentiated, hidden chaos, as some theories say, nor was it blurred and indistinct, as others incoherently say. Confucius rarely spoke about mandate and humaneness because he did not carelessly issue forth his most sincere, root intention. Hence Zi Gong said, "The Master's brilliant explanation and orderly display may be heard, but his discourses about nature and the way of Heaven cannot be heard" [*Analects* 5.13]. It was Confucius's grandson who spoke of this for the first time: "What Heaven mandates is nature; following nature is the way" [*Mean* 1]. These two clauses are the great origin of the Learning of the Principles, but unfortunately, they are difficult to penetrate thoroughly. Later scholars do not have the same opinion because they have different root natures. How then is it possible to obtain unity?

Mencius: "Nature is good."
Xunzi: "Nature is evil."
Yangzi: "A mixture of good and evil."
Hanzi: "All three levels."
Chengzi: "Principle and vital-energy."[86]

---

85. This is a more literal translation of the saying of 'Alī mentioned in 1.1.
86. These are all well-known Chinese thinkers: Xunzi 荀子 (3rd c. BCE), Yangzi 楊子 (or Yang Zhu 楊朱; 4th c. BCE), Han Feizi 韓非子 (3rd c. BCE), and the Neo-Confucian Chengzi 程子 (11th c. CE). The last may refer to one or both Cheng brothers, Hao 顥 and Yi 頤.

People today take Chengzi's opinion as the best. They consider good as the nature of principle and evil as the nature of vital-energy. They do not know, however, how vital-energy and stuff come to be at the root. When there is that kind of seed, there will be this kind of fruit. Apricot kernels never produce plums. The mentioned opinions are all unsettled theories, for they do not penetrate the fountainhead.

From the time of the Song Dynasty, everyone says that the principle is the same and the vital-energies are different. Some in Nature and Principle say that nature is one, but in the midst of its flow there are hard and soft, dark and bright, and these are not nature. For example, there are three people who have eyes with which they can distinguish the five colors. One is in a closed room, another inside a tent, and the third in a spacious garden. Their opinions concerning dark and bright will be different. It is not their eyes that are different; it is rather their dwelling places that are different.

Someone said that three people may dwell in one place, but they are not the same concerning dark and bright. How is this to be understood? Another analogy is not far from this case: Together three people encounter the calamity of rebellion. One fully realizes loyalty, one follows the rebels, and one compromises and procrastinates. Good is good, and evil is evil. We can see that their natures are not the same. How would it be possible for no one to differentiate between jade and stone and everyone to take advantage of a disorderly world and become rebellious?

As for the distinction to be drawn between principle and vital-energy, it is like that between branches and knots, so there is still no settled discussion.

A scholar who inquires into the root and thoroughly investigates the fountainhead may ask, "What is heaven? What is mandate? What is nature? What is following?" He would surely be given the answer that heaven is the supreme ruler, mandate is like its command, nature is the mandate, and following is like complying with it.

He may further ask how the supreme ruler comes to be and who receives heaven's mandate. Moreover, if heaven's mandate is like a ruler's mandate or a general's command, then it is not known how the mandate or the command is able to become nature and who are the ones who follow their nature. To this extent no explanation emerges that everyone will cherish in his breast.

Only the true teaching of Islam explains that natures are not the same and vital-energies are also different. They are pure and unmixed, undifferentiated yet distinct. If someone thoroughly investigates the principles and fully realizes nature, he will reach the mandate. This is real knowledge.

Why do I say this? Because the Former Heaven is the mandate, and the Latter Heaven is nature.[87] The mandate is the seed, and nature is the fruit. The mandate is not nature, yet it is not apart from nature. Nature is not the mandate, yet it is not apart from the mandate. Without the mandate, there is no nature, and without nature, [the mandate] is incomplete.

Today people talk about the principle of both nature and mandate but heedlessly do not differentiate between the two. They speak foolishly about "one principle." They know that it is really one, but they do not know that it is also two. If you already know that it is two, you will certainly know why it is one.

Someone said: Nowadays, following nature is the way, and this is possible if nature is good. But what if nature is not completely good?

I said: The knowledge of those who know affairs but do not know themselves is by no means real knowledge. If you wish to know the good and evil of human nature, you must first know what nature and mandate and good and evil are.

Nature and mandate are the root suchness of each thing. Good and evil are the issuing functions of nature and mandate. Of these two issuing functions, good is the root function—such as seeing, hearing, smelling, and speaking, which cannot be increased or decreased and cannot be given to another person. Evil is the working function, such as various skills like copying, drawing, and all sorts of artisanry, which can be owned jointly and taught to others and learned.[88]

---

87. In other words, the Former Heaven (all that precedes the manifestation of forms) is determined by the divine command, and the Latter Heaven (the ascending ladder of forms going back to the Real) displays the stages of nature (inanimate, vegetal, animal, human). Liu Zhi presents this relationship schematically in diagram 0.6.

88. The distinction between the two functions correlates with discussions of the ambiguous status of the soul (*nafs*) in Islamic psychology. The soul's root reality is the spirit or intellect, and to the extent that it conforms to its root it is good. But its faculties are engaged with the body, and to the extent that it allows the body to dominate over it, it is evil. This explains the constant criticism of the *nafs* in Sufi texts, meaning not the soul per se, but, to use the Qur'anic expression, "the soul that commands to ugliness" (*al-nafs al-ammāra bi'l-sū'*). On the various dimensions of the human soul, see Murata, *Tao*, chapter 9.

When there is nature and mandate, there is surely the root function, for without the root function, nature and mandate would be defective. But, when there is nature and mandate, a working function is not necessarily there, for without the working function, it would not be defective. Still, outside nature and mandate, there is no working function.

The methods and teaching of Islam are for the sake of the common and ignorant people, not for the sake of the sages and the wise. The sages and the wise embody the root function and rectify the inclination toward the working function. It is not that they do not have the working function, but that their knowledge of it is innate. The common and ignorant people incline toward the working function and are dark in their embodiment of the root function. It is not that they do not have the root function, but that their knowledge of it is gained by learning.

As for people's origin, it is the same, but not one. This is like the deep ocean and shallow water, or like pure and turbid in the same flow.

There are three degrees: sage, worthy, and ignorant.[89] Sages are those who are awake and not asleep. Worthies are between wakefulness and sleep. The ignorant are slumbering deeply and have not awoken.

The Real Lord is the utmost humaneness who made the Classic descend and sent the sages to direct and guide the perplexed to the path, so that they may return and go home to the True Way and reach the root origin directly, climbing back to the Heavenly Country.

When the worthies are summoned, they immediately wake up. When the ignorant receive the call, they do not respond. This is the meaning when the Classic says, "Even the Sage cannot command the dead to hear and listen."[90] When someone grasps this principle, he will differentiate between movement and stillness. Then he can talk about the goodness and not-goodness of human nature.

Each thing belongs to its own kind. Things of the same kind have the same nature, and things of different kinds have different natures. Only the nature of the human has the ability to beget and

---

89. Liu Zhi adds another category, the wise, and explains the relationships among these four human types under Diagrams 4.7–4.10.

90. "Surely thou dost not make the dead to hear, nor dost thou make the deaf to hear the call when they turn away, retreating" (Qur'an 27:80, 30:52).

grow, the ability of knowledge and awareness, and also that of deducing the principles.[91] The human's begetting and growth make him distinct from metal and stone, his knowledge and awareness make him different from grass and trees, and his deducing the principles gives him excellence over birds and beasts.

When man makes deductions about affairs and things, this is not only to clarify the principles, but also to discriminate the secret that demons and spirits cannot fathom. Seeing the beginning, he can grasp the end. Relying on the outward, he can penetrate the inward. The ability to deduce the principles belongs uniquely to mankind, distinguishing them from other things. In actual fact it is the nature and mandate of man.

When the root substance of nature and mandate is discussed along with its functions, which are the feelings, then both [substance and function] emerge from the Real Lord's creative transformation. When the principle is the root [substance], then people can enjoy and love them [i.e., the functions] in themselves, because the root is good without evil. But when the feelings are discussed as functions, then they are based on individual selves, and individual selves do both good and evil. The actions of individuals are distinct and different because the feelings, which are the functions, are between good and evil. This is like a sword and seal bestowed by a sovereign king. Those who receive them use them publicly and privately according to their own convenience.[92]

What are called feelings issue forth from nature. Were there no private selves influenced by external things, the feelings would of course listen to the mandate of the principles and there would be nothing but good. When people cling to their unjust selves, of course they do not attain to the truth, and there will be nothing but evil.

---

91. In books on Chinese thought "deducing the principles" (*tuili* 推理) is often translated as reasoning or reason. As noted in the introduction, for this specific quality Islamic texts typically use the words *'aql* (intellect, reason) or *nafs nātiqa* (rational soul).

92. The relationship between nature and feelings (*qing* 情) is much discussed in Neo-Confucian thought. Feelings are said to be "nature when aroused" and nature and feelings together are the heart's substance and function (see *Sage Learning* 262–63). Wang's discussion here is reminiscent of the contrast drawn by Islamic texts between *'aql* and *nafs*, intellect and soul. "Private self" is a good Chinese way to express the quality of the *nafs* inasmuch as it "commands the ugly."

This is like the time when a person is healthy and the various tastes all accord with the truth. When he becomes sick, sweet becomes bitter and bitter sweet. When the nature of the feelings is tainted, it is no different from this.

Someone said: If the nature of the human is good at root, where does evil come from?

I said: A person's nature has the ability to do both good and evil. It is not that nature has evil at root. This is like a noted painter who is good at drawing images of the multitudes, the old and the young, the ugly and the beautiful, just as they are. It is not that he has the ability only to draw one kind.

Evil is not a real thing.[93] It is like still water that is left in a pot for a long time and changes. How can it be so at its fountainhead?

As for the nature of birds and beasts, it is not similar to the nature of the human, which has the ability to do good and act with evil. Birds and beasts cannot establish the real endeavor of virtuous activity, so by themselves they cannot reach the glorious nobility of climbing up to the Heavenly Country.

Good, however, has two parts. The good of nature is the root good, and the good of activity is practiced good. The root good is the original virtue of nature and mandate. It is transformed and begotten by the Real Lord, and the human has no share in this. As for human good, it is the piled-up virtue of meritorious deeds practiced by oneself.

For example, mothers love their infants, and birds and beasts are the same in this, as when mothers kneel to suckle or birds disgorge to feed their young. If the people of the world, whether good or evil, see an infant sitting or standing in a dangerous place, they will always think of rescuing it.[94] All this is the root good. This has nothing to do with the fact that birds and beasts are similar to people who have no good.

Acting on righteousness immediately upon seeing it and loving any good when meeting it are called practiced virtue. In general,

---

93. A point often made in Islamic philosophy. Ibn al-'Arabī provides a subtle classification of the sorts of evil based on their rooting in nonexistence ('*adam*). See Chittick, *Sufi Path of Knowledge* 290–92.

94. This is the famous example offered by Mencius (2.1.6.3) to prove the goodness of human nature.

when people are first born, they are like beautiful women, and all is originally inherited from their parents. It is not that they have such abilities by practice. This is like Xizi,[95] who was covered by filth, so everyone who saw her despised her. Then, after they had waited for her to take a bath and put on makeup, her outside tallied with her inside. Then people began to know her perfect virtue.

You should know that mandate is one kind, but nature is differentiated into two kinds. These are called real nature and endowed nature. Real nature emerges from the origin of the mandate. In reality it is the utmost principle of the Former Heaven. If it is able to issue forth and be disclosed, it will be single-minded loyalty and chastity. It will face the Lord with one heart and put aside everything under heaven like worn-out shoes. It will see wealth and nobility as floating clouds.

Endowed nature emerges from the corporeal body, which is rooted in the four elements. It is like a vicious horse. Gain and loss are related to the manner in which people use it and take care of it. If they let it follow its nature, it will run wild and flee recklessly. If they tame its nature, it will attack boldly and destroy the enemy. When you have the endowed nature, foolish boastfulness is born, but if you do not have it, there will be deficiency and weariness. Why would you be wrongly attached to it?

Everyone receives one of the mandate's seeds, in which are contained their different selves. Peach pits produce peaches, plum pits produce plums. The myriad kinds are all different because of what they bring upon themselves. The seed of the mandate joins with the bodily ground, which is affected by time and season, cause and effect. The seed with good fortune does not fall on unfortunate ground, and unfortunate ground does not receive the seeds of good fortune's fruit. Each has its own native place in the Former Heaven, and there cannot be the slightest irregularity.

Where do things begin and where do they end? Although illusory images melt away, the principles are preserved and do not decay. In general things have three stages without being apart from their root soil. When affairs reach the end, they return to the old depending on their origin. This is the secret of the Powerful One.

---

95. Xizi 西子 or Xi Shi 西施 (7–6th c. BCE) is considered one of the four most beautiful women in Chinese history.

Predetermination and free will are secrets determined by the Former Heaven. When they arrive here, both give forth their red and purple. Each has the true nature and mandate, which is evidence of the seed. Giving forth red and purple is evidence of flowers and fruit. "If you want to discern the real seeds of the Former Heaven, look at each of the roots and sprouts issuing forth before your eyes."

Once the explanation reaches this point, the man of wisdom should be aroused and awakened as a matter of course. He will carefully observe his own actions and never make any of the errors and mistakes before his eyes. How will regret be of any use?

The principle of nature and mandate is concealed, subtle, and unfathomable. Portraying it with utmost effort will give nothing more than shadows and echoes. An easy and agreeable description would not be different from mercury grasped in the hand. When someone's intention is stable, the mercury will not move in the slightest. When someone's heart is careless, he will not keep hold of it.

Thus we see that those who obtain it will obtain it by themselves, and those who lose it will lose it by themselves. Nothing is strange here.

1.12. The Real Heart

The Classic says, "Heaven and earth are not able to receive and carry the Real Lord—only the heart of a true person."[96] The meaning of the true heart is that a man goes home and recognizes the Real Lord, not that everyone has the true heart.

Scholars discussed this heart from the outset, but in the end no one has ever explained what it is. Some may say that this heart is nature and mandate, but it is not nature and mandate. Some may say that this heart is wisdom and intelligence, but it is not wisdom and intelligence.

There are three hearts. These are called the animal heart, the human heart, and the real heart. The three hearts altogether have seven levels: the level of desire, the level of wisdom, the level of humaneness, the level of seeing, the level of joy, the level of mystery,

---

96. This is a *ḥadīth qudsī* cited by Rāzī in *Mirṣād* (*Path* 219): "Neither My heaven nor My earth embraces Me, but the heart of My faithful servant does embrace Me."

and the level of the utmost. Worldly people have only the three levels of desire, wisdom, and humaneness. Only true people can have all seven levels completely.[97]

The animal heart dwells in the level of desire, which is grounded in the nature of awareness. Inside it is like a young man's bravery and courage in relation to the measure of his strength, and outside it is like the light of a lamp in relation to its oil.

The human heart dwells in the two levels of humaneness and wisdom, which follow the nature of the spiritual. Inside it is like knowledge and awareness in relation to movement, and outside it is like roaming fish in relation to rivers and seas.

The real heart dwells in the four levels of seeing, joy, mystery, and the utmost. It has no self, so it complies with the clear mandate. Inside it is like subtle clarity in relation to purity and cleanliness, and outside it is like the sun's brightness in relation to a clear sky.

The natures of the human heart are not the same at origin, so the cultivation of the way cannot be one. When a child is first born, it has not yet practiced good and evil, even though there is evidence of good and evil at the origin. If the nature is good, then following it will be the true way. If it is evil, then following it will be the unjust way.[98] The various scholars are confused about this; they are not united because they themselves conform with their natures.

Islam teaches that the selfishness of the private self must be conquered and that people should not be self-determining. When someone is not self-determining, the real heart will begin to disclose itself. Then he will come to have the real heart, without self and without self-determination. He will comply with the Real Lord's clear mandate, cultivate the way, and establish the teaching. From ancient times until now, from near to far, all have complied and venerated, so they have been united, for they have not conformed with and followed their own natures.

Lowly and ignorant people give rein to appetites and desires. They incline toward the animal heart, which pertains to the nature

---

97. The seven levels of the heart are probably based on Rāzī's discussion (*Path* 195–97, 208). Liu Zhi also depicts seven levels (diagram 4.2), though he names and describes them differently. Petersen provides the broad context of Wang's discussion in "The Heart of Wang Daiyu's Philosophy."

98. Wang is again referring to the first sentence of *The Doctrine of the Mean*: "What heaven mandates is nature; following nature is the way."

of awareness, so they do nothing but damage other people and profit themselves, having only greed and anger.

Those of higher wisdom act in keeping with humaneness and righteousness. They conform with the human heart, which pertains to the nature of the spiritual, so they do nothing but regulate the family, govern the country, observe loyalty, and have filial piety.

Only true and great people comply with the clear mandate and embody the selfless, real heart. They always direct the perplexed to go back to the truth and to work for the Lord alone.

Someone asked the honorable Rābi'a, "Are you joyful with the Lord?"

She said, "Yes."

"With the devil?"

She said, "No."

"Why not?"

She said, "I have only one heart. How could I have two?"[99]

You should know that the real heart's *seeing* is seeing things while also seeing that they do not exist, so it sees only the Creator. Its *joy* is not the selfish joy of worldly people, but the real joy that is granted only in the Original Being that has no beginning and no end. This is not put to use in the emptiness and nothingness of the myriad affairs and things, for things and affairs cause success and failure, cutting off and continuity, without the permanence of real joy. The level of *mystery* is the secret of recognizing the Lord. The level of the *utmost* is the subtlety of selflessness. When you arrive at the position of this ground, you do not know that there is a country, a house, or a body, for you are dedicated to the Real Lord, the Unique One.

This is because the human body has form and spirit, and the heart has color and subtlety. The human body is the concealed quintessence of the forms and colors of heaven, earth, and the myriad things. The human nature is the ultimate pivot of the origin of heaven, earth, and the myriad things. The color of the heart is the outstanding essence of this body, and the subtlety of the heart is the mysterious secret of nature.

---

99. The story is told by 'Aṭṭār (*Tadhkira* 80; *Memorial* 106): "It was said to Rābi'a, 'Do you love the Exalted Presence?' She said, 'I do.' It was said, 'Do you hate Satan?' She said, 'I do not turn away from love of the All-Merciful toward hatred of Satan.'"

The Classic says, "Those who are not born again, for a second time, will not be able to enwrap heaven and earth and permeate everything from antiquity until now."[100] This is because as long as a fetus is not separated from its mother, it will be contained in the mother's belly. If nature does not emerge from the body, it will surely be bound to the body. If the nature of the spiritual is unable to conquer the self, how will the real heart issue forth and be disclosed?

When the heart reaches the time of issuance and disclosure, it will totally cast off these three births. Then it will begin to have no inside or outside, no antiquity or now. Thus a worthy said, "The myriad things are provided inside the real heart, for it is vast with nothing outside. The real heart is embedded in the midst of the myriad things, for it is tiny with nothing inside."[101]

This is the great meaning of enwrapping heaven and earth and permeating everything. It is not like what the various scholars say—that it is enough to clarify the heart of the human way and to see the original nature. They think that what you recognize as the root nature and the root heart is the Lord Ruler. What a delusion!

Only the true person surpasses the heart of the human way and reaches the selfless, real heart, conquering the nature of the root spiritual. Then the great nature of the sage, called the seed of the Non-Ultimate, will become manifest, and it will bring forth the perfection of the Non-Ultimate's fruit.

In general, when the nature of awareness in the animal heart sees things, it has appetite, but if it does not see them, it does not.

When the nature of the spiritual of the human heart sees things, it is able to obtain the real and the false of the things' forms. After seeing this, it is able to embrace the spirit and feelings of the things' subtlety, but when it does not know or see something, it falls into guessing and sees only shadows and reflections.

When the great nature of the real heart obtains the knowledge and vision of the sage, everything in the universe—what has gone before and what will come in the future, what is seen and what is not seen—will appear before him as the same because of this heart's

---

100. Probably Wang has in mind the Arabic translation of Jesus's saying in John 3:3, often cited in Islamic texts: "None will enter the dominion of the heavens unless he is born twice."

101. Compare Liu Zhi's discussion of small and great in diagrams 5.8 and 5.9.

function, which complies with and attains to the clear mandate. This is like a minister who makes an imperial inspection in place of the ruler. None of it is his own affair, but everyone will honor and venerate him. The authority is conferred upon him by the emperor, but if he were called "emperor," that would bring about perplexity.

You should know that this principle does not belong to the sort of theory that says that someone who fully realizes the heart will know nature and know heaven.[102] Why? Because those who argue for this say that the heart is the substance of the spirit's clarity and that nature is the principle embedded in the heart and emerging originally from heaven. Their root text goes from shallow to deep and from rough to refined, but when we look at the commentary, there is distinction in names, but in reality there is confusion in the principle. Therefore they say that there is no nature outside the heart and no heaven outside nature.

One can say that there is no nature outside the heart, but to say that there is no heaven outside nature is false awareness. Why? Because, if there are billions of people, then there are billions of hearts. If there are billions of hearts, there are billions of natures. If there are billions of natures, there are billions of heavens. But how can one say that?

If we say that there is no light outside the mirror, or that there is no water outside the ocean, then the beautiful woman would certainly be inside the mirror and the clear moon would be revealing itself from the ocean's depth. Certainly one cannot say that there is no one outside the mirror's light or that there is no moon outside the ocean's water. A person can have a form in a mirror, but the mirror is not the person. The moon can emerge in water, but the water is not the moon.

Without penetrating the nature of the heart, how can one talk about heaven? With such a great root and great origin, how can one proceed simply on the basis of practiced knowledge and practiced vision?

1.13. Life and Death

The Sage said, "If you have this world, you will have an afterworld, and if you have the floating life, you will have sudden death." You

---

102. Liu Zhi talks about realizing the heart and knowing nature in the context of describing the path to enlightenment, with a view toward the Buddhist notion of gradual and sudden enlightenment (*Sage Learning* 485–86).

should know about this. It is difficult to talk about the secret of life and death, but let me try to do so briefly.

Life and death are called being and nonbeing, but being and nonbeing have various meanings. Being has three levels: Being without beginning and end is the being of the Real Lord, the Unique One. Being with beginning but without end is the being of the Numerical One, the heavenly immortals, man, and spirits. Being with both beginning and end is the being upon which those in water and land rely—flyers and walkers, grass and trees, metal and stone.

Nature and mandate also have three levels: The lowest level is called the nature of begetting, the middle level the nature of awareness, and the highest level the nature of the spiritual.

The mandate of begetting and growth is the nature of grass and trees, which can support the begetting and growth of grass and trees. When grass and trees wither and decay, this nature disappears and perishes.

The mandate of knowledge and awareness is the nature of birds and beasts, which can adhere to the begetting and growth of birds and beasts and allow them to see, hear, smell, taste, know, and be aware through eyes, ears, nose, tongue, body, and heart. They are not able to deduce principles, however, and when they die, this nature also perishes.

The mandate of the spiritual and intelligence is the nature of the human. It combines the two natures of begetting and awareness, supporting people's growth and nourishment and allowing them to know and be aware and also to deduce the principles of affairs. Although the body dies, this nature exists everlastingly.

Affairs of knowledge and awareness that rely on the body are useless once the bodily form ceases to be. Since the natures of grass and trees, birds and beasts, take the body as root, when the body dies, the natures accompany the body and perish. But the nature of deducing and clarifying principles has no necessity to rely on the body for its evidence, so this nature can operate by itself. Even when the form of the body has perished, the spirit still has the ability to function by depending on its origin. This is why the human is greatly different from birds and beasts, grass and trees.

When the heart of someone who wants to clarify the principles of things receives something's form, he must cast off the form and extract the pure essence. Then he can contain it in his heart. This is like the eye that takes in the greatness of mountains and rivers and easily lays it out in its own square inch. If the heart had no utmost spirit, how could these huge things be put into its tiny container? Thus, if you have the spirit, you have the ability to receive, but if you did not have the spirit, it would be impossible to receive.

Someone asked: What is "relying on the body" and what is "not relying on the body"?

I said: If the ability to beget and rear the bodily form had no bodily form on which to rely, there could be no begetting and rearing. Seeing, hearing, smelling, tasting, knowing, and awareness are housed in eyes, nose, tongue, body, and heart and are caused by scent, taste, sound, color, cold, and warmth. If these six affairs were not there, then seeing, hearing, smelling, tasting, knowing, and awareness would be of no use whatsoever, for all of these are servants of form.

To say that the nature of begetting and awareness relies on the body means that when the body dies, it follows along and perishes. As for the root function of the nature of the spiritual, it does not rely on the body. If it relied on the body, it would be a servant of the body. How then could it distinguish between right and wrong? When birds and beasts see edible things, they want to eat them and cannot hold themselves back. How can they be expected to discriminate between right and wrong, propriety and modesty?

When someone is hungry and thirsty and sees unrighteous food, his heart will of course not be perplexed. No matter how delicious it looks, he will certainly scorn to eat it. Moreover, when he recognizes the Lord, has loyalty to the ruler, is filial to parents, regulates the family, governs the country, and enriches everyone under heaven with virtue, then his fragrance will flow for a thousand ages. Even if his body does not move, his spirit may travel the universe, functioning in everything according to its ultimate. How can it be a servant of the body?

In general, living things have only one heart. The human alone has two hearts: the heart of the human and the heart of things. He also has two natures: real nature and endowed nature. When he encounters unrighteous wealth and beauty, he loves it but considers it improper. The heart of things would make him follow it, but the heart of the human makes him reject it. This is like two streams of water side by side, one pure, the other turbid. Even if you have not seen their fountainheads, you know for certain that they are not the same.

Birds and beasts have the heart of birds and beasts, but they do not have the intelligence of the spiritual to distinguish between right and wrong. Their hearts issue forth in willful intentions without the ability to control them. Moreover, they themselves do not know that their acts are good or evil. Their knowledge of form is such that their feelings cannot penetrate anything but the outward form. How could they reflect upon themselves and return to knowing their nature? Hence from antiquity until now there has been no law of reward and punishment for birds and beasts.

Only the human is not like this. He has the ability to distinguish between good and evil and to investigate thoroughly the subtlety of being and nonbeing. By himself he is able to act or stop and to extend this to other things. How can bodily form be a barrier to him?

When a person dies, this is the death of the nature of awareness that belongs to the bodily form, not the nature of the spiritual. In the body the nature of the spiritual is restrained as if in prison. When the body dies, it is as if the prisoner emerges from restraint. Then the spiritual is doubled.

Those who know the mandate do not see death as difficult. When they go home and return to their original place, each of them will have his fixed position, and they will no longer be able to shift by themselves. It may happen that someone will receive the mandate and return home, and then he will meet with the people of the world by becoming manifest again in the form and capacity that he had when alive and he will encourage his posterity to do good and not do evil. This also demonstrates that after people die, the nature of their spiritual exists everlastingly and does not perish, for it is distinct from the nature of awareness that belongs to birds and beasts, which scatters and perishes and does not go home.

For those who wish to clarify the principles of things and affairs, there is no other way but to reach the inward from the outward. They should verify that which has not yet come on the basis of what has gone. This is like looking at a house that has collapsed, its hedge ruined and broken—you know that no one is inside the house. When you see heaven, earth, and the myriad things, the ascending and descending of sun and moon, the waxing and waning of the four seasons, all without alteration and change, then you will surely know that there is a Lord of the creative transformation. Given that man has an ability to act with endeavor that has not decayed for a thousand ages, this is evidence that in fact his spiritual and spirit do not perish and that he has a final resting place without end.

Although the spiritual will not perish, yin and yang are still connected with each other. In their midst are found the distinction between the Original Being and the newly born. All things that have come into being from yin and yang, one after another, have come from the being of the Numerical One. So time is never apart from day and night, and man is never apart from waking and sleeping. Day and night are evidence and proof of yin and yang, and waking and sleeping are evidence and clarification of life and death. The secret of the two worlds of being and nonbeing is wholly included in the document that is the human body, verifying that it has received the mandate.

If there were no distinction between recognizing the Lord and recognizing self, this would be outside the way. The alterations and changes of having the body and not having the body let you know about the ruling authority of the ability to let live and the ability to bring about death. When you see black night, you actually come to know broad daylight. It is because of life and death that you will begin to awaken to the constancy of the Real.

You should know that life is not life, for it also has death, and death is not death, for it circles back to life. At root there is neither life nor death. All day you have been afraid to die and greedy to live, and now you are sleeping in confusion. Once you wake up, you will actually know that you were dreaming. The floating clouds of wealth and nobility will be cast aside and given to other people.

In true reality good and evil are not apart from your own body. Life and death are two paths that belong originally to the dwelling places of travelers. When you leap beyond being and nonbeing, you will be sustained in a realm where there is neither death nor life. Once you reach that ground, you will certainly recognize and obtain the Real Lord, the Unique One without beginning and end. He alone is the Original Being without beginning and end, He who has the actual ability to make life into death and to transform death into life. This is why the Real Lord does not fall into being and nonbeing. Man and spirits must experience the life and death that are not in fact life and death. This is the great meaning of Lord and servant.

If you wish to investigate thoroughly the Utmost Principle by means of writings, not only will you not be able to obtain the Principle, but also the text will be lost to you. Unless you empty your heart and understand through the spirit, you will never be able to attain It.

1.14. The Level of the Human

The Human Ultimate is the mysterious pivot that enwraps the myriad images. The rare secret of the creative transformation of being and nonbeing was fully recorded in the ancient document of this body.

At the time of the great beginning, the Real Lord turned the Non-Ultimate and opened the Gate of All Subtleties, which is the root of human nature and principle. He used the Great Ultimate to create the forms of heaven and earth, which are the root of human stuff and vital-energy.

Heaven, earth, and the myriad things are like one great tree. The human is the spiritual of the myriad things, and human nature and principle are the seed of the tree. The human is the noble of the myriad things, and the human corporeal body is the fruit of the tree.

If we talk about the tree as one, unified in both its roots and its branches, its refined and its coarse, it is called the human, and the human is humaneness. When he is only one and not yet differentiated, he is the Human Ultimate. When one is transformed into two, these are husband and wife. At origin the Human Ultimate is one human, but husband and wife are two humans (二人). One human is human (人), and two humans are humaneness (仁). Hence the Three Bonds, the Five Constants,[103] ruler and subject, father and son—all are based on the humaneness of husband and wife.

Before heaven and earth, the human became the root origin of the myriad beings; as the embodiment of the Real One, he became the firm principle from antiquity until now. After heaven and earth, he will be the origin to which the myriad laws go home.

When he goes beyond the myriad levels, he will begin to go home to the Real One. Among the myriad things, he is second to the Real One, so nothing has greater honor than the human. Just as the flourishing of grass and trees and the abundance of flowers and fruits are all contained in the seed, so also the greatness of heaven and earth and the manyness of the myriad things are all included in the Human Ultimate.[104]

If there were heaven and earth without the human, this would be no different from a makeup stand without a mirror. If there were the human without heaven and earth, this would be like a precious

---

103. The Three Bonds (*sangang* 三綱) are the proper relationships between ruler and subject, father and son, and husband and wife. The Five Constants (*wuchang* 五常), discussed in the introduction, are the five constant virtues of Confucianism, though Wang could also have in mind the five pillars of Islamic practice (the topic of chapter 2.1).

104. Compare Liu Zhi's description of "the nature of continuity," one of the names he gives to the level of the Human Ultimate (diagram 3.12).

mirror without a stand. Just as the human is not able to abide by himself without heaven and earth, so also the myriad things are not able to exist by themselves without the human. The myriad things are for the sake of protecting[105] and guarding the human, and the human is the pivotal secret of the myriad things. The myriad things exist through the spiritual of the human, and the human is preserved by the forms of the myriad things.

This is like water and fish. Water will surely spoil without fish, and fish will not survive without water. At root, heaven, earth, and the myriad things are made for human use, but humans do not know their own honorable level. Instead they toil for wealth and nobility, bending their knees to the myriad things. Is it possible to say that they know the human?

The Classic says, "The Real Lord manifested His great power by creating and transforming heaven and earth, but heaven and earth do not have that power. When He wished to make His own self manifest, He created and transformed the Human Ultimate, but the Human Ultimate is not that self."

The differentiation between Lord and servant is that between the Real One and the Numerical One. If you say that the human has the same level as the Real One, this is a great transgression. If you say that the human has the same level as the myriad things, that would be a great denigration.

The Real Lord created and transformed heaven, earth, and the myriad things. Some are of the same class but with different kinds, some are of the same kind but with different bodies, and some are of the same body but with different functions. Insisting that there is one body would conceal the complete power of the creative transformation.[106]

Things are beautiful in their own many ways. If the various things under heaven were all of one color, who would not hate that? If the five colors were all mixed together, no one would enjoy looking at them. The same is so for the five tastes and the five sounds. If things are such outwardly, how can all of them be the same inwardly?

---

105. The 1904 and 1922 editions have "seizing" (*huo* 獲) instead of "protecting" (*hu* 護).

106. Here and in the next few paragraphs, Wang has in view the theories he criticized in chapters 1.8–1.10.

Variations of kinds and natures do not always mean difference in guise. For example, a living person and a wooden person have the same guise, but at root they are different kinds. A wooden person and a wooden horse have different guises, but at root they are the same kind. One should not confuse the distinctions between kinds and bodies. When things stand by themselves, those that pertain to the same body are surely of the same kind, but those that pertain to the same kind may not be of the same body.

In general, affairs of the same body all belong to the members and bones of the body. If the mouth can give advice and if it can make people act good and change their mistakes, then the whole body is designated as humane and righteous—it is not the mouth specifically that is praised. If the hand is able to steal skillfully, the whole body is called a thief. This is firmly so because of the principles.

If the myriad things under heaven were indeed one body, we could say that when Dao Zhi stole alone, Xiahui also stole. When King Wen acted alone according to humaneness, we can also designate Shang Zhou as having humaneness, for if they had one body, their reward and punishment must have been the same. If you see things like this, is it not because you are confusing the root suchnesses of things?

When we discuss the distinctions among the myriad things, some have the same body and some have their own bodies. How can it be that the myriad things are united as one body? Those that are connected with each other have one body, but those that are distant from each other have different bodies.

Moreover, man is one kind, but he has more levels than an ox has hairs. Birds and beasts are by no means limited to a thousand sorts, or grass and trees to a myriad varieties. This is to say that those of the same kind do not have the same body.

If you are still caught up with the explanation of the myriad things as one body, you will make light of the creative transformation, confuse the reward and the punishment, conceal the same and the different, unify the high and the low, and take away the right and the wrong. The sin of foolish words like this is not insignificant.

Just as man's body and behavior are rare and special, not similar to the myriad things, so also his nature has more spirit and wisdom. For example, if you want to create sailing ships, you must have bamboo and wood. If you want to mold cauldrons and pots, you must have brass and iron. When the utensils are not the same, the materials you use will surely be different. When you already know that the body and behavior of man are different from those of the myriad things, then surely his nature and mandate are not of the same kind. This is the great cause and effect of rising and falling from ancient times until now. The person of knowledge knows it by himself, and the person of ignorance is ignorant by himself. What a difference between the two!

Worldly people today are greedy for the illusory shadows of name and gain. They are deluded about where they will return and whence they originally came. They do not know who has transformed them or what kind of being is their root. They do not know what affairs they should do or where they will return and go home. They do not know whence they came in the beginning, nor do they know where they will go in the end. Merely having the guise of man, they are probably not human. This is extremely lamentable and painful.

First you must know the human level, and then you will start to know the activity of the human. If you do not know the principle of the human, how can you travel the human way? As for the fact that the human is different from birds and beasts, there is no more powerful and greater evidence for the human level than the root wisdom. It is this root wisdom that allows you to discern the real from the false, distinguish right from wrong, know self, and recognize your Lord. Then you can hardly be cheated by teachings that lack the principles.

Moreover, wisdom is embedded in the human body like the sun in the world. The light of clarity is universal—there is nothing that is not illuminated. To abandon the clarity of the root wisdom is to betray the purport of the clear mandate and to fall into the unjust propagation of heresy. This is no different from putting aside the sun's light and illuminating things with a lamp.

You must wash your heart, cleanse your consideration, and be able to put aside meritorious name, which is like dew and lightning, and reject your plans to live like floating clouds. You should examine and peruse the ancient document of your own body. You must wipe and polish the clear mirror of your root body so that it will illuminate all of heaven and earth as if they were tiny dust motes, running through from antiquity until now in the twinkle of an eye. If your own body brings the true fruit to perfection, you will leap so far above that nothing will be beyond you. You will lead the myriad beings and continually establish the Creative and the Receptive. Only then will you not betray the great meaning of the Real Lord's creation of the human.

1.15. Husband and Wife

How great is the Non-Ultimate, the beginning of husband and wife, and the Great Ultimate, the origin of the myriad images!

The Non-Ultimate manifests nature and mandate, and without nature and mandate, there would be no spirits and demons. The Great Ultimate forms the two wings, and without the two wings, there would be no heaven and earth. The beginning of the Non-Ultimate and the origin of the Great Ultimate are summarized in one great human. What is called the Human Ultimate is the heart of this great human. This is what it means to say that the human is the spiritual of the myriad things.

The Human Ultimate embodies the principle of the Non-Ultimate and continues the function of the Great Ultimate. When he was transformed, he became husband and wife. Without husband and wife there would be no ruler and subject, no father and son. Hence in the true teaching marriage is the Real Lord's clear mandate, and those who disobey are rebellious.

Cold is unable to beget cold, and heat is unable to beget heat. Only cold and heat can beget cold and heat. This is the secret of the transformation of yin and yang.

Celibate men and women are a class who disobey the mandate of the Lord above and betray the five human relationships below. Although they have come from yin and yang, they foolishly think that they will rise above the common things, thereby ruining the root and stopping up the fountainhead. Ignorant and self-determining, they are no different from those who seek ice inside fire or want to drag the moon out of water. They take extinction and not begetting as a true act. Why then did the Lord of heaven and earth transform and beget man and woman and propagate mankind? This is as different from that as heaven is from earth. Which one do men of discernment regard as right?

They also say that the way of husband and wife is rooted in lustful desire, so it is not a righteous activity. But they too were begotten from lustful depravity. They warn people about killing living things, but then the kinds of animals would increase daily. If they stop people from marrying, the constant human bonds will be cut off. In the end their intention is to wipe out mankind and to hand over everything under heaven to birds and beasts. How can this be allowed?

Looking at great things like heaven and earth, humans and spirits, and looking at small things like insects and worms, grass and trees—both those that have feelings and those that do not—nothing has ever been successful[107] or gained benefit without obtaining yin and yang.

When the essential vital-energy of your own body is complete, yin and yang will be in harmony, but when it is increasing or declining, you will be ill. If you are lacking in either yin or yang, you will die. This proves that your body's yin and yang were imbalanced. How much more so is this the case when husband or wife is lacking!

Usually you see that celibate men and women are withered and rough in appearance, and the intentions of their hearts have a thousand divisions. Wrongful ideas grow luxuriantly, and affairs that lead to loss of chastity are many. All this is only because they have lost the order of yin and yang.

The principle of the true teaching is that the widow and the widower should not stay alone. Why? Because it is better to remarry with clear justification than to stay clean outside and lewd inside. Which is light and which heavy, which is right and which wrong? This is already clear without the need for discrimination.

It must be known, however, that these affairs can enable one person to be good and another to be evil. Why? The good person is true in sexual relations, and the evil person depraved in sexual relations. The Classic of Poetry says,

> The modest, retiring, virtuous young lady
> is a desirable match for the profound person.[108]

This is what is meant by "obtaining this and forgetting that." For example, if you eat a meal and drink soup until you are full, then, even if a rare delicacy is offered, you will pay no regard. Hence there must be people who are true in sexual relations. The Classic says, "The way of husband and wife is to protect[109] and guard each other."[110] This is the meaning.

---

107. Yang-Yu has "enjoyed" (*xiang* 享) instead of "been successful" (*heng* 亨).
108. Legge, *Classics* 4:1.
109. The 1922 edition has "seize" (*huo* 獲) instead of "protect" (*hu* 護).
110. Wang may have in mind the verse, "And of His signs is that He created for you, of yourselves, spouses, that you might repose in them, and He has set between you love and mercy" (Qur'an 30:21).

Sexual depravity and lewd talk have the utmost power to enable a person's evil. Thus it is said, "Look not at what is contrary to propriety; listen not to what is contrary to propriety."[111] In general, readily looking at a woman will easily move thoughts of lewdness and bring harm to real virtue. Much more so is this the case for those who have improper intimacy all day long. Should they not be warned?

Salt emerges from water and melts when it sinks into water. Man is born from woman and may be deluded by encountering woman. When water that is clear and pure at root is given to soil, it becomes mixed and turbid by uniting with soil. Men and women are both good, but when they come close to each other, their natures and feelings become disturbed.

This is why you should avoid depravity in sexual relationships. The Classic says, "Wild beasts can be tracked, and poisonous snakes can be tread upon, but men and women must not readily approach each other." Evil things harm only one's own body, but women can poison the gate of the heart and mandate. Beware, beware!

Liu Xiahui held a woman in his lap and was not distracted. He cannot be compared with the man from Lu, who closed the door so as not to receive [the woman].[112] Why was this? Xiahui was not distracted because he could guard himself. The man from Lu's not receiving is a sufficient law for all generations.

According to the teaching of Islam, a woman goes to her husband's house at marriage and comes out of the house when she dies. Even if her father and mother are in danger of dying, she would not herself dare to go home to see them in their illness without her husband's command. This is because of the rules for meeting relatives in person. When a girl reaches ten years of age, she no longer meets with men, even the closest relatives, except her father, mother, father's elder and younger brothers, brothers from the same parents, and brothers of her mother. Thus a profound person remains far from suspicion.

Long ago Fāṭima, the daughter of our Sage, accidentally encountered a blind man, so she hid. The Sage said, "Why did you hide?"

---

111. *Analects* 12:1.

112. The contrast between Xiahui and the man from Lu 魯 is found in *Kongzi jiaoyu* 孔子家語, *The Family Sayings of Confucius* 10.16, a supplement to the *Analects*. The man from Lu apologizes to the woman for not giving her shelter by saying that he does not have the virtue of Xiahui.

She said, "Although he could not see me, at root I should not see him."

If a man and a woman who are not relatives come face to face and look at each other while laughing and talking, how can this not be shameful?

The Sage said that once the leader of the devils approached him and said about himself, "The thing for which I use the least strength but which is quickly and greatly efficacious is simply that I make men and women encroach on each other by complimenting and flattering each other."

For example, when a man is awake and looks stealthily at the fragrant chamber of a woman, he will dream of sharing her pillow in conjugal harmony. Is this not how the devil brings them together? You must comply with and guard Islam, running toward truth and escaping deprivation, following good and leaving evil.

When the Creative and the Receptive have peaceful intercourse, the myriad things all pervade. The root of the creative transformation, the principle of issuing forth and nurturing, the prosperity of human relationships in expanding the way, the Three Bonds and Five Constants—all have revolved ceaselessly from antiquity. All are based on and established by husband and wife. But these principles cannot be explicated in their entirety.

1.16. Immortals and Spirits

Immortals are the heavenly immortals, and spirits are the spirits and demons. They are different in kind from the human.

The root body of the heavenly immortals was created from clear light, which is pure yang without yin. They dwell in heaven everlastingly, neither young nor old, neither male nor female. They have no likings and desires, they do not multiply or beget, doze or sleep, eat or drink, disobey or sin, tire or become lazy. Heaven is everlasting and earth long-lasting, and they will remain as long as the world. The nature of their spiritual exists forever without perishing, but they also will be resurrected.

The evil demons belong to pure yin and dwell everlastingly in the earth. They are depraved, so they are not upright. Only humans have both yin and yang completely, whereas half of the spirits are pure and half turbid. If humans and spirits are good, after death their spirituals will ascend to heaven and bond with the heavenly immortals, though they will not become heavenly immortals. If humans and spirits are evil, after death their souls will descend into the earth and become the neighbors of the evil demons, though they will not become evil demons.

Among the myriad classes, the heavenly immortals are the most spiritual of the formless things, but they are partial because of their weightlessness and purity. Among the myriad classes, the Human Ultimate is the most spiritual of the formed things, because he is complete and equipped with everything.

There are nine levels of humans and nine levels of heavenly immortals.[113] However, the heavenly immortals obtain only purity, whereas the Human Ultimate is fully embedded with forms and subtleties. It is because of this secret that the human is uniquely able to expand the way, and the way is assigned specifically to him. The human is the most complete and noble of heaven, earth, and the myriad things. All the heavenly immortals as well as the spirits and demons came into being because of the human.

Generally speaking the heavenly immortals in their nine levels have three degrees in their official duties. Their power can reach both the inside and the outside of things without probing and thinking, with spontaneity and thorough illumination. Those who have the upper office descend to transmit the clear mandate and to arrange life and death. Those who have the middle office make the various heavens revolve and regulate the coming and going of the sun and moon. Those who have the regular office control the wind, thunder, clouds, and rain and safeguard the great earth, the mountains and rivers, reaching the smallest things—insects and worms, grass and trees. If the crash of thunder does not frighten infants, and if scorpions and snakes do not encroach upon the blind, this is all connected to their protection and guarding. Without traveling they can reach all the affairs under heaven attained by the eyes' strength, and without discriminating they can attain all the affairs reached by the heart's thoughts. Their act of transmitting the Lord's mandate is as swift as the heart and eyesight. When they come down from heaven to earth, nothing whatsoever gets in the way. Each has its own governance and complies with the clear mandate, and none acts on its own.

---

113. Liu Zhi describes the nine levels of humans, drawing from both Rāzī and Nasafī, but he does not talk about levels of the angels. See especially diagram 1.6.

Although they are obedient followers in this way, they have no ascent or reward because they have no likes or desires. Let me explain this in detail: Their level is high, pure, and clean, but they are perfect only as part of the Human Ultimate. Were there no Human Ultimate, the heavenly immortals would have no function. Thus the nobility of the sages surpasses the heavenly immortals of the upper level, the nobility of the worthies surpasses the heavenly immortals of the middle level, and the nobility of true persons surpasses the heavenly immortals of the regular level. Although man has likes and desires, he also has the ability to discriminate the proper activity of likes and desires so as not to become their servants.

Someone asked: The Real Lord made the heavenly immortals His representatives in heaven and earth. Is this like a sovereign king who makes civil and military officials govern the country as his representatives?

I said: A sovereign king is certainly honored, but he belongs to mankind; his knowledge and discernment are no different from that of the multitudes. The Real Lord stays the same and His knowledge and power always exist, whether or not heaven, earth, and the myriad things exist. Man's limited knowledge and power are not like that, because the more they become differentiated, the more they become scattered; the more affairs increase, the more his spirit becomes weary.

A ruler must rely on the skills of civil and military officials, who work on his behalf. In contrast, when the Real Lord bestows power on the heavenly immortals to manage and guard the myriad things, He is not allocating His responsibility to them, but at root He is rather manifesting His honor. It is not that they assist His strength, but rather they specifically manifest His completeness. You should know this principle.

The spirits are beneath the Human Ultimate and the heavenly immortals. Their root body was created from the light of fire, which is turbid in the midst of purity and pure in the midst of turbidity, so they do not reach those two. They have life and death, male and female, likes and desires. They multiply and beget, drink and eat, sleep and doze. Some obey and some disobey, some are true and some depraved. They carry out endeavors and tasks, and they have their own affairs and occupations. Each has its own duty, but this is not like the public affairs of the heavenly immortals.

Among them is a huge spirit named Iblis, whose achievements surpassed that of the heavenly immortals. He had the spiritual penetration and power of his own willful intention. He excelled the various spirits and gained a position dwelling at the level of the immortals. But when an arrogant thought was suddenly born, the secret of resistance and disobedience was immediately revealed.

The Real Lord created the Human Ultimate with water and soil and took him to a dwelling place above the immortals and spirits. All the immortals and spirits received the mandate to pay courteous respect to the Human Ultimate. Only this huge spirit resisted the mandate and did not pay respect. He said, "I was made of fire, and the human was formed of soil. I am high and he is low. I am prior and he is posterior. How is it fair for me to pay respect to him?!"[114]

He did not know the Real Lord's mysterious secret or His subtle function of settling and arranging. Although flowers and leaves are prior to the fruit, in reality the fruit is nobler than flowers and leaves. Although fire is outwardly clear, inwardly and originally it is black and dark. Moreover, things can hardly be entrusted to it, because a spark of fire is able to burn away a mountain of a myriad *qing*,[115] quickly reducing it to ashes. Although soil is indeed outwardly turbid, its inward root is clear and luminous. Things can be entrusted to it, so one seed-grain increases to hundreds of thousands of millions, all of them turning into the beauty of fresh greens. The Real Lord has given it the mysterious secret of entrusting, so it has the great virtue of being able to receive benefits with humility.

When Iblis resisted the mandate, he led various spirits to rebel against the Lord and follow him. Most of the spirits refused to follow, and all those who did follow were blamed as evil demons. They fell down and were reduced to the ultimate low, never again to ascend on high. In the human world he is pleased when people do evil and envious when they do good. He is intentionally presumptuous about his own spiritual penetration and conveys his teachings by becoming manifest in bodies, speaking of himself as uniquely honored. The ignorant and deluded respect him and have faith in him. Those who are far from him establish images, and those who are near come to him face to face. Sometimes he commands the various demons to conceal themselves inside images and to speak wildly so as to perplex the multitudes. Sometimes he makes them shine or leave traces. The ignorant, those in drunken dreams, become fearful of calamity and

---

114. Reference to the Qur'anic verse in which Satan explains why he did not obey God's command to prostrate himself before Adam: "I am better than he: You created me of fire and You created him of clay" (38:76).

115. *Qing* 頃 is a unit of measure equivalent to about 7 hectares or 16.5 acres.

harm and they rely on him for protection, quickly forgetting the Pure and True. Then he stirs up recklessness among worldly people and they recognize him as the lord, and together they go home to the Earthly Dungeon. This is his utmost desire.

Someone said: The Real Lord created and transformed the Human Ultimate and he is nobler than the immortals and the spirits. Why is this evil demon allowed to act recklessly and to cause perplexity and confusion? Why is he not cut off and made to perish?

I said: There are three principles behind preserving him and not making him perish. One is that this makes it possible for man to back away from him and to be spared and forgiven by the Lord. Thus it is said that there are demons and devils in the world for many reasons and there is a subtle arrangement in this.

Second is that he makes it possible for people to manifest their achievements. Thus it is said that if the endeavor of bloody battle had no merit, no one could obtain appointment to nobility and the allotment of land.

Third is that he makes it possible to discriminate the real from the false. Even when the appearances of real and falsehood are the same, there are distinctive differences in the midst. Without his constant attacking and tormenting, hidden and concealed thoughts would be too difficult to fathom and measure. Many people deceive themselves by taking falsehood as good and then they deceive the people. Real gold is proven by fire, and human virtue becomes true by going through difficulties.

You must look into the hidden details, all of which are the subtle meanings of becoming human. At root mankind has two seeds: good and evil. Good seeds will bring forth good fruit, and evil seeds will certainly give rise to evil flowers. Without question good and evil do not change, but it is necessary for the seeds to be cultivated and tended to so that their contents may issue forth entirely. The true teaching and real transmission cultivate and tend to true people. Evil demons and heterodoxy nourish depraved people.

People who obtain the truth become sages and worthies. When they leave the world, they ascend to the Heavenly Country. People who lose the truth become deluded and rebellious. After death they fall down to the Earthly Dungeon and are jailed in a dark prison along with evil demons. Evil demons, however, are there at their own convenience, whereas sinful people are not able to come and go. This is like criminals in the world, restrained by bonds and chains and unable to enter and leave by themselves; even more so are those in the afterworld who were deeply and greatly deluded and rebellious.

At present there are ignorant and beclouded people who incoherently say that people can become immortals and spirits and live everlastingly in this world. But they are extremely perplexed. Why? Some of them talk about gathering the yin to strengthen the yang and nourishing cinnabar to refine the elixir—if one attains this, he will become immortal. Some talk about preserving spirit and nourishing vital-energy, inhaling dew drops and exhaling wind, and then being able to walk on air and abstain from food. They make people forget and reject the covenant of life and death and the just judgment at going home to the Real. Their sin is profound.

If it were indeed possible to live everlastingly in the world, how would this be different from a runaway child who does not go home? A subject who decides[116] to reject the original root is disloyal, and if he is a son, he has no filial piety. Much more so is the case of those self-determining fellows who rebel against and disregard the Real Lord of heaven, earth, and the myriad things, not wanting to go home to the origin. What kind of sin will that be!?

Moreover, the heavenly immortals were created from light, the spirits and demons from fire, and the Human Ultimate from soil. The origin of the creative transformation is not clear to these people, so they are incoherent in themselves and become confused concerning their own firm positions. They do not know that in fact the human is honored and noble, surpassing the myriad levels. How can they regard themselves as so trifling that they want to dwell in the ranks of the immortals and spirits?

1.17. The True Teaching

The Classic says, "The way of the true teaching is nothing but loyalty and sincerity."[117] When we investigate this principle, the meaning

---

116. Instead of "decide" (*pan* 判), Yang-Yu has "rebel against" (*pan* 叛).

117. This is probably a translation of Qur'an 3:19: "Surely the religion with God is the submission (*al-islām*)." Before modern times the word *islām* was rarely used as a proper name; classical texts analyze it rather as the first step in "the religion" (*al-dīn*), namely the surrender to God's command that is the necessary precondition for becoming fully human (see Murata and Chittick, *Vision*). Translating *islām* as "loyalty and sincerity" is not far from the typical explanations found in the sources.

of *true* is to be real, eternal, and just. The meaning of *loyalty* is to be devoted to the Unique One alone. The meaning of *sincerity* is to be pure and clean without taint.

Some go too far and speak of "silent perishing" and "empty nonbeing." Others do not go far enough and speak only of what is before their eyes. How can you say that these are true?

The Real Lord established the origin of the true teaching at the very beginning of creation. He ordered the heavenly immortals to descend to the human ancestor Adam and to transmit the clear mandate to him: Adam should represent Him to establish the ultimate and to open up and elevate the utmost way. First the Constant Bonds[118] were established, and then the teaching came into being, giving the mandate that people should have genuine faith in nothing but the Real Principle and exert efforts in nothing but true tasks. It prohibited heterodoxy, base acts, and affairs that violate righteousness. If anyone betrays this and walks on some other, false path, not only will he be unable to decrease in transgression, but also he will advance and increase in error. This is like someone facing east who wants to go west. The more haste he makes, the farther away he will go.

When those who have the will to cultivate virtue and establish good do not rely on the true teaching, they may exhaust the strength of their hearts, but this will not be sufficient to conquer the self and go home to the Real. This would be like a fish net, which is unable to fend off the cold.

Thus followers of the true teaching speak about the beginning in order to know where they came from. They speak about the end in order to wake up to this body's final resting place. And they speak about the laws so that these will guide them to the utmost principles of becoming human.

For countless generations before and countless generations after, the principles found in the universe have been and will be as clear as arranged dishes of meat and fish. There is no doubt about them whatsoever, but they certainly cannot be established by human strength. If you constantly examine the classic books and the histories by the various scholars, you will hardly see and hear matters concerning

---

118. The Constant Bonds (*gangchang* 綱常) are the Three Bonds and the Five Constants.

the original beginning and the essential end. As for talk about the real traces of ancient peoples before the three dynasties, that is vague and doubtful.

You should know that ever since the begetting of mankind, only reliance on the real transmission has been trustworthy, whether people were close to the origin or far from it. How can someone deduce it by depending on principles? In this country you can depend on the records in the books of history from the Five Emperors onward, but before that there is nothing to be examined.[119] Thus we have the theory that there were tens of thousands of years between the time of the first differentiation of the chaos and the time of Fu Xi. Examination easily shows this to be unreasonable and uncanonical.

During the time of the Five Emperors, people and things were still scattered. At the time of Tang of the Shang dynasties, when less than a thousand years had passed,[120] people and things had become extremely crowded. How could it be that the people and things begotten over hundreds of thousands of years not be as many as those of several hundred years? When we carefully examine the explanation of tens of thousands of years, is there sufficient evidence?

When we examine the sources transmitted by the classics of the true teaching, these give reasons why the regions came to be demarcated and truth came to be divided from falsehood. From the time of the human ancestor Adam, people and things prospered for three thousand years inside the boundaries of the Tianfang country, with years of abundance and success. Some officious people talked among themselves and said, "The people of our country are multiplying daily and as a matter of course will be separated and scattered in the future. Why do we not make bricks and quarry stones so as to construct one great city and establish a high tower, the peak of which will reach the Milky Way? Thus we will display talented people's prosperity in this time. Will that not be beautiful?"

All agreed with these words, for they had lived in peace and forgotten danger. They began to create the tower without cease. The Real Lord knew the people's proud thoughts and their desire to complete the task. They all spoke in the same tongue and had the same

---

119. The Five Emperors are said to have ruled from about 2850 to 2200 BCE.
120. Tang 湯 overthrew the Xia 夏 dynasty and founded the Shang 商 dynasty in around 1600 BCE.

heart, so everyone wanted to do this absurd task and would not cease until they finished. It was necessary that their tongues be made different and confused so that they would no longer have one heart and would stop what they were doing. Hence He gave the mandate to the heavenly immortals to attack and destroy the tower. It broke into three pieces, and the sound made the earth tremble. Mountains fell and rivers broke open, and all the myriad kinds were frightened. The people were faint and giddy, and when they came to themselves, the tongues of the multitudes quickly changed into several kinds. After this each kind gradually changed until it became one thousand branches. Thus we can know why we are different in this eastern land.

The work of the high tower was stopped only because the languages were different and the hearts distinct. People became suspicious of each other and could not be united. From then on they became close to those who shared the same tongue and migrated to other realms from near to far. This is why they reached everywhere.[121]

Thus the people of ancient times became differentiated under heaven, but their root origin was the Tianfang country. At the time of the differentiation of the tongues, they were located twenty thousand *li* west of the eastern land. After several hundred years of moving their abodes, they gradually began to reach this land. According to the records of the Tianfang country, that time was the same as the time of Shennong and Fu Xi. Also at this time people came together and established other countries outside Tianfang.

When the real records of the various countries in the four directions are examined, there is nothing before the time of the moving of the abodes. As for the explanations that are now and then given about that earlier time, they are nothing but additions to make up for the deficiencies and omissions, not the real record.

Those who had the same tongue as Fu Xi accompanied each other and moved to the eastern land. They began to reestablish language and characters and opened up the new territory, creating and erecting everything in their own manner. The other three directions were also like this. It is not that the former people were totally ignorant and began to establish things when they arrived here. The vari-

---

121. There is no mention of the Tower of Babel in the Qur'an, but historians like Ṭabarī (d. 923) make reference to it (*History* 2:22). Given the length of Wang's account, he is more likely to have heard it from Christian sources, such as the Jesuits who were active in Nanjing during his time.

ous regions were gradually moving farther from Tianfang, but at this time they still had similarities with Islam. They were serving only one supreme ruler and never had two Ways or the heresies of the Daoists and Buddhists.

In later time people longed for and remembered the mercy of parents, and with gratitude they looked up to the virtue of the ruler and the kindness of great people. Finally they made portraits and images of them, burning incense to pay respect and to display the thoughts of loyalty and filial piety. The time of antiquity was so far away that they lost the intention of their ancestors and did not know that they were making images of dead people, foolishly calling them spirits and spirituals. This is why the chief devil mounted on the people's distraction and was easily able to put forth evil doctrines. Thus the heterodoxies of the immortals, the buddhas, the demons, and the spirits prospered.

Moreover, at root the sages, worthies, immortals, and buddhas came from yin and yang. Leaving life and entering death are received only from the Real Lord's creative transformation. All that is created is related to human portions and has nothing to do with the Original Being. Success and failure, gain and loss, do not rely on people's free will. How could they abruptly establish Ways and teachings in order to govern the world?

First you must know that the Original Being is the Real Lord, the true teaching is the real transmission, and our bodies are of delicate subtlety. Only then can the heart's intention be pure and real and the human way begin to be firm. If this is put aside, what sort of benefit can come by other routes?

When jade and stone are mixed together, it is impossible to distinguish their differences without clear eyes. When the true and false stand together, how can the real transmission be obtained without true awareness? I can only hope that the true and profound person will pay attention to this matter.

1.18. The True Learning

The Sage said, "The clear mandate for the man and woman of the true teaching is to study and learn."[122]

---

122. Translation of the hadith, "The search for knowledge is incumbent on every Muslim."

Learning is not that you learn in vain. It must be for the sake of action. You certainly cannot act without learning. Why? Learning without action is like a flower without fruit, and action without learning is like a house without a gate.

You should know that you cannot further your learning of what you do not know if you have not compliantly acted upon what you have already learned. Not only will you not attain what you have not yet attained, but you will also harm what you have already learned. This is not the meaning of true learning.

True learning means not to consider oneself intelligent or to follow self-nature, but to take the Honorable Classic as first ancestor and the sage teaching as wet-nurse. There is no learning outside this meaning.

If you abandon compass and square, you can still make circles and rectangles, but the people of the world will not put them into practice. If you abandon weights and scales, you may make only the smallest mistakes, but the people of the world will not accept. Why? Because someone's self-determination alone can never be trusted. Only the firm rule can be put into action publicly. The way of Islam is the midmost, utmost truth, without increase or decrease, alteration or change. It is the same everywhere, in heaven above and earth below, inside and outside the six directions, from ancient times until now, because it is not based on self-determination.

The root of establishing oneself is not outside of learning, which is like a compass with which you pass over the ocean, or the accurate marking-lines of a great master. Without a compass, how can you discriminate among north, south, east, and west? Without accurate marking-lines, how can you settle long and short, bent and straight? In no way can you be without them.

The law of the teaching is that man and woman, prince and subordinate, old and young, must all follow the way of learning right up to the point when the body actually and fully comes to its end.[123] One should not interrupt it for even a day, for the way of doing good has no end. Someone may say that he has reached it, but in fact he has not. Someone may say that he has progressed to the utmost good, but in fact he has come to a halt between good and evil.

---

123. Reference to the well-known hadith, "Search for knowledge from the cradle to the grave!"

Hopefully those on the path of learning will first discern between truth and falsehood and have the root intention of why they must learn. Otherwise they will toil in the path without knowing where it will take them. Some learners study for the sake of great erudition, but this is vain knowledge; some for the sake of selling, but this yields base profit; some so that people will know them, but this is crooked diligence; some for the sake of admonishing people, and this is humaneness and righteousness; and some to govern themselves, and this is the great wisdom. Thus the highest aspiration in learning is to learn only for the sake of recognizing self, and this is the True Way.

The meaning of the True Learning is not simply to emulate fully the conduct of those who formerly gained awareness or to record their writings. Within it is also certainly found the learning of the true awakening[124] of your own body as well as the learning of thorough understanding by consulting and observing heaven, earth, and the myriad things. A man of wisdom will never suffer from a lack of classics and masters, because his masters and classics will be heaven, earth, and the myriad things.

The meaning of the affair of this learning has great importance. Truth and falsehood, profit and loss, large and small, high and low—it contains all of them completely. Here I have no time to expound the other learnings in detail, so I refer only to the True Learning.

The True Learning is three: the great learning, the middle learning, and the constant learning. The great learning is going home to the Real. The middle learning is clarifying the heart. The constant learning is cultivating the body.

You can recognize the Lord by going home to the Real, you can see nature by clarifying the heart, and you can govern the country by cultivating the body.

The learning of recognizing the Lord is like nature and mandate, for without nature and mandate, people would not be alive. The learning of clarifying the heart is like clothing and food, for without clothing and food, people would surely die. The learning of cultivating the body is like physicians and medicine, for without physicians and medicine, illness would not be cured. One must not lack any of these.

---

124. In place of "awakening" (*wu* 悟), Yang-Yu has "feelings" (*qing* 情).

Generally the people of the world are ill because they are forever drowned in possessions, lust, and reputation. If someone is still deluded by lust after knowing the learning, how can he be courageous? If he is still arrogant, how can he be humble? If he is still perplexed by unrighteous possessions, how can he be pure? If he is still drowning in wealth and nobility, how can he follow the way of virtue? If he is still murmuring against the Lord and blaming others, how can he comply with the mandate? He who knows his own evil-doing will perceive the germ of good and may easily enter into virtue.

People today honor the other learnings and thereby forget the Real. They study hollow literature so as to gloss over their own faults. If this is indeed learning and literature, how sad it is! Ships are for the sake of carrying things, and literature for the sake of delivering over to the way. If a ship does not carry things, it is certainly unworthy, and if literature does not deliver over to the way, it is certainly void.

Someone who penetrates the way will always be good at literature, but one who penetrates literature does not necessarily have the way. When literature and the way are in balance, that is the True Learning. When the Creative and the Receptive are dark and obscure, the bright light of sun and moon needs to come back. When the heart-ground is ambiguous, it must be opened up thoroughly with the True Learning.

Although the real knowledge of the True Learning is rooted in the profound purport of the Heavenly Classic and the real transmission of the Utmost Sage, it must issue forth from the fountainhead of nature and mandate. Having intelligence, a good memory, extensive reading, and wide experience and knowledge is not sufficient. A precious mirror illuminates forms, but it will not obtain bright light without wiping and polishing, though the bright light exists at root without polishing. In many people of the world the heart's secret is not alive, so they vainly read a myriad volumes of classic literature. They do not plant seeds in their own fields, but they wander around and pick up dregs from other people. How can they learn real knowledge?

The Classic says, "Real knowledge rests in one point."[125] When someone obtains the learning of this one point, it will never be exhausted even if it is put to use time after time. This is what is

---

125. This may be a reference to a saying attributed to 'Alī: "Knowledge is one point made many by the ignorant" (*al-'ilm nuqṭa kaththarahā al-juhalā'*).

meant by the saying that a pond will be pure and clean when it has a fountainhead of living water flowing into it.

When a true person explains the large, heaven and earth fit inside. When he explains the small, a dust mote will be outside. What is inside the dust mote can enwrap heaven and earth. What is outside heaven and earth can be enclosed in the dust mote. The alterations and transformations are unfathomable, but whether they are large or small, their cause is one.

You should know that just as the True Learning is vast, so also evil practices are great. Given the general illness of the world's people, you cannot fail to observe this. Why? Right and wrong are upside down, real and false are confused.

A profound person is such that inside he is clear and decisive, but outside he appears to have neither knowledge nor power. A small person is such that outside he is talented and eloquent, but inside he is truly ignorant and dull. Those who have an excessive fondness for thinking are like wild streams, finding their pleasure in teaching others. Those who day by day make essential progress in studies are not ashamed to ask questions. A wise man examines and inquires with an empty heart, for how can the ocean of learning be exhaustively measured?

The Sage said, "My greatest fear for those of the true teaching is that their learning will not correspond."

The people asked, "What is not corresponding?"

He said, "Someone who has the tongue of the knowers and the heart of the ignorant."

A worthy said, "There is a class of learners like flies and mosquitoes. They do not seek for the clear light of the True Way, nor do they tread in the reality of the evidence. They follow only sounds and scents in the air."

Know that people's seeing, hearing, smelling, and speaking are lodged in eye, ear, nose, and tongue. Their functions, however, are not the same. Why? If the heart follows self-nature, it will not observe the real and the false, so it will not discriminate between worthy and stupid. If the eyes depend on the function of the ears, which can only hear sounds, they will not differentiate between black and white. Even when people say that they are searching for worthies, they will regard as right those who are the same as themselves and will regard as wrong those who are different from themselves. They surely will not become worthies and they will want to regard the worthies as the same as themselves. This is like someone who wants to unite the illumination of the sun and the moon with the light of a firefly. It will never happen.

Ancient peoples regarded the known as that which they knew and the unknown as that which they did not know. This indeed is the secret of coming to know. People today do not know, but they do not consider themselves unknowing. Rather, they regard themselves as knowing, so they remain unknowing all their lives. This is mere self-deception.

If those who become teachers envy those of superior talent and do not share their learning with others, they will not think that the ground of their teaching is to mold and edify people. When those who become scholars go fishing for name and praise and do not examine and seek, they will not awaken to the utmost principle of learning. They will be like a deaf man and a blind man meeting in a hall. Though face to face, they remain as far apart as a thousand *li*. They do not know that the gate of learning is prepared in the mutual assistance and inquiry of teacher and disciple. It is this that is actually beneficial.

Even if there is material for large beams, how can they be completed without an ax? Even if there are refined and skillful hands, how can they alone create something without precious stones and rare gems?

In ten houses there will surely be one loyal and faithful person. How can it be possible that there be no one who knows himself in the universe? But you should not share subtle words with the ignorant and confused. Rather, share elucidation of principles with those who have achieved great clarity.

Someone who should talk but does not talk is like water held back from a precious tree. Someone who should not talk but does talk is like fresh dew soaked up by creeping weeds. If masters are like this, how can you hope to share with them in advancing your studies?

Someone with high aspiration will go against the flow and search for the fountainhead. He will be willing to dive deeply after the pearl, seeking clear indications with diligence, and he will face up to going home.

Someone else will have the urge to put himself among the masters, concealing the subtlety of Islam and glossing over the ignorance of his own heart. When he meets dull and dark people, he will confuse and perplex them with foolish explanations, and when he encounters those with superior talent, he will imitate the general direction and make excuses.

Know that those who conceal others' intelligence with both hands definitely do not know that they themselves are already in the shade. My hope is that good teachers will open up the mysterious subtlety of the true teaching and remove the obstructions that block the heart and breast. Then good learners will not be able to stop even if they want to. Let them go home together to the utmost truth in the midst of the great. Perhaps that is possible.

1.19. *Huihui*: The Returning Returners

How great are the returning returners, the mirrors of Islam! Heaven and earth are their mold, and the myriad things support them to complete the forms of the mirrors. Cleaning and polishing by the way's teaching bring forth the light of the returners' mirrors.

Those who return have two lights, one for the return of the body, the other for the return of the heart. The body has two returns, one circling back to return, and the other going home by leaving.[126]

The body circles back to return because of its root. The four greats [the elements] perfected its form, and it was united with the two companions, yin and yang. Turning around, it lodged in the father's essence and the mother's blood. Nature and mandate begot metal and pulled together the black lead of the corporeal body, uniting the high and low without differentiation. This is the root cause for the unmixed real to become dispersed and disconnected

Liking to eat and sleep belongs to the action of horses and cows, and relying on the strong and oppressing the weak are the function of tigers and wolves. You need to restore the four natures[127] to their original purity and cleanliness so that they will once again give light and clear away the causes in this world; thereby you will return to the Original Being as you were before.

---

126. Islamic texts commonly refer to these two returns as voluntary and compulsory. The first is to return to God by following the religious command, and the second is to return by way of death and resurrection, which are necessitated by the creative command.

127. By the four natures Wang seems to have in mind the mineral, plant, animal, and human natures.

Once you overcome this barrier, you will begin to perfect the human way. This is like a piece of jade contained in a stone, or gold concealed by sand. The precious jade will come forth once the stone is cleaned away, and the pure gold will appear once the sand is removed. If you do not awaken to this secret, you will not understand what should be accepted and what should be rejected and you will also disavow advantage and disadvantage.

The return of going home by leaving is that we came from somewhere in the Former Heaven and will leave for somewhere in the Latter Heaven. We came, but how did we come? We will leave, but how will we leave?

Know that the time of coming was when the seed was planted in this body's ground. The time of going home will be the issuing and disclosing, when each person harvests both good and evil. The seed must be drenched and nourished with the water of the True Way; it must never be nourished and watered with your own selfishness. That which is drenched and nourished with the water of the True Way will give the fruit of Islam. That which is nourished and watered with your own selfishness will blossom with the flowers of error and falsehood. Hence great caution is necessary in going home to return.[128]

The return of the heart is also two. When people live in this world, all of them love wealth and nobility and hate poverty and meanness, but then they come to be tainted by these two affairs. Foolishly giving rise to anger and greed, they fall into the ocean of suffering and quickly forget their original beginning. They may suddenly wake up and become aware that profit and name are like dreams and that the body is not their own possession, not to speak of things outside it.

When they think again about the Origin, they will quickly search for the path to go home. They will mold feelings and desires to act in keeping with the principles of heaven. They will transform the myriad images to take them back to emptiness and nonbeing. This is the return of the true heart. This is the very moment of seeing Thusness,[129] perfecting the Great Ultimate, opening the Gate of All Subtleties, and attaining the way of being and nonbeing. This is what

---

128. In other words, since there will be a compulsory return, one should prepare oneself by means of the voluntary return.

129. "Thusness" renders *zhenru* 眞如 (literally "the real as such"), the standard translation of Sanskrit *tathātā*, a Buddhist term designating things as they truly are.

is meant by saying that no one can advance beyond the True Real, above which is nothing.

If you want to advance one more step, you must tear away the curtain of Thusness, pierce and crush the circle of the Great Ultimate, and break and smash the Gate of All Subtleties. Then you will go beyond the way of the Three Teachings. Outside this way is a house that people do not discern, for they are searching leisurely for the nest inside the way. If you can once again obtain the nest and arrive at this house, you will certainly return to the no-heart. When you return to the no-heart, the fountainhead of the mandate will become manifest and you will attain the Non-Ultimate. When you embody the Non-Ultimate and recognize the Real Lord, that is the utmost return.

Most people today falsely take on the name *huihui* and do not devote their attention to the reality. When asked about the principles, they know nothing at all. Are they not ashamed before the meaning of *huihui*?

At the time when the Utmost Sage was returning to the mandate, he gave this command to the worthies: "Take my robe and hand it over to Uways."[130]

They asked, "Who is Uways?"

He said, "Inquire after him and you yourselves will find out."

By and by they complied with the command to inquire and search. They reached him in a mountain field. They gathered together and asked, "Why did you not visit the Sage?"

He said, "I and the Sage are together such that there is not the space of one breath between us. What do you mean by not visiting? When you were together with the Sage, you saw only his beard and eyebrows. How could you have seen his real original face?"

1.20. Bearing Witness

The true teaching of Islam is that the gate of human virtue demands first to recognize the Lord by saying one sentence: "I bear witness."[131]

---

130. Uways Qaranī lived in Yemen during the time of the Prophet and is said to have become a Muslim through an invisible rapport with him. The anecdote here may be based on 'Aṭṭār's account in *Tadhkirat* 20ff. (*Memorial* 53ff.).

131. This of course is a reference to the Shahadah, the first of Islam's five pillars, which is to say, "I bear witness that there is no god but God and I bear witness that Muhammad is God's messenger."

Why? Because recognizing the Lord necessitates recognizing self. When you recognize self, you will actually be able to recognize the Lord.

Your own being is the words and sentences of all the subtleties of the heavenly suchness. It is the ancient document of the mysterious secret of the creative transformation. When people look back at the ancient document of their own body and read carefully its words and sentences, how intimate and simple it is! If you put this aside and follow another plan, it will always be a wrong path.

Thus it is that this one sentence, "I bear witness," has awakened people from drunken dreams from ancient times until now. Without regard to location in the Former Heaven, it talks directly about the origin of what we are at present after the interaction and coupling of yin and yang and of our father's essence and our mother's blood. But who after all bestows and grants the causes and effects of the bodily apertures and spiritual clarity?

If we suppose that things come into being from emptiness and that there is no Lord Ruler at the origin, then everywhere can beget wombs and eggs, and mountains and hills can produce fish and the scaled. That would be like a house that does not wait for the lord of the house to create it, but, all by itself, suddenly rises up as rooms and corridors. That will never happen.

If the abilities of father and mother were the basis, then they would beget male and female as they pleased, many or few according to their willful intention. Begetting or not begetting, likes and dislikes, large or small—all would accord with their own wills. If these relied on one's own self-transformation, there would be no calamity and harm whatsoever. One's body would exist everlastingly, wealth and nobility would never alter, and progeny would have everlasting well-being. But since the creation of heaven and earth, who has been able to avoid passing over the crossroad between life and death? Who can preserve forever wealth and nobility, influence and power? You need to observe the details, for nothing at all depends on self.

Even though the human is more spiritual than the myriad things, who can come to be by himself? If we suppose that there is something that can come to be by itself, then there must be a self beforehand to be regarded as the ancestor of this self-creation. If there is already a self, then recreating the self is useless. If there is no self beforehand, then the one who makes the self will not be the self. Hence things cannot come to be by themselves.

Once a Buddhist monk had an audience with a king in a country of the true teaching. The king inquired about the original beginning of the creative transformation. The monk said that ever since beginningless time, the stillness moves when it reaches its ultimate, and movement becomes still when it reaches its ultimate. One movement and one stillness—each is the other's root. Just as flowers in the sky arise and perish, so also life and death turn and revolve. All are so in the self-so.

The king could not submit to this, so he called for his chief minister, but it took a long time for him to arrive. The king asked him why he came so late. The minister said, "My dwelling is north of the river, and a bridge had suddenly collapsed, so it was impossible for me to cross the stream. Then I saw an empty boat, no one poling it, crossing back and forth by itself. I waited until it unloaded on the other side and came back. Then I got on the ship to cross the river. That is why I came late."

The monk said, "He is trying to make fools of us. Who has ever heard of a ship crossing by itself without someone in control?"

The minister said, "If a ship without someone in control cannot cross by itself, how then can it be as you say, that heaven, earth, and the myriad things come to be by themselves without a Lord of creative transformation?"

He was ashamed and could not answer.

It is not only the greatness of heaven and earth, but also all the kinds of living things, whether begotten from wombs, eggs, or seeds, that surely had first ancestors that came before. Only then can there be these three. When you extend this to the first ancestor of every kind, you will never find a kind that came to exist by its own power at root. Before the things existed, there had to be a reason why the kinds of things were completely different. Only then could the myriad things be created and begotten.

Although a mirror can be shaped by a mold, it still relies on the ability of the workman. Who can say that it is the mirror's mold that shaped it and not the workman? Only when you take this as a clear proof will you begin to awaken to the Real Lord who transforms and begets your body. You will sweep away entirely the wrong transmissions with their many errors.

You will not recognize the mysterious secret of the Lord until you look carefully into your own allotment. Who but the Real Lord could have arranged and laid out the delicate subtlety of your own body? How sad it is that the ignorant and dull possess the utmost principle of their own body but do not investigate it thoroughly. They steal the dregs of others and regard them as jewels. They read widely from the ancients and the moderns, but what does that have to do with the root body? This false literature puts on a show, but how does it benefit their own nature and mandate?

If there were not the mysterious purport of the Heavenly Classic and the real transmission of the Utmost Sage, who would be able to discern and open up to the utmost principle of this ancient document? Only by these kinds of heavenly characters, which do not belong to voice and sound and are not similar to written characters, will you recognize the Real Lord who has no similars, standing beyond howness.

Know that it is possible to recognize self by means of talk and the elaboration of words, but at root it is impossible to recognize the Lord by letters and words. If you could come to understand the mysterious subtlety by seeing and hearing, this would be no different from storing the ocean's water in a cup. Though it is difficult to talk about the Real One's subtlety, if someone attains this subtlety, then heaven will flow by itself and become manifest in the measure of his knowledge and in keeping with his activity. But if he attains this, he will surely do so on the basis of realized practice.

Realized practice means to comply with the clear mandate of the Real Lord and to follow the real transmission of the Utmost Sage. On the inside it is to clarify the heart's nature and to manifest once again the origin of the mandate, and on the outside it is to regulate and cultivate the body and to differentiate ritually between Lord and subject.

This is why, when someone overcomes himself by a fraction, he increases the real by a fraction. Once the self has been dissolved completely, the subtle clarity is suddenly disclosed. Without relying on the elixir of the true teaching, how can anyone reform his own self-nature? Once the causes and effects of nature are eliminated, the light of the Great Nature will be clarified. Once you have arrived at this ground, you will know that heaven, earth, and the myriad things are solely for the sake of one person. You will attain the actual recognition that the self is the beginning of heaven and earth and the mother of the myriad things.

Today everyone recognizes wrongly that this one grain, which is the seed of the Non-Ultimate, is the True Real above which is nothing. Suddenly they have forgotten the Real Lord, who planted it. How sad!

Book Two

2.1. The Five Constants

The Five Constants of the true teaching, which are the clear mandate of the Real Lord, are five affairs: remembrance, giving, abstaining, worship, and assembly.

The human outside and inside accompany each other in color and subtlety. They are interconnected and secured with a lock. The lock has five springs: eyes, ears, nose, tongue, and body. The springs can be undone only with the five keys that are the Five Constants. Once the lock is opened, you will penetrate everything as a matter of course, and no doubts will remain. If the lock remains shut, you will stay in a drunken dream.[1]

The *first* of the Five Constants is called remembrance and is of two sorts: the remembrance of intention and the remembrance of praise.

The remembrance of intention is constantly to remember and not to forget the Real Lord. Forgetting is to lose the heart, and remembering is to have the heart of humaneness. Death is lodged in forgetting, but forgetting itself is not death. Humaneness is lodged in remembrance, but remembrance itself is not humaneness. Remembrance means to remember going home to one's homeland and to long for and look to Islam. Forgetting means to forget the memory of one's native place and to rebel against and disobey the original beginning. Remembrance is the root of the myriad actions, so all affairs issue forth from it. The sincerity of one remembrance can pierce metal and

---

1. The analogy of the five senses as a lock to be opened by five keys, namely the Five Pillars of Islamic practice, is based on Rāzī, *Mirṣād* 163–64 (*Path* 180–81).

stone, surpass the ancient and the modern, and enwrap heaven and earth. How can one not be careful? To forget the fountainhead and be self-determining is to be transformed into ignorant and deluded. To preserve the real and overcome self is to be established as sage and worthy. Body and heart, household and country, sage and ordinary, depraved and true—their tight connection lies in this one initiative, so its merits and demerits are surpassingly great.

The remembrance of praise means to praise and be grateful for the overflowing mercy of both the Real Lord and the Utmost Sage. Why? Because body and life come from the creative transformation of the Real Lord, clothing and food are granted by the Real Lord's solicitude, the myriad things support and tend to the nature of your spiritual, and heaven and earth cover and carry the bodily form. Are these not overflowing mercy? In the former heaven and earth the Utmost Sage is the root suchness of the Non-Ultimate and the fountainhead and root of the human. In the middle heaven and earth he governs and establishes the human way, which has been the firm principle from ancient times until now. In the latter heaven and earth when everything returns to the mandate and goes home to the origin, all will depend on his pulling and promoting. How can you not praise him? When drinking water, you must think of the fountainhead and not forget the root. This is the humaneness of recalling and remembering the true teaching.

The *second* of the Five Constants is giving. There are two kinds of giving: giving self and giving things. Giving self is to give one's body, heart, wisdom, and intelligence to Lord, parents, ruler, and empire. Giving things is to give the various sorts of things, like money, silk, and grain, to those who live in danger and poverty, saving them from hunger and cold. This is why in the way of Islam no one is left uncovered, no one needs to beg, and no one has an unkempt appearance. There is no difference between kinfolk and distant, no difference between near and far, no difference between ancient and now. Travelers under heaven need not spend any money at all, since all those who live surrounded by the four seas are siblings. One's body and life, money and things, are granted by the Lord's solicitude. Things received from solicitude should be given away so as to reach fellow humans who are undergoing dangers and difficulties. Thereby you will not betray the mercy of solicitude from above, and you will love all those whom He loves here below. This is the meaning of giving in the true teaching.

The *third* of the Five Constants is worship. There are two kinds of worship: the propriety-worship of the Real Lord and the propriety-worship of ruler and parents. These are the propriety[2] of the self-so. The due degree is called propriety, and indeed propriety is the root of being human.

When we look at other teachings, all disavow the root and forget the fountainhead. This is like a fugitive who flees his native town. When he faces great hunger and cold and sees someone, he immediately salutes him, but he does not know the outcome. Is this propriety?

The great way of Islam is to worship and respect the Real Lord, who is pure, clean, formless, and without directions and positions. Each act of worship unites the proprieties of the seven heavens. Each has twelve clear mandates in accordance with the allotments of the twelve mansions, which are the twelve heavenly principles that embody the number of months in a year. When united, they make the twenty-four divisions of the year, and when differentiated, they measure one revolution of heaven.

The propriety-worship is five times a day, and its principle embraces each of the five agents. When a person bows once and puts his head on the ground twice, his body is an image of the everlasting revolution of heaven's wheel along with the ascent and descent of sun and moon. The twenty-eight sage acts in succession are the tiers of clouds and stars.[3] When the five members of the body touch the ground, the forehead is facing straight ahead with dignity. This is the root of propriety.

Someone said: The Real Lord is the utmost honorable. Why does He hope for man's worship?

I said: The Honorable Classic says, "Your Real Lord is the Unique One, without guise."[4] This one verse aroused people who

---

2. Yang-Yu has "principle" (*li* 理) instead of "propriety" (*li* 禮).

3. The twenty-eight sage acts refer to the twenty-eight movements that are embraced by the four-cycle ritual prayer (each cycle includes standing, bowing, rising to a standing position, prostrating, rising to the knees, prostrating, and rising to the knees). By the tiers of clouds and stars Wang may have in mind the twenty-eight levels of the cosmos—fourteen on the arc of descent and fourteen on the arc of ascent. Liu Zhi puts them together in diagram 2.5.

4. Probably a reference to the verse, "Nothing is as His likeness" (42:11).

had been deluded for a thousand ages from their drunken dream. It refuted the fallacies of silent perishing and empty nonbeing and swept away and rejected evil and false images. They came to know only the Real Lord, the Pure and Clean. Moreover, the people of the world have never considered it strange to respect and serve heaven or to worship and remember buddhas. All the more should this be so with the Real Lord, who created and transformed heaven and earth, man and spirits. When someone dwells in the human level and has received Islam, how could he not worship and respect Him?

Nonetheless, there are two principles in worship: On the Lord's part, merciful solicitude directs the people toward the truth and makes them reject evil. On man's part, worship with propriety prevents forgetfulness of the Root and ingratitude toward Him. You should know these meanings.

Here merciful solicitude is of two sorts: one is that of principles, the other that of forms.

The merciful solicitude of principles is that the form of the human level was perfected from the principles of grass and trees, flyers and walkers. In order to go home and return from the human level and position, man must once again go beyond the natures and desires of flyers and walkers, grass and trees. You must rectify remembrance in the heart's intention and you must toil with the body's muscles and bones. Only then can you reach the original beginning. This is why no one has ever become a sage or a worthy without suffering and difficulty. Thus you must pay back whatever has been borrowed, you must go back and return to the original beginning, and you must go beyond the crossroads of the myriad beings. Only then will you attain the origin, the Non-Ultimate.[5]

---

5. By saying that people must pay back what has been borrowed, Wang is alluding to a practical consequence of returning to the One. In the descending stages of the Former Heaven the human essence moves from simplicity and unity toward composition and multiplicity. As it returns to God in the ascending stages of the Latter Heaven it discards the multiple components of the self. This is to say that in order to become manifest in the world, the human spiritual essence must successively assume the forms of animals, then plants, and then minerals; in going back to the origin, it must discard these forms in the reverse order. For a nuanced exposition of the stages of assuming and discarding forms, see Chittick, "Qūnawī, Neoplatonism, and the Circle of Ascent."

When you stand in service in the midst of the propriety-worship, your head is toward heaven and your feet on the ground. This is the human guise that surpasses all things, so you should be grateful for the mercy of spiritual nobility. When you bow, your back is up, and it comes and goes at your own willful intention. This is the guise of the flying and walking kinds, so you should be grateful for the mercy of turning and moving. When you prostrate yourself and put your head on the ground and then move from low to high, this is the guise of grass and trees, so you should be grateful for the mercy of begetting and growing. When you sit on your knees at the end of the worship, having completed the various affairs, this is the guise of the origin, so you should be grateful for the mercy of the original beginning. Indeed, this is what is meant by the saying that you came by this path, and there is no other path by which to go home.[6]

This is sufficient to see the Real Lord's solicitude. He gave the mandate of propriety-worship to the people, clearly pointing out the principles of going home and returning, lest they forget the root origin. If you do not awaken to its secret and consider this too difficult, how will you know the merciful solicitude of the Real Lord?

The merciful solicitude of forms is that human beings living in the world are never exempt from disobedience and mistakes. Thus the proprieties of the seven heavens were united and made into one rite of worship such that each time of propriety-worship embraces all the endeavors of the myriad kinds, thereby letting people redeem their mistakes and errors.

The rite of propriety on man's part is also two: the principle of propriety and the form of propriety. What is called the principle of propriety is that the heart maintains respect and awe such that this principle issues forth and appears from the heart. This is like red and green inside a seed, which by themselves issue forth to the tips of the branches. This principle is unchanging.

What is called the form of propriety is that the Real Lord created and transformed heaven, earth, and the myriad things for the sake of the human, who is responsible for the subtle function of the mysterious secret of the Real Lord and who keeps the universe standing continuously. His spiritual surpasses the myriad levels, but his

---

6. This paragraph seems to be inspired by Rāzī, *Mirṣād* 167–68 (*Path* 183–84).

bodily form, clothing, and food are all granted by the Real Lord's solicitude. This overflowing mercy cannot be repaid with property, nor can anything be given to compensate for it. People are put to shame because the myriad affairs do not belong to them. Were it not for the body's standing to serve, its bowing and kowtowing, its kneeling and rising in the rite of propriety-worship, how could one attend to Him with reverence?

If man disobeys the Lord's mandate, the Lord's honorable greatness will lack nothing. If man obeys the Lord's mandate, the Lord's honorable greatness will be increased by nothing. Those who think carelessly that the Real Lord hopes that people will worship Him are base indeed.

Know that the Real Lord's love for man is such that He was afraid that man's inner humaneness would be disturbed by outward evil. Thus He gave a special mandate to the Sage to make these outward rites so that these would open up people's inner virtue while they preserve it constantly and reflect upon it. Hence they perform the propriety-worship daily and are grateful and do not forget Him. It clarifies man's origin and purifies him of mistakes and transgressions. It indicates to him his final resting place and makes him increase his virtuous endeavors so that in the afterworld he may receive the real reward of complete bliss.

So when the Real Lord calls people to propriety-worship, is this for their sake or His sake? If someone does not worship, is he human or inhuman? Those who perform the propriety-worship know mercy, and those who know mercy are human. Those who do not perform the propriety-worship do not know mercy, so they are birds and beasts. From the outset birds and beasts have no responsibility. When they die, that is it. But birds and beasts with human faces have a connection with the clear mandate and a relationship with the Constant Bonds. Their punishment will be heavy indeed. They will neither be born nor will they perish, without end and without rest.[7] So in fact they should not be compared with birds and beasts.

The *fourth* of the Five Constants is called abstaining and sustaining. Abstaining is to abstain in one's self-nature, and sustaining is to sustain wisdom and intelligence. The Classic says that you must

---

7. Probably a reference to Qur'anic mentions of hell, wherein people "neither die therein nor live" (20:74, 87:13).

use the sword of opposition to make your self-nature surrender. Self-nature has six roots: eyes, ears, nose, tongue, body, and heart. Self-nature also has two assistants: being well fed and well clad, and having wealth and nobility. Violence and fierceness emerge from being well fed and well clad, and pride and extravagance emerge from wealth and nobility. In order to make your self-nature surrender, you must know the causes of hunger and thirst so that violence and fierceness will disperse by themselves. If you embody the recognition of midmost action, you will rely firmly on the propriety of modesty and frugality. Then pride and extravagance will come to an end by themselves.

Abstaining and sustaining have three great meanings. There are few worthies at present who have not done immoral things in the past, and there are few now on the path who did not formerly betray the way. People who make progress on the path are usually those who not only know their former mistakes, but also are truly ashamed and deeply repentant. With simple food and coarse clothing, they willingly take upon themselves the suffering of toil in order to redeem former transgressions. You must examine yourself attentively so that nothing may stay dark and obscure. This is the first meaning.

Those who act without wisdom and intelligence, following only the pleasure of lustful desires, are human in countenance, but in reality their actions belong to the animals. The harm of other diseases stops with the body, but the taint of lust's poison penetrates the heart and bones. When people wish to cut off desire while fully nourishing the body, they are like those who desire to stop a fire but keep on adding reeds. How is that possible? If a servant is too strong, he will surely disobey his lord. When blood and vital-energy flourish and become strong, this will certainly upset the heart's will. If savory and delicious tastes are not allowed into the body, and if silk brocade is not placed upon it, then blood and vital-energy will be balanced harmoniously and the whole body will be constrained by itself. This is the second meaning.

In addition, the bodily world in front of your eyes is an inn for visitors on the everlasting path, not a place for tarrying and enjoyment. You should anxiously busy yourself with the True Way. How can you leisurely busy yourself with the crooked path? The joy of the way's virtue can let you be of the same rank as the heavenly immortals, but the delicacies of food and drink put you on the same path as the animals. The virtue of the way allows people to clarify their heart and lets the benefit reach the body, but food and drink cause the body to be lazy and allow burdens to reach the heart. The hearts of the people of the world are diseased, so they know nothing of the beauty of virtuous deeds. When you know the joy of such deeds, all kinds of taste are frivolous. The Classic says that those who know the principle of abstaining and sustaining do not think about food and drink during their lives. This is the third meaning.

When you perfect the three meanings, you will have the true wisdom of Islam. There is still the Ultimate Way, however, beyond this true wisdom. The Ultimate Way begins with this wisdom and ends by going beyond this wisdom.

The Real Lord's imperial proclamation says, "The sustainers and abstainers are like Me, and I will personally show them solicitude."[8] At root the Lord is pure and clean and at origin He does not have causes like feelings and desires, food and drink. If man can in fact cut himself off from the various causes and practice the Lord's purity and cleanliness, that is the meaning of the saying, "The sustainers and abstainers are like Me." It does not mean that the Lord Himself sustains and abstains. The meritorious deeds of people will all be rewarded with the Heavenly Country, but this one affair alone is not the same kind as the myriad activities, for it is an affair that man cannot reach by himself. It has the level of the utmost pure, so the Heavenly Country cannot be its recompense. It must be granted by His personal solicitude in its own measure.

The meaning of being granted personal solicitude is to see the Lord. At root the Lord has no guise, so eyes cannot observe Him. Only the heart is able to see Him. Someone who attains the Real Being, the Pure and Clean, does not know that he has body and life. At that very moment there is an undifferentiated suchness without "I," so how can there be talk? When his heart cherishes the virtue of the way, he will have an intimate bond with sages and worthies. When he continues to practice the Lord's pureness and cleanness, he will be near the Lord as a matter of course. This is the ultimate meaning of abstaining and sustaining.

The *fifth* of the Five Constants is called assembly. Assembly is called the covenant, and the complete covenant is called faithfulness.

---

8. Reference to the sound hadith, "Every deed of Adam's child belongs to him except fasting, for it belongs to Me and I will give recompense for it." The paragraph is based on Rāzī, *Mirṣād* 169 (*Path* 185).

The covenant is of two kinds: the covenant of the Former Heaven, and the covenant of the Latter Heaven.

When heaven and earth were cleaved apart at the beginning, the human ancestor descended to the Heavenly Chamber, which is located in the true middle of the four poles, as shown by the evidence of the shadow thrown by the sun, which is as evident as that a country has a ruler, or a body a heart. Then the human ancestor Adam complied with the clear mandate of the Real Lord, at which point the true teaching came to be. The teaching exercised its influence daily, and people and things increased day by day. Then they poured outside the country of the Heavenly Chamber and poured forth even further. Daily they rushed toward delusion, and from there began offshoots and outgrowths.

The Real Lord in His kindness had pity because people went away, became scattered, and forgot their own origin. He gave the human ancestor Adam an imperial mandate to be presented to the multitudes: Once in a lifetime you should pay a visit to the Heavenly Chamber, having given up what you treasure and departed from home. From antiquity until now this has continued so that people will not forget the first root. They will follow the traces handed down by the true teaching and comply with the clear mandate of the Real Lord. This is the covenant of the Latter Heaven.

When you reach this place and go into the courtyard, you will not see those who preceded you, but when you visit the Heavenly Chamber with respect, you will again think about the Original Lord. It will suddenly be opened up to you who it is that has created and transformed heaven and earth and where the predecessors went home when they returned. Being and nonbeing will be like dreams, wealth and nobility like dust motes. You will recall the Former Heaven whence you came, the Latter Heaven where you are going, and the fact that the scenes of this place are only the illusory circumstances of the traveler's path, not your eternal abode. At this time you will be watchful and wakeful and at once you will cut off connection with the myriad causes surrounding you. You will leap beyond the crossroads of life and death and recall the return to the Village of the Non-Ultimate. This is the completion of the covenant of the Former Heaven. You will return to the mandate and go home to the Real, facing the Lord with one heart. This is the assembly of faithfulness in the true teaching.

Although we talk about the outside and inside of the true teaching's Five Constants, at root they flow from the fountainhead and provide direct indications to body and heart without regard to the others or the "I." This indeed is called the fountainhead of purity, and what flows forth is pure by itself. The fault of those who know this way and yet do not compliantly act by it is doubled, and their hearts will be further perplexed. They are like a person who is able to eat, but the food is not digested, so it stagnates and he feels bad. Not only will it have no benefit, but also it will be harmful. How can you not pay attention to this?

2.2. Real Loyalty

The Real transforms and extinguishes various evils, and loyalty cuts off and sweeps away the myriad beings. This is the great root of the human, and this is why the profound person attends to the root. When the root is established, the way is begotten. If the root is not established, how can there be the way?

Ever since people have followed our teaching, they have not worshiped idols and have extinguished the various evils; thus it is called pure and clean. They have honored the Unique One, the Lord without twoness; thus it is called real loyalty.

One country has one ruler. Were there two, that would be wrong. Heaven and earth have one Lord. Were He to be regarded as two, that would be the greatest crime in the world. Thus the true teaching esteems the One.

In discussing the One, there are three: the Unique One, the Numerical One, and the Practicing One. The Unique One is the Real Lord, the Numerical One is the Seed, and the Practicing One is the Real Human Being.

The Real Lord turned the Non-Ultimate and opened the Gate of All Subtleties. With the Great Ultimate He perfected[9] the bodies of the myriad images. He surpasses the Non-Ultimate and the Great Ultimate, so He does not fall into yin and yang. This is the Unique One.

The Seed means, "The nameless is the beginning of heaven and earth; the named is the mother of the myriad things" [Laozi 1]. This is the Numerical One.

Although the body of the Real Human Being is placed between heaven and earth, he does not suffer the obstructions of heaven, earth,

---

9. "Perfected" (*cheng* 成) is missing from the Yang-Yu edition.

and the myriad things. He faces the Lord with one heart, not two hearts. He is the Practicing One.

Here it becomes clear that the great root is real loyalty. This is the basis for destroying the diverse idols and evils. It is like the sun in the midst of heaven, reducing the vital-energy of yin to its minimum. How can a trivial, halfway loyalty, small and insignificant, be talked about in the same manner?

Hence you need to recognize self, cultivate the body, be loyal to the ruler, serve parents, manage husband-and-wifehood, make friends, govern the country, and regulate the family; all of these rise up from this root. If you discard it and want to find another way, there will be the sadness of crooked ways.

When you are loyal to the Real Lord and also loyal to ruler and father there can be the True Way.[10] When the fountainhead is pure, everything will be pure. Those who are loyal to ruler and father but not loyal to the Real Lord are merely heterodox. Why? If you worship this and that, if you pray to Buddha and to spirits, each of them is a lord. How can you be loyal to the One? Those who have no father and no ruler are even worse.

Life and death, longevity and young death, wealth and nobility, merit and name—all are based on the Real Lord's predetermination. So also punishment and virtue, hardship and bliss—all are entrusted to the Lord of men. Ignorant people say that all these rely on Buddha, who usurps the secret of the creative transformation and steals the authority of the Lord of men. The harm of this is not shallow.

If we suppose that the Buddha's doctrine were to be fully acted upon, then people would have no fathers and their offspring would be cut off, so no one would be able to act on the Buddha's dharma. If people had no ruler, they would fight to deprive others and attack to kill, injuring and destroying each other, so the Buddha's followers would not be able to establish themselves.

He prohibited people from marriage, thereby cutting off the origin of the way. He warned against the killing of living things so

---

10. In this section Wang sounds much like the Neo-Confucian philosopher Wang Yangming 王陽明, who writes, "When this heart, which has become completely identical with the Principle of Heaven, is applied and arises to serve parents, there is filial piety; when it arises to serve the ruler, there is loyalty; when it rises to deal with friends or to govern the people, there are faithfulness and humanity. The main thing is for the heart to make an effort to get rid of selfish human desires and preserve the Principle of Heaven" (Chan, *Source Book* 667).

that birds and beasts would increase daily and the world would be possessed by animals. Indeed, he discarded the Three Bonds, the Five Constants, heaven and earth, the three sorts of light, the myriad things, and the myriad affairs.

I humbly think that when dealing with a friend among worldly people, if you hear one or two lies from your friend, in the end you will hardly have faith in his opinion. Things like this are wrong and foolish, but people still have respect for them and faith in them. How can they be so ignorant? A fountainhead of black water does not give forth pure blue waves. How can a root of thorn trees produce pine and cypress fruit? Except for wise men of real loyalty, it is rare for people not to be perplexed.

You should know that the great root of real loyalty begins with the son of heaven. The ruler cannot make himself a ruler; only the Lord can grant him rulership. Thus it is said that the son of heaven cannot grant what is under heaven to the people; only heaven grants. Hence the loyalty of ruler and father [to the Lord] is a precious jewel, the loyalty of subject [to ruler] and son [to father] is gold, and the loyalty of friends is silver. The name of loyalty is one, but the reality is not the same.

You must recognize the Lord, then your heart will be true. When your heart is true, your loyalty will be real. The taproots of all of the myriad good things issue forth from this loyalty. You must keep the due degree so that your propriety may actually be complete.

Someone asked: What is the utmost ritual propriety of real loyalty?

The Classic says that nothing other than the Real Lord, the Unique One, should be worshiped. Dwelling in the world, man has three great and true affairs in life: obeying the Lord, obeying the ruler, and obeying parents. Disobeying them is of three sorts: disloyalty, unrighteousness, and lack of filial piety. Affairs, however, have heavy and light, and righteousness has different degrees. Ruler and parent will never have the same degree as the Lord, for to Him belong the greatest relationship and the ultimate loyalty; you cannot but know this.

When you pay the utmost respect by putting down your head in worship and reverence, ruler and parent have no share in that, for this is the utmost ritual propriety. Why? Man has no greater obligation than recognizing the Lord. As evidence for having recognized the Lord, nothing is greater than worshiping the Lord. In the rite of worshiping the Lord, nothing is more important than putting down the head. The Real Lord is honorable and great, pure and high, and

He does not hope for anything from man. When we serve the Lord, we cannot use our wealth and property for this purpose. Though we have a corporeal body, it cannot toil for that. This propriety-worship alone differentiates us as subjects and servants.

Moreover, the Real Lord created and transformed heaven, earth, and the myriad things, but the utmost nobility belongs only to the human. In the human body, the utmost nobility belongs to the head. It is most suitable that you worship the utmost, honorable Lord Creator with the head, which is created with the utmost nobility. Who below Him is suitable for this?

As for honoring ruler and parent, they were created and transformed by the Lord, so their authority is given and taken by the Lord. Life and death, failure and success, old age and youth, peace and danger—all of these listen to the Lord's mandate. Who can obtain a share of honor, greatness, purity, and highness so as to desire propriety equal to His?

In addition, when a subject serves the ruler and a son[11] serves his father, they can exert strength and devote the body, and there are many other things that suffice as proof of respect. As for the rite of putting down the head in worship, if it were necessary to share it with all, how could you clarify the meaning of honor and highness and distinguish the propriety of subject and servant? If the propriety-worship of putting down the head and placing the head on the ground were to be used in all cases—for a ruler serving the Supreme Ruler, for a subject serving the ruler, for a son serving the father, for a commoner serving the noble, and for a young person serving the old—how could we differentiate between light and heavy and how could we discriminate the various ranks?

So also the servants, who are created, are firmly differentiated from the Lord, who is the Original Being. How can you fail to distinguish the Lord, the most honorable, from the human, the most mean, and offer them equal propriety? How can this be propriety? Can this be called real loyalty? Those who have discernment certainly know that this is impossible.

When people who are wealthy, noble, and arrogant and those who are mean, lowly, and obsequious encounter [idols of] soil and wood, they bend the body. When they encounter evil spirits, they put down their heads. They also worship those who sit on high platforms and talk of dharma, pretending to be buddha-ancestors, though all of

---

11. Yu-Yang has "profound person" (*junzi* 君子) instead of "son" (*zi* 子).

them bring disorder to the five human bonds and rebelliously disobey the Creator. I cannot bear to talk more about this.

Rulers and parents should know that the noble cannot make themselves noble and the elderly cannot make themselves elderly, but there is someone who makes them noble and elderly. Thus they will not dare to accept with ease the rite that is for the most noble and most elderly. This is the real loyalty of ruler and parents.

As for mean and lowly people, they do not dare to hope and scheme for good favor. By seizing the happiness of the moment they become confused about the propriety of taking the noble as noble and treating the elderly as elderly. This is the real loyalty of mean and lowly people.

All of these are propriety, and all are of the utmost propriety. Today, however, the people of the world are such that they cannot serve ruler and parents without making mistakes. When they see people who do not perform the worship [of bowing the head], they regard them as not having propriety. Since they do not know loyalty, they also do not know propriety.

You should know that generally the rite of propriety has four levels, each of which should be observed in due degree. When you meet people of the same rank, you should pay respect by bowing with hands clasped. When you see the honorable and the elderly, you should pay respect by kneeling down. When you serve rulers and parents, you should turn the edge of your ear toward the ground and pay respect with the side of your head. Only when you serve the Real Lord of heaven and earth, man and spirits, should you pay respect facing straight ahead. Such is the greatest and most honorable propriety. If you serve the people in the same way, you will bring about transgression in this and that. This damages not only the loyalty and filial piety due to them, but also what is due to the supreme position. How can this be a minor affair?

2.3. Utmost Filial Piety

The Classic says, "You should worship the Lord and have filial piety toward your parents."[12] So after serving the Lord nothing is greater

---

12. "Thy Lord has decreed that you worship none but Him and, toward parents, beautiful-doing" (17:23; cf. 2:83, 4:36, 6:151).

than serving the parents. Filial piety is the human root. You serve the Lord by means of the virtue of the way and you serve your parents by means of humaneness and righteousness. Those who have real loyalty will surely have filial piety, and those who act with filial piety will surely be loyal. When loyalty and filial piety have both been completed, the true teaching is perfected.

The Classic says that the Real Lord's joy is lodged in the happiness of father and mother with the child. If the father and mother are not happy, it does not matter if the child does a myriad deeds.

Someone asked: When someone attends to his parents who suffer sickness for a long time and does not harbor resentment, can this be called filial piety?

I said: In three general ways the kindness of parents and the filial piety of children are as far apart as heaven and earth. When parents cherish and nurture, this is rooted in the thoughts of the heart, but when children show filial piety and care, this is mostly to preserve ritual propriety. This is one way.

Even if you have no resentment when attending to parents who are suffering from sickness, when it lasts a long time you will look forward to their death. But when parents cherish children during the calamity of a disease, even when they suffer the utmost toil and it lasts a long time, they still want to keep them alive. This is the second way.

Parents' thoughts of their children have no time or limit, but children's affection for parents has a limit and measure. This is the third way.

Thus we see that when we compare the caring of children with that of parents, the former is not one-hundredth of the latter.

Know that filial piety has three levels: body, heart, and mandate. When people nourish only the parents' bodies, this is not filial piety, for they also nourish dogs and horses, and this is not called filial piety.

The will of the heart to be filial toward parents is common filial piety, but this also is not the utmost filial piety. Why? Because heaven and earth are man's lodging place, and wealth, nobility, and long life before the eyes last no more than one hundred years. When the body dies, filial piety is cut off. How can this be sufficient filial piety?

The utmost filial piety is that you should have all three levels. You should serve parents faultlessly so that you do not let them fall into disobedience and rebellion. You should help them avoid the suffering of recompense and receive immeasurable happiness; at the end of each of the five daily acts of worship, you should pray for them, and you should assist and aid them when they are poor and in difficulty. And you should have the intention of remembering your ancestors. This is the utmost filial piety of nature and mandate.

In the way of the true teaching, there are five ways not to have filial piety, but cutting off descendants is greater than all. First is not to recognize the Lord, second not to embody the sages, third not to be intimate with the worthies, fourth not to earn one's livelihood, and fifth not to practice the learning.

When you recognize the Lord, your heart will be true.

When you embody the sages, your intention will be sincere, for the level of sagehood is sincerity itself and hence also clarity. The worthies are clear in themselves and thus have sincerity. This is why a worthy cannot be sincere apart from sagehood. But how then are sages distinguished from worthies? The sincerity of the worthies is like the light in a mirror that has a little bit of filth and dust. It needs effort to wipe away the dust, and then it can be transparent and penetrating. It is not that there are two kinds of sincerity.

When you are intimate with worthies, your body will be cultivated.

When you earn your livelihood, your family will be regulated.

When you practice the learning, the country will be governed.

As for what is called "cutting off descendants," this does not mean cutting off children and heirs. Rather, it is that descendants lose the learning. Why? If someone has the learning, he will keep his body good even when he is impoverished. When he is successful, he will keep the world good. When his good reputation flows for a thousand ages, the people of the whole country will honor and venerate him. When he dies, it will be as if he is still alive. How could this be the same as cutting off children?

If one has children who lose the learning, they will not recognize the Lord, not be filial toward parents, not embody the sages, not know the laws, and will easily violate statutes issued by the authorities. Their burden will reach the clans, and its stench will last a myriad years. They will be detested by everyone. While they are still alive, they will be as if dead. Is this having descendants? Even if one desires such descendants to die quickly, perhaps they will not perish at once.

In the Real Teaching, cutting off descendants means that children lose the learning, and the responsibility goes back to fathers and mothers. No sin is greater than this.

This cannot be compared to the [Confucian] statement that not to have filial piety is of three kinds, and cutting off descendants is the worst. Why? A man of wealth who possesses all under heaven may have a hundred thousand concubines and desire a child, but it may not be possible. A poor man with no house to live in may have many sons and daughters and desire to cut off pregnancy, but it may not be possible. When you observe carefully, ascribing the gravity of cutting off descendants to human responsibility is not a solid conclusion.

Someone said that this meaning explains why Shun got married without telling [his parents]—in order not[13] to cut off descendants. Even if this argument is right, that may not have been the intention in Shun's heart. Moreover, there are still six possible doubts. If the meaning of cutting off descendants is "not married," then these two words, "not" and "married," should be used at the outset, for these are straightforward and clear. Then the scholars of later generations would not make mistakes and have wrong understandings. This is one possible doubt.

Why is it necessary to replace "not married" with "cutting off descendants"? Does this not harm the meaning by using the wrong characters? This is the second possible doubt.

If we suppose that the root intention was cutting off descendants, not the fact of not being married, then later scholars made a mistake in understanding it as not being married. It is possible to say that their commentary does not accord with the subject. This is the third possible doubt.

If we suppose that not being married is certainly the lack of filial piety, then Shun's father Gusou clearly must have commanded him to marry. If Shun disobeyed him intentionally and did not marry, then he acted without filial piety. This is the fourth possible doubt.

If Shun was not commanded to marry and had not dared to marry, then this would have been an act of filial piety on his part, not a lack of it. This is the fifth possible doubt.

If Shun wanted to act with filial piety by getting married but did not tell his parents, one can say that he lacked filial piety for the sake of filial piety. This is the sixth possible doubt.

When you investigate this in detail, it is not a sound argument to explain Shun's marriage without announcement only by the grav-

---

13. The 1873 edition has *wei* 為 instead of *fei* 非, which makes the verb affirmative instead of negative.

ity of cutting off descendants. A puzzle like this has probably not arisen for a thousand ages. I simply tried to talk about it as a sound argument while expecting intelligent men to share in the discussion.

It is possible that Shun did not make an announcement only because he was afraid that Gusou did not approve of his wives [the two daughters of Emperor Yao] and that he might disobey the ruler's command [to marry them] and become disloyal, thereby greatly damaging the nation's dignity. Rather, Shun made himself responsible for a lack of filial piety by not making the announcement because he could not bear to place the sin of disloyalty to the ruler on his parents. Thus he further completed the propriety between ruler and subject. Not only did Shun have complete loyalty and filial piety, but also, by resisting his parents' command, he was loyal in concealment. This is the utmost loyalty and filial piety of the Eastern Land.

2.4. Listening to the Mandate

To listen to the mandate is not to follow self-nature and to conquer one's selfish heart. The Real Lord set down a simile and proclaimed, "A servant put to use cannot have any affair of his own." This indicates clearly that He commands people to listen to the mandate and conquer themselves, not to be self-determining. The disobedience and transgression of the world's people result from the partiality and selfishness of their own willful natures. If they do not listen to the mandate, they will not be able to conquer their selves. If they do not conquer their selves, they will not be able to go home to the Real and enter the way.

Listening to the mandate is the way of heaven, and conquering self is the way of man. These are each other's outward and inward, issuing forth from one heart and lodging in four affairs. Obeying the Lord and being loyal to the ruler lodge in intention and thought. Praising the Lord and praising the Sage lodge in mouth and tongue. Worshiping the Lord and being filial toward parents lodge in the corporeal body. Being grateful to the Lord and helping the people lodge in money and things.

It may be that people obey only the Lord, praise the Lord, worship the Lord, and give thanks for His kindness, but they are not able to be loyal to the ruler, praise the Sage, be filial toward parents, or aid the people. Then the first half of these four affairs cannot be regarded as having any merit. In the same way, people may be loyal only to the ruler, praise the Sage, be filial to parents, and aid the people, but they are not able to obey the Lord, praise the Lord, worship the Lord, and give thanks for the Lord's mercy. Then the first half of these four affairs will still be regarded as the path of heretics.

It is not only this, however. In all these matters—filial piety and respecting elders, loyalty and faithfulness, propriety and righteousness, modesty and shame—if there is any lack and deficiency, then the way of heaven and the way of man will not be complete. We cannot call this listening to the mandate.

When you observe this in detail—intention and thought, mouth and tongue, corporeal body, money and things—there is not a single affair that does not need listening to the Lord's mandate, nor is there a single, tiny affair that can be done with the disorderliness of one's own nature.

Generally speaking, those who conquer self will not lose one in ten thousand, but those who hold on to self will not gain one in ten thousand. This is why forgiving people belongs to the sages and worthies, but forgiving self pertains to a heart that is unjust and partial. Only by conquering self and forgiving people will you enter into the True Way. By holding on to self and forgiving self you will gradually end up in heterodoxy. Forgiving people is because of not having self, and knowing only to forgive self is because of holding on to self.

Forgiving self brings harm in seven[14] ways that you should know about. Forgiving your heart brings about the fall of will. Forgiving your nature gives free rein to desire. Forgiving your body produces laziness. Forgiving your falsity yields a great deal of oppression and injustice. Forgiving your poverty produces the lowliness of flattery. Forgiving your learning puts you at ease with ignorance and vulgarity. Forgiving your wealth means that you have concealed something evil [by not paying alms].

Those who desire to complete the way should suppose that all the people of the world surpass them. With the heart of honoring self, they should respect the people. This is not far from the way. A worthy said that someone who knows who created and transformed his body will of course not dare to look down on the people, and someone who knows whence his body came into being will of course not dare

---

14. The 1873, 1904, and 1922 editions have "eight."

to dwell presumptuously in high nobility. Those who compare their own excellence and deficiency with others and dwell happily in high nobility do so only because they do not know self. When someone knows his own mistakes, he will meticulously observe his private heart and guard against evil deeds. How will he find the leisure time to compare himself with others?

There was a worthy in ancient times who cut himself off from mixing with friends and dwelt alone in seclusion. Someone asked him, "Why do you live like this?"

He replied, "With my every breath the Lord shows the solicitude of mercy to me, but my own self adds a veil. When I am thanking the Lord for this mercy and removing this veil in the midst of my breath, how can I find the leisure to interact with people?"

A man's life is lodged between breathing in and breathing out. If breathing in and breathing out should stop, his intention to live will suddenly be cut off. Alas! If someone who exists by these uncertain moments of breath should absurdly become anxious to remain one thousand years, how can you say that he knows self?

When you think about this, then you must be like an office-holder. You must get along harmoniously with others when you conduct yourself in the world. You must be modest when you make friends. Even though life and death cannot be fathomed, since they change and shift with the speed of an eye's twinkling, you should still act like this.

Moreover, you should not stop here. If you cannot listen to the mandate and conquer self, you must mix with worthies and good people. Then, even if you cannot fully realize the good, you will certainly not reach evil. A worthy said, "You should interact with the Real Lord, and if that is not possible, you should interact with the friends of the Real Lord."

When someone disobeys the Lord's mandate, fails to comply with the Sage's words, and does not approach worthies and good people, how is he different from birds and beasts?

The honorable Baṣrī said, "People are not as good as sheep. Why? Because sheep led to pasture scatter in the mountain fields, but they all come back at once when they hear the shepherd calling."[15] The human spiritual excels the myriad kinds. The Classic descended

---

15. Ḥasan Baṣrī (d. 728). 'Aṭṭār, *Tadhkira* 43 (*Memorial* 77).

and the Sage was sent to direct and guide those on paths of delusion. Though they received advice, they did not awaken, nor were they willing to turn their heads. Thus we see that they are not as good as birds and beasts.

Shaqīq asked the honorable Adham, "What should the servant do?"

He answered, "When he has something, he should be thankful for His mercy. When he has nothing, he should be patient and enduring."

Shaqīq said, "That is what a dog does. When it receives food, it guards and protects the house, and when it does not receive food, it does the same. This is not the meaning of servanthood. The one called a servant is he who, when he has something, gives it to the people, and when he has nothing, is still grateful and thankful."[16]

Thus, when he has something, he aids the people, and when he has nothing, he keeps his heart pure and clean. Having nothing does not mean receiving no mercy, so he is thankful in every case. The common people, however, are the contrary of this. When they have something, they are greedy and angry, and when they have nothing, they are perplexed and reckless.

The Classic says that on the day when people are called to justice in the afterworld, the Real Lord will put the various kinds of cattle among those who obeyed and disobeyed, and this will be sufficient proof against the people. At that moment He will proclaim to those who disobeyed the mandate, "Did not the Real Lord command the cows, horses, and so on to submit to you?"

Everyone will say, "Indeed He did."

Again He will proclaim and say to them, "Did the cattle ever disobey and transgress against you?"

Everyone will say, "Never."

"Why then did you disobey and transgress the Lord's mandate?"

No one will be able to answer this question.

Then again He will proclaim to the people who obeyed the mandate, saying, "You commanded cows and horses to do the cultivation and carry things on their backs. During that time did they ever fail to do so and act against your command?"

Everyone will say, "Never."

---

16. Shaqīq Balkhī (d. 810) and Ibrāhīm Adham (d. ca. 782). 'Aṭṭār, *Tadhkira* 236.

Again He will proclaim and say, "Were you able to obey each of the mandates of the Lord?"

Here the obedient people will have no answer. At this moment those who obeyed the mandate will be ashamed while pleased and happy. Those who disobeyed will be afraid of punishment while sad and miserable, but it will be too late to repent.

You should also know that when obedient people reach this point, they will be ashamed not simply because they could not fully realize the Lord's mandate; they will also be ashamed even if they did fully realize the mandate.

In olden times there was a hermit who abandoned the world and retreated into the deep mountains. When he was thirsty he drank from flowing springs, and when he was hungry he ate fruit from trees. He totally forgot worldly matters and worshiped only the Real Lord. For a long time he kept his body and heart pure and clean. He obtained great spiritual penetration but was not aware that a bit of self-esteem was appearing in his heart. He thought that he had excelled the people of the world. Suddenly the water dried up and the trees withered, so he had nothing to sustain his body. Then he became fully aware that it is absurd to see oneself as surpassing others. He came to know that his meritorious deeds did not come from his own self-power.

You should pay careful attention to this. If the Real Lord's universal compassion were to stop, all of heaven, earth, and the myriad things would turn completely into nonbeing. How can anyone depend on this tiny human body?

2.5. The Chief Leader

The Sage said, "You are all like shepherds, and in the future you will be asked about your duty to those with whom you were charged."[17]

Let us examine this with care. The sovereign king has responsibility for all under heaven. The district magistrate has responsibility for one area. The head of a family has responsibility for one family. Someone who lives alone has responsibility for his own body.

Although all these are equal in responsibility, of most concern are the people and things of your own body, for they are the most

---

17. For the full text of the hadith, see p. 19.

important root. The heart is the lord-ruler of the whole body. Intention, deliberation, memory, and wakefulness are among its close attendants. Seeing, hearing, smelling, and speaking are its ministers of state. The four limbs and one hundred bones are its people and things. As one body the whole of this body is a country. If the heart is unjust, then the whole body will be unjust; if the heart is true, then the whole body will be true.[18] How can this be a small affair?

The sovereign king has a heavy responsibility and an honorable position. He must begin with the soil of the country of his own body. If his body is in disorder, then the country will surely be in disorder. When the body is regulated, then the country will surely be regulated. It has never been the case that the body is regulated but the country is in disorder.

You should know that the essentials of regulation and disorder lie only in justice and injustice. Even if everyone under heaven is a heretic, this will not be an obstacle to regulation. But, if laws are bent and activities are failures, it will not be possible to regulate. Thus the Sage said, "The way of justice in the world is the scales[19] of the Real Lord. On the future day of bringing justice, someone who regulated the world with justice will of course not meet the ultimate punishment of the unjust."

Generally, retribution for injustice and lack of humaneness is of three sorts: First is everlasting punishment without forgiveness. Second is the possibility of forgiveness without punishment. Third is waiting for full punishment and then being released.

Those who are never forgiven are the ones who do not recognize and discern the Real Lord, the creator and transformer of their own selves, or who know Him but are doubtful, perplexed, and unsettled. They are like those who dwell in a king's land, eat from the king's salary, but still communicate in private with another country. Or they look ahead to prosperity and decline, so they keep both sides. These are sins that cannot be shown any leniency.

Those who are forgiven and not punished are the young who lack knowledge and sometimes disobey the clear mandate. When they

---

18. Allusion to the hadith quoted near the bottom of p. 19. Muslim scholars often discuss the heart as the king of the microcosm, aided by its vizier, the intellect, and so on. See, for example, Ghazālī's discussion of the heart as king, quoted in Murata, *Tao of Islam* 242–43.

19. In place of "scales" (*tianping* 天平) Yang-Yu has "impartiality" (*gongping* 公平).

reach adulthood, they regret and repent their former transgressions. If they are sincere and do not sin again, they will be forgiven without punishment.

Those who have full punishment and then release are of three sorts: One sort is such that the same is appropriate for both sides, as they were equal in the world and opposed to each other. But when human power in money and things, or in blood and vital-energy, was not equal in strength and weakness, the retribution and punishment for the oppressors will be twice the measure of their wrongdoing. Then there are those who were under someone else's control and bonds, as in the case of rulers and subjects, officials and the masses, fathers and sons, husbands and wives, elder brothers and younger brothers, masters and slaves. If those controlled received nothing but unjust treatment along with utmost suffering and hardship, but they held back the grievance and put up with the insult, not daring to challenge, then the retribution [for the oppressors] will be many times their suffering.

The Sage said, "You must have sympathy for the classes of people under you, for all of them are created and transformed by the Real Lord. Their bodies and lives are the same as yours, and their joy and anger are also not different from yours. That which you yourself cannot put up with should never be given to others. Otherwise, on the day of bringing justice in the afterworld, both the Real Lord and the I will give witness to that."

This concerns not only those who wrong people. Those who wrong the animal kinds—the cows, camels, horses, and mules—will receive retribution beyond description. Why? When people are unable to put up with their own suffering, it is still possible to complain to superiors, to ask parents and friends to relieve them, or to run away and be done with it. But sometimes the various kinds of animals find cold and heat unbearable, and sometimes they have the utmost hunger and thirst. They carry heavy things for long distances, they cultivate and plough without rest, or they are so sick that they cannot rise—yet people still strike them with whips. How can they put up with their circumstances? The retribution for this sort of thing is most serious.

The Classic says, "Servants and the various sorts of domestic animals may not be put to use at three times: At the time of suffering from sickness, at the time of sleep, and at the time of drinking and eating."

Once there was a man of high position whose hard nature did many crooked things. He visited a physician seeking a cure. The physician said, "Sir, you should have much disease and sleep, or you should want a quick and violent death. Then you will be healed."

The man was displeased and his face turned color. He said, "What kind of talk is this?"

The physician answered, "Of all the varieties of good medicine, nothing is better than this. When you have much disease and sleep, you will not be able to interact with others, and thus your defects and crooked deeds will of course decrease. Then there will be no cause for retribution. If you die a quick and violent death, the people will forever be at peace from your crookedness and defects, and that will prevent endless retribution for yourself. What can surpass this medicine?"

At this he was pleased and said, "Bitter medicine and good words! You correctly indicated the disease of my heart. There is nothing worthy of your reward, but I will give you whatever you ask for."

He said, "Two servants of mine are two lords of yours, so what should I ask for?"

He said, "How can that be?"

He answered, "I can use both anxiety and greed as servants, but you are bound by both of them."

The king finally repented and wept with grief.

When you reach this point, you will surely know that at root treating people wrongly is to treat self wrongly and forgiving self is not equal to forgiving others. You cannot but observe this.

The people of the world all know that unsuitable punishment is crookedness, but they do not know that unsuitable forgiveness is also crookedness. When someone unsuitably forgives the one who should be punished and does not punish him, does this not give rein to evil? Hence the Sage said, "If those who are sovereign and superior have no excess and shortcoming and if they govern the world only with justice, when they leave here they will ascend to a quiet heaven and climb to a precious throne of clear light. Dwelling in the highest, they will look down on the various heavens. Nothing can compare to their happiness. As for those who make the laws crooked, when they leave here they will fall down to the lowest and be restrained in a restricted, pitch-black prison, trapped in the midst of a myriad sufferings. Nothing can surpass their hardship."

I earnestly think that if your willful nature is unjust and seizes the happiness of the moment, you do not know that you are stirring up the anger of the Real Lord. Your just punishment will last forever. How sad! The Classic says, "If affairs are done with harmony and warmth, they will be in good order; if with force and violence, they will be broken to pieces." Thus true people will take justice as the way and harmony as beauty.

Someone asked: What is the most fearful and frightful thing between heaven and earth?

I said: The anger of the Real Lord.

He said: How can I avoid it?

I said: You can avoid it by not turning your own anger against others.

The Real Lord proclaimed to a former sage, "You should eat whatever you see!" At that moment he saw something far away, its form as great as a mountain, its color deep black. Having received the mandate, he took himself forward to eat it. The nearer he came to the thing, the smaller it became. When he met it face to face, it was only a mouthful. He swallowed it and it tasted delicious. After all this, he still did not know what it was. Then again it was proclaimed to him, "That was your anger. At the beginning, it was very difficult to accept it, but if you are determined and are able to eat it, it will be most delicious."

Thus it is that sages and worthy rulers have no need to rule over the people, for the people's hearts submit to them by themselves. Although someone who keeps to his own calling can rule over the people, he cannot necessarily rule over himself. Those under heaven will comply only with his regulations and activities.

This is why there are two levels of courage: the courage of talent and wisdom and the courage of vital-energy and blood. The courage of talent and wisdom is the ability to suppress one's self-nature so that the vital-energy of harmony flows freely and everyone is influenced by the benefit of virtue. The courage of vital-energy and blood is having the force to suppress a myriad people, but imposing one's influence for a time will be nothing more than the people's fearing the law and its statutes.

The Classic says, "First transform self, then transform others!"[20] If you do not, will you not be ashamed of yourself?

It is often the case that someone has the urge to transform others throughout his life, but he cannot open up a single person. Someone

---

20. Probably a reference to the hadith, "Begin with yourself!"

else may hear one word by chance and then forcefully overcome self; at that moment he transforms himself without any explanation.

You must know that sages and worthies bite back their own anger when someone should be punished but is not punished. This is not comparable to the case of someone who is equal to others or lower and inferior to others. Why? Those who are equal to others sometimes accept injustice and appease anger only to save vital-energy and preserve wealth. If someone inferior and low shows endurance while he wants to retaliate but it is impossible, that is because there is no alternative. In these cases forgiveness is not the root intention.

How could this be like the generosity and endurance of the ruler and elder based on the magnanimity of self-control? Thus the generosity and endurance of the sages and worthies are like the great earth: All unclean things are poured upon it, but it issues forth and discloses only flowers of red and blue, fragrance and scent. The tiny capacity of worldly people can never be comparable with this.

2.6. The Way of Friendship

The Sage said, "Give what pleases you to others and keep for yourself what you do not want, and always act like this."

You should consider this fine and subtle point in detail. When someone harms others to benefit himself, even his family will become his enemy and hate him. When someone overcomes himself and helps others, everyone surrounded by the four seas will be his brother. If you do not treat your brothers and sisters with righteousness, they will be a thousand *li* away from you even if you are face to face. If you act with humaneness toward those with different surnames, they will be your neighbors even if they are at the ends of the earth.

When the source of ancient peoples is traced back, they originated from one ancestor with one way. They lived simply and plainly in undifferentiated suchness, and there were no distinctive differences among them. Then they scattered and gradually became distant from each other, migrating to the myriad places, and various heresies arose in clusters. They became different branches and quickly forgot their original beginning. Only Islam's teachings do not darken the fact that we were originally of one vein. Thus it is said that the Heavenly Classic is your original ancestor and true people are your brothers.²¹ This is the clear edict of having the same ancestor and one way. Hence in the constant bonds of the true teaching, the ways of elder and younger brothers, friends, relatives, and neighbors are all provided with principles.

Evil is caused by a single crack, but good is caused by complete perfection. Precious things become worthless with slight damage; white jade is devalued by a tiny flaw. Do not fail to avoid evil because it is small, and do not fail to do good because it is small. You should only be afraid that you have not acted sufficiently.

The intention established by the sages and worthies issued forth from the root origin and has been complete from beginning to end. The intention established by ignorant people arises from human affairs; they pay attention to branches and forks. The Classic says, "The noblest things for you are mostly the least with the Real Lord, and the least things for you are mostly the noblest with the Real Lord."²² Since the Real Lord's pleasure is hidden among a myriad deeds, you must not be partial to one action, whether the meritorious act is large or small. Only true sincerity of intention is noble. The proverb says, "Traveling to a nobleman's house is not equal to going to a poor scholar's house."²³ In other words, being connected with a person of noble rank is not equal to visiting a wise and good person.

The friendship of a profound person is like pine and cypress; it does not disappear because of poverty and humbleness. The friendship of a small person is like peaches and plums; it is fresh and beautiful for the sake of influence and profit. Gold needs to be smelted a hundred times in order to become pure. Calamity and hardship perfect the friendship of men. It is not like the friendship of worldly commoners, which is only for the sake of name and profit.

In ancient times the honorable Shiblī became sick and stayed in a sanatorium, and his intimate friends went to see him. He asked, "Who are you?"

---

21. Compare the earlier passage: "True learning means . . . to take the Honorable Classic as first ancestor and the sage teaching as wet-nurse" (134).

22. Perhaps a translation of the verse, "It may happen that you dislike a thing that is better for you; and it may happen that you love a thing that is worse for you; God knows, and you know not" (Qur'an 2:216).

23. Wang may have in mind this saying of the Prophet: "The worst of scholars is he who visits noblemen, and the best of noblemen is he who visits scholars," cited by Rūmī at the very beginning of *Discourses* (*Fīhi mā fīh*).

They all replied, "We are your friends. We have come to ask about your health." Then that honorable man threw stones to strike them, and they all hid or ran away.

He laughed and said, "You all lied to me. Those who are sworn friends will go through boiling water and fire for each other and not shrink away. But you, with a tiny difficulty, all ran away. Have you not deceived yourselves?"[24]

The way of friendship has the utmost eminence. One must certainly choose it with care. For instance, when a sick person seeks a physician, he will certainly visit a physician of the highest skill. If he is treated by someone of ordinary ability, not only will his root illness not be diminished, but new diseases will also be added.

The honorable Ṣādiq said that there is one with whom you should have friendship, and six from whom you should cut yourself off; you should know them all. You should have friendship with the one who reminds you when you forget and guides you when you are mistaken. You should not go near someone who lies, for he will always cheat you and harm everyone; even if he has something good, he also has evil. You should not go near someone who is ignorant and dark-hearted, for he may want to benefit you but he will harm you instead; in reality he does not have self-knowledge. You should not go near someone who is niggardly, for he will treat people harshly without humaneness and go far from the good way. You should not go near someone who has no faithfulness, for he will abandon you on dangerous ground at the most important time. You should not go near someone who gives weight to mouth and stomach, for he will throw people away even if they are his relatives for the sake of a single meal of bean soup. You should not go near someone who covets wealth; regardless of nearness or distance [in kinship], when he sees profit, he will forget righteousness. These are the six people from whom you should cut yourself off.[25]

You should also know that those with whom you should have friendship can help you avoid losing the moment, and then you will always be at ease and happy. Those with whom you should not make

---

24. 'Aṭṭār tells this story in *Tadhkira* 617.

25. A version of this saying given by 'Aṭṭār in *Tadhkira* 18 (*Memorial* 52–53) and by Ghazālī in *Iḥyā'* 2:249 mentions only the five sorts with whom one should not have companionship (*ṣuḥba*).

friendship can make you neglect the truth, and later you will lament and regret, for the lost moment cannot be recovered. The thing of utmost nobility is nothing but the present moment. Losing it and neglecting it are worse than death. Why? Because death cuts you off only from people, but losing and neglecting the present moment betrays the Lord. This is because disobeying the mandate and losing the moment are caused mainly by losing friends. Having friendship with good people is better than good affairs, and having friendship with evil people is worse than evil deeds. Why? Because each affair of good and evil has but one part, but both good and evil people have been provided with everything. Should we not be cautious?

In ancient times, someone advised a man to become the friend of a certain worthy. The worthy met him but treated him as if he had not met him. It was said to the worthy, "A friend came to visit you. Were you not pleased?"[26]

He replied, "My parents gave birth to my body, and good friends increase my will. This is not a small affair. When you choose people, you must see with your heart. How can friendship rely on other people? If someone befriends you because of someone else's opinion, he will cut you off because of someone else's opinion, since the reason for nearness and distance will be from others, not from himself. Right and wrong will be in his ear rather than in his heart. When you think about this, it is better for you not to become acquainted with him than to be close. This is right for this situation."

Know that the heart of a sage is like a mountain peak that does not sway or move when high wind stirs up the sea. The heart of a worthy is like a forest tree whose root does not move when its branches and trunk sway as it encounters sudden and violent gales. The heart of a common person is like a flower or a leaf that becomes dispersed and scattered when it meets even a tiny wind. Is this not dangerous?

Only great sages and great worthies have nothing to do with the taint of customs. Covering and carrying all things, they cannot be gauged by ordinary measures. This is like the healing of disease by Bian Que.[27] No matter the depth or shallowness of the disease,

---

26. Wang may have in mind the reference to friends coming to visit in *Analects* 1.1.

27. Bian Que 扁鵲, also known as Qin Yueren 秦越人, was a famous 4th c. BCE physician and practitioner of acupuncture.

he always achieved the expected result, though there were hopeless patients who could not be cured. Thus the Sage said, "The true person is the mirror of the true person."[28] He sees clearly and discriminates even the most hidden and tiny thing. This means not only that he can scrutinize the true person, but also that the depraved person fears his clarity and keeps away from him. This tells us about those who are like-minded.

The face is the verification of the heart, the tongue is the clear evidence of the intention, and what emerges from the mouth and is done by the body follows in sequence. When [the true person] sees the face, he knows the heart; following the face, the intention becomes manifest to him. How sad that the people of the world start avoiding affairs only at the last moment. As for sages and worthies, as soon as a thought moves, they overcome it.

Without the guidance of the sages and the wise and without the admonitions of good friends, how will the common and ignorant people come gradually to virtuous tasks? In general, among the regulated principles of the Constant Bonds, none is more important than having masters and friends, because they will correct your mistakes daily until you come to a halt at the utmost good.

The worldly commoners befriend only people, but sages and worthies do not neglect the things. Why? Because the utmost[29] person makes friends with the sun and the moon in order to imitate their highness and clarity, which illuminate the universe. He makes friends with the earth and soil in order to imitate their modesty and lowliness, which undertake what is proper. He makes friends with the mountains and forests in order to imitate their purity and cleanliness, which take part in the creative transformation. He makes friends with the rivers and seas in order to imitate their kind-heartedness, which has nourished from ancient times to the present. He never holds on to only one part.

In ancient times, the honorable Shaqīq's heart was sincere in all affairs. Someone asked whether or not he had a master in sincerity. He replied that his master was a walnut: "Once I saw walnuts at a feast. I chose the largest, the outside of which was shiny. I cracked it open,

---

28. Reference to the hadith, "The believer [mu'min] is the mirror of the believer."
29. In place of "utmost" (zhi 至) Yang-Yu has "sage" (sheng 聖).

but it was empty and without fruit. I was shocked and thought, 'How is this different from the deeds of ordinary people, who have no sincerity?' Although the body does good deeds, at root the heart has no sincerity. What then is the benefit of toiling in pain throughout life?"

What the ignorant and dark-hearted regard as meritorious deeds, the possessors of clear insight regard as vain toil. If you investigate this in detail, you will see that there are masters and friends everywhere, but only people with the right intention will find them.

Nonetheless, you should know that there are near and far, roots and branches. If you cannot be harmonious and pleasant with your family, or cordial and friendly with your ancestral clan, and if you cannot have overflowing love toward all the members of your home town, then there will be no place to discuss the way of friendship.

2.7. Taking and Putting Aside

The Classic says, "The myriad things decay; only what belongs to the Real Lord does not decay."[30] It also says, "When you have lost yourself, you will come home." The general meaning is that you must get rid of this world's causality. Only then can you be united with the Original Being.

The Original Being of the Real Lord exists constantly, creating and transforming the myriad things. The myriad things are interlaced with being and nonbeing and with entering and leaving life and death. Distinct beings are born newly moment by moment, but they do not recognize themselves as previously dead things. He who admits only himself will not know himself, nor will he recognize the Real Lord. He will dwell in the utmost extremity of foolishness and disorder, for by recognizing his own nature he will turn it into his lord. When someone conquers these two kinds of ignorance with two kinds of knowledge, he will have great wisdom.

Knowing self gives birth to modesty, and modesty is the fountainhead of the myriad good things. Its streams are humility, veneration, fear, emptying the heart, and submitting to the good. Ignorance of self gives birth to pride, and pride is the root of various evils. Its branches are bullying, jealousy, and fishing for praise and reputation. Without modesty, how will you overcome pride? When you are mod-

---

30. "All that is upon [the earth] undergoes annihilation, and there subsists the face of thy Lord, Possessor of Majesty and Generous Giving" (Qur'an 55:26–27).

est, you will be without self. When you are without self, you will receive good just as the ocean receives all streams.

A person's body is formed from the impurities of seed and blood and emerges from the lowly gate of begetting. Entirely chaotic, it knows nothing; completely naked, it has nothing. Little by little it is clothed and fed and gradually it increases in knowledge and discernment. Life and death, failure and success, peace and danger, gain and loss—none of these is based on self.

You should think quietly and carefully about the details. When your genuine heart issues forth and is disclosed, as a matter of course arrogance will be destroyed. Then you will awaken to the Real Lord, who transformed and begot you. Once you know Him, you will obey the mandate. Obedience to the mandate is the root of the myriad good things. These are the two kinds of knowledge.

When you are proud, you have self. When you have self, you do not know that there is the Lord. This is like a tree's shadow, which never sees the sunlight in its whole life, for its obstacle and veil is itself. Thus you know only that there is self, but you do not know that there is the Lord. If you do not know that there is the Lord, you will be deluded and rebellious. Delusion and rebellion are the taproots of all evils. These are the two kinds of ignorance.

Moreover, when someone has pride, it sticks to him quite early and separates from him quite late. It is like underwear—you put it on first and take it off last.

The critical crossroads in being human lies in discriminating between these two [knowledge and ignorance]. Hence the Real Lord had compassion and pity on the people of the world, who are upside-down in right and wrong. Specifically He sent down the Honorable Classic to guide the deluded so that they could enter the truth. By recognizing the Real Lord, they will go home to constant existence. By casting away empty nonbeing and abandoning self-being, they will go beyond the gate of life and death and tread the way of Islam, perhaps not falling into confusion and error.

In reality self-being is the root from which are born the various causes. Someone who overcomes the various causes outwardly but does not overcome self-nature is like a precious bottle filled with stinking and rotten things. Although its outward appearance is beautiful, its inside[31] has not been purified and cleansed.

---

31. Instead of "inside" (li 裡), Yang-Yu has "heart" (xin 心).

The learning and discernment of the people of the present time gives them the knowledge to desire things. It busies and binds them, so they do not wake up to the obstacles blocking the principles. The obstacles blocking the principles are attachment to the cultivation of the body and exertion of effort to an excessive degree. This is like adding flowers to silk brocade, or taking medicine after curing the disease. If they do not grasp the moment properly, what they do will not be good. Thus the people of the world follow the way in name, but their principles lead to the path of delusion. Many people regard themselves as having left the world, but this is only because they do not have real knowledge.

When you should put something aside but do not, this is called miserliness. When you should not put something aside but you do, this is called foolishness. When you should take but you do not, this is called ineptitude. When you should not take but you do, this is called greed. When neither taking nor putting aside is clarified, there is much distress.

Once you fully recognize that all the affairs of the world alter and shift as rapidly as surging water, that your own moments are ceaselessly and forever passing away, and that the original being of the Real Lord has neither beginning nor end, then you will verify the evidence of true reality only by prompt action [in taking and putting aside].

A long time ago the honorable Bāyazīd said, "I finished with pure and modest meritorious deeds in three days. On the first day I put aside the wealth and nobility of the lodging place that is this world. On the second day I put aside the glory of the eternal abode that is the afterworld. On the third day I put aside my own self, and then there was no-self."[32] His will was to empty himself of all beings so as to honor and attain the One Real.

How sad that the people of the world have forgotten the fountainhead and instead follow the streams. In the midst of the ocean's waves they demand comfort. In thunder and lightning they foolishly look forward to everlasting life. It is only the wise who take this side as frail and the other side as solid. They enjoy the way's virtue and are at ease with poverty. They reject wealth and nobility like rotten things.

---

32. Probably a translation of this saying: "Renunciation [*zuhd*] has no worth. I renounced for three days—on the first day this world, on the second day the afterworld, and on the third day everything other than God" ('Aṭṭār, *Tadhkira* 197; *Memorial* 228).

Wealth and nobility are means that invite people to strive for them. Those who achieve their desires have the myriad kinds of annoyance and anxiety. Even when sleeping and eating they are not at leisure. Why? All those who seek wealth compete constantly with others, for they have pretexts to compete with each other and deprive each other. The poor, who live alone in the meanest places, are the most at peace, because no one competes with the poor, so they alone attain happiness. The status of the poor is low and there is no further lowness. The status of the wealthy is high, but they think it should be higher. Is this not dangerous?

I seriously think that nothing shifts and alters as easily as wealth and nobility. Holding on to desires is like grabbing a loach. The harder you squeeze, the quicker it slips away. Or it is like black clouds that spread suddenly, striking with lightning and rolling with thunder, and people all run away. Then the rain suddenly stops, the clouds disperse, and the majesty and severity of lightning and thunder cease, with only mud and mire remaining. This is how nobility, position, power, and influence suddenly fall away.

Someone asked: What is the utmost perplexity of human hearts and what is the greatest weariness of the corporeal body?

I said: Striving for wealth and nobility. When you do not have them, you seek to gain them and are not at peace with yourself. When you do have them, you are afraid of losing them, so you still cannot be at peace with yourself. Before you receive the happiness of a position, you experience the difficulties of the position. Is this not the sadness and joy of a play? Once you wake up, you will see that you were dreaming. How sad that the people are not at all awake to the real knowledge of how to become wise and the true meaning of taking and putting aside.

2.8. Preparation

The Classic says, "You should die before you die."[33] If death presses against you and you are confused about it, this is only because you have not prepared for it.

Time is the root of making preparations for death, and this world is the ground for planting the seeds of going home to the Origin. If

---

33. This saying is commonly cited as a hadith.

you have not prepared yourself, how can you cross over the wind and waves of this ocean of dust? If you have no meritorious deeds, how can you be received into the boundless Heavenly Country?

If you plant seeds at the right moment, you can harvest in the autumn. If at that moment you take your ease, you will suffer hunger and cold. Fruit trees give fruit, and thorn branches beget thorns. Those who act with good will have a good reward. Those who act with evil will receive an evil retribution. Good and evil follow in a circle without any mistake whatsoever.

This is not the same as the world's laws, in which you can sometimes have a lucky escape. Only the Real Lord has unmixed clarity and utmost justice. In this world you can do good deeds and evil deeds as you please, but the reward and punishment that come later will not change. If you repent while still alive, you can benefit. If you weep blood after death, that will be a vain lamentation. When you reach that state, remorse will be of no use.

Someone said: The utmost way does not talk about meritorious deeds. It is concerned only with the cultivation of virtue without talk of reward. It prohibits evil by talking about sin but not about punishment. It talks about humaneness and righteousness but not about benefit and harm. Why is this?

I said: All these are the deviated opinions of the people of our time. From ancient times the classics and the teachings held that you cannot encourage people to do good without rewards, and you cannot stop people from evil without punishment. Moreover, the Canon of Shun codifies punishments with imagery and says five punishments are pardoned by banishment. It also says that the services of officials should be examined every three years. After three examinations, the inefficient are to be demoted and the intelligent promoted.[34] All these are explained in the great canon, so it does indeed talk about reward and punishment along with benefit and harm. Who says there are no reward and punishment? Mencius begins his teaching with humaneness and righteousness to encourage the ruler of the time to govern humanely. His goal was to attend to everything under heaven with the king's way. Is this not benefit?

Affairs need regulations and arrangements, and governance needs what comes before and what comes after. All of this is because

---

34. For these passages from the *Shun Dian* 舜典, part of the Classic of History, see Legge, *Classics* 3:38, 50.

the people of the world have long been drowned in name and profit. If profit is not used to encourage them and harm to warn them, what will make them follow guidance? This is like making a garment with silk brocade. You must stitch it with a needle. Without the needle, the thread will never be able to enter by itself. If the needle goes through only once and then comes out, that thread alone will be preserved in the garment.

The true teaching arouses and awakens the people of the world with the real benefit and harm of the afterworld, so that in the end they may recognize the Lord. When the high intention is fulfilled, there will be no room for low thoughts.

Today people of the world talk about benefit and harm on three levels: the benefit and harm of the body, which are ease and suffering, longevity and early death; the benefit and harm of wealth, which are gain and loss, increase and decrease; and the benefit and harm of name, which are praise of one's honor and mention of one's faults.

When the true teaching talks about benefit, this is firmly rooted in real benefit, which brings about the harmony of righteousness, not in the benefit of name, which brings about forgetting the fountainhead and betraying the root. The *Yijing* says, "Benefit is the harmony of righteousness."[35] It also says, "Making use [of knowledge] to pacify the body is exalted virtue."[36] How can there not be benefit in the harmony of righteousness and exalted virtue? The wealth and nobility of this world do not pass beyond the realm under heaven, and reputation and name do not surpass the emperor. These are unreal benefits that do not last.

The benefit of the true teaching goes beyond these three levels. It alone talks about the prosperity of the afterworld's real eternity. Even if all the people should attain this, no one would be competing with anyone else. Those who count the afterworld's benefit as great certainly see the benefit of this world as trivial.

Someone said: Why do you put aside the nearness of this world and make yourself suffer by thinking about the farness of the afterworld? I am afraid that this is not wise.

I said: Those who are not farsighted will certainly have immediate worries. The more wisdom people have, the more their thoughts

---

35. From the commentary on the first hexagram, *Qian*, *Wenyan Zhuan*.
36. From the Great Commentary 2.5.3.

will be farsighted. The more ignorant they are, the more they will be shortsighted. From the beginning of history, countries have been defeated, families have perished, and people have lost their lives and been disgraced, all because they were not farsighted and they acted vainly on the plan before their eyes.

Someone said: People may be farsighted in this world, but they are concerned only with the present time. I am afraid that talk of affairs after death is too impractical.

I said: When the Sage established the teaching, he carefully considered the future for a thousand myriad generations. From ancient times until now, no one ever considered this impractical. When true people engage in activity for themselves, it is for the sake of both worlds. Can you say that this is impractical?

Know that the human root has two affairs. That which exists everlastingly is the nature of the spiritual. That which decays is the corporeal body. True people take the everlasting as real, and worldly people take the decaying as reality. True people take the native place as the root, and worldly people take the lodging place as their house. Who is impractical here?

Benefit and harm right now are simply examples of benefit and harm. The affairs of this world are either good luck or bad luck, neither of which is worth talking about. This is like actors in a theater who put on makeup and become emperors, statesmen, scholars, servants, and maids. The actors look exactly like real people, yet all of them have put on temporary adornment. The clothes they wear are not at root their possessions. The benefit and harm they pass through do not in fact reach them. Once the acts of the play are completed, they take off the makeup and costumes, which have no relation whatsoever with themselves.

A one-hundred-year human life is a one-time drama. When compared with the unlimited, endless years of the afterworld, it is not enough for one day.

Moreover, how can the money and things obtained here be real things? Why do you have to obtain them to be happy and lose them to be sad? No matter if you are a sage, a wise man, or an ordinary, ignorant person, you were naked and empty-handed when you came, and you will be naked and empty-handed when you go. Even if you have all the wealth under heaven, when you die you cannot take the tiniest part of it into the soil. The false affairs of this world simply come to an end, and the real affairs of the afterworld begin to arise. Then everyone will take the real honor or disgrace of what he has earned.

Someone said: The recompense of good and evil should remain with the person in this world. If it does not remain with the person in this world, then it should be given to the children and grandchildren. Why should it have anything to do with an afterworld?

I said: The recompense of this world is not sufficient to make manifest the Real Lord's acknowledgment of the endeavor of perfect virtue, nor is it sufficient to make people satisfied with the measure of perfect virtue. Why not? Anyone who thinks of the joy of perfect virtue should take a broad look and observe heaven, earth, and the myriad things. He will see extraordinary scenes before his eyes, making him sigh and praise without end.

Here, however, the different kinds of people, good and evil, dwell together. If a place of complete happiness is to be made for a man of perfect virtue, should it not be more suitable than this? For example, when a rich merchant carrying money enters a market and encounters small things, he will pay the price. But if he comes across precious articles and does not carry enough money, he will surely promise that he will pay the price when he goes home.

When worldly people do small acts of good, their reward is trifling, so the Lord compensates them with corresponding worldly happiness. But if someone serves the Lord with a sincere heart, his endeavor will have great weight. How could worldly happiness be sufficient to pay for the utmost virtue?

Ah! Ignorant people count what their eyes do not see as nonbeing. This is like a blind person who does not see heaven, so he does not believe that there is a sun in heaven. Although at root there is the light of the sun, his eyes do not see it. How can it be possible that there be no sun?

Also, there are always some people in the world, both those with humaneness and those without it, who are alone and have no children. How can their good and evil be compensated?

A grandfather is a grandfather for himself. Sons and grandsons are sons and grandsons for themselves. If all the good and evil of the grandfather came back to the sons and grandsons, how could this be called just? When good can be rewarded and evil punished, why should recompense be given to the person's sons and grandsons rather than to himself?

Moreover, sons and grandsons have their own good and evil. The grandfather may do good and the son and grandson may do evil. If the reward deserved by the grandfather were given to the evil-doing son and grandson, how could this be called righteousness? So also, the grandfather may do evil and the son and grandson may do good. If all the punishment deserved by the grandfather came back to the good-doing son and grandson, how could this be called humaneness?

In both the laws of a king and the laws of the mighty, punishment must not reach innocent people. This is much more true in the case of the Real Lord, the most just and the most humane.

Generally good is rewarded when it reaches its utmost limit, and evil is punished when it reaches its utmost limit. If we suppose that when you do one act of good, you are rewarded, and when you do one act of evil, you are punished, and that throughout your life half the acts of one day are good and half evil, then at one moment you will be rewarded and at the next you will be punished. That is not the view of an intelligent man.

If you want people to act with good and stop evil, but you do not show them the final resting place of good and evil, this would be as if they were undertaking the affairs of farming without expecting the harvest. Their will would have nothing on which to depend. Is this not the meaning of silent perishing and empty nonbeing? In the floating life, which is like dewdrops and lightning, there is no leisure to award merits and punish demerits.

Were there no Heavenly Hall and Earthly Dungeon, the small person would have a great advantage and those upright in conduct would receive no gratitude. If good is to be done and evil stopped, there must be reward and punishment with the utmost justice. This is the authority of the Real Lord in His governance of the world. If we dismiss it and do not talk about it, not only will the Real Lord's justice fail to become manifest, but also people's fitness and unfitness will not be differentiated. Would this not block the gate of good-doing and assist small people in not being fearful?

When someone reaches the point where evil has been exhausted and good completed, there is still the greatest affair of [the Real Lord's] governance. Not only will he receive measureless purity and happiness, but also he will be rid of body and mind and start to come out from the mold of the Creative and the Receptive. The glorious light of the precious mirror will then appear refined and beautiful without guise.

Once you turn your head, you will become aware of your tardiness. The red sun is about to set, and you are late in beginning the journey. As soon as you close your eyes, all your money and things will turn into instruments of punishment and all favor and love will turn into acts of enmity. Everything will alter and shift in the twinkling of an eye. This place, unlike the place of everlasting life, is like a spark from a stone, a flash of lightning, or the things and affairs of a dream. You must not consider it real. Those who are loyal and righteous will make use of this world to extend humaneness and will attain immeasurable joy through this fleeting life. Those who are ignorant and muddled will allow their feelings to work evil for the sake of a moment's cheerfulness and receive the suffering of eternity.

You may pass through the present time in confusion, but you can hardly go home to the Real in concealment. Why do you not hasten to arouse yourself from sleep in order to avoid extraordinary regret?

You should know that preparing for death in life is always of the utmost importance, but only those with great wisdom are able to do it. When the time of death has almost arrived and your body is about to be separated from life, what benefit is there in wanting to act hastily with good?

When cows, horses, sheep, and pigs are pulled, the first three follow. Only pigs are frightened and disobedient, crying out madly such that they can be heard far away. Why is that? The horse is being called for riding, the cow for cultivating, and the sheep for shearing wool. Each has an important function and does not have doubts about being harmed. Only the pig roams the whole day in the enclosure with nothing taken from it. At the moment of being pulled, it guesses that it will be killed, so it twists obstinately trying to escape.

Those who act with good look forward to immeasurable happiness after the body dies; they will feel at ease with themselves in the midst of perils and will look forward with pleasure. Those who are insolent and lazy will act all day long in accordance with their own desires and have no endeavor upon which to depend. Having done evil deeds for which they grieve, they will not be happy in the midst of happiness. When at ease they will have doubts in their breasts, and when slightly ill they will be afraid to die. These indeed are not auspicious people.

2.9. Observing the Moments[37]

The human body has the subtleties of seeing, hearing, smelling, and speaking, all of which are enclosed in the principle of the true heart. If the heart-principle is not clear, then the eyes, ears, nose, and tongue will not be governed, nor will the whole body and the one hundred bones.

Looking at things with the eyes is not like observing them in their principles. What the eyes see may have discrepancies and errors. When you observe them in their principles, nothing is lost in itself, nor is anything hindered.

For example, there may be two things whose bodies are large and small and whose positions are near and far. The one with the large body may be far and the one with the small body may be near, like the sun and the moon. The sun is many times larger than the moon and much more distant. When you look at it with the eyes, the one with the large body becomes small and the one with the small body becomes large. This is because of the farness and nearness of position. But, when they are observed in their principles, at origin the large is large and the small is small. You will not be confused about their small and large bodies because of the near and far positions. Thus you should not look at affairs simply in terms of outwardness. You must observe the substances in their principles in order to perceive them.

One day has twelve two-hour periods, which include hundreds of minutes and thousands of seconds. Whether in noise or in silence, there are internal and external actions and daily matters and ordinary affairs in homes. In seeing and hearing they are externally the same but they are different. There are many similar affairs when there is no discrimination, so at this very moment you must observe carefully. If there is still confusion and error, this is like taking a thief for a good man. This is not a small mistake.

Contrast these: Recognizing the I and recognizing the Lord, the Real One and the Numerical One, the heart's faithfulness and the tongue's talk, deceiving others and deceiving self, real knowledge

---

37. Instead of "observing the moments" (*chashi* 察時), the text of 1873 and the table of contents of 1922 have "observing the principles" (*chali* 察理).

and practical knowledge, arrogance and contentment, humility and vulgarity, thriftiness and miserliness, courage and ruthlessness, taciturnity and stammering, circumspection and fearfulness, bold speech and reckless interruption, harmony and conspiracy, giving way to others and flattery, straightforward loyalty and untamed foolishness, righteous charity and extravagance, patience and bowing to the inevitable, taking upon self and blockheadedness, serving obediently and seeking to please, leisureliness and negligence, judging and suspecting, attending to and fawning, examination to the end and annoyance by questioning, good words and disparagement, real action and false reputation, experienced perfection and dull hindering, joyful ease and wandering about, uprightness and attachment, accommodating and constant shifting, assisting those in distress and supporting evil, abiding in stillness and snatching moments of leisure, taking precautions and suffering in poverty, disregard and profligacy, broad humaneness and crooked forgiveness, acting for others and interfering with others, bending to follow and heedless promising, remonstration and ridicule, encouragement and slander, just law and cruel punishment, firm opinions and aversion to correction, dwelling in the world and governing the world, outward cleanliness and inward lewdness, the heart's ease and the body's ease, moderation for the sake of purity and moderation for the sake of name, discarding and escaping, gazing on transformation and roaming around for amusement, sincere devotion and habitual practice, pure stillness[38] and silent perishing, real being and empty nonbeing. All these are similar to those. I have listed a few examples, but it is not possible to mention them all.

You must clearly differentiate each from the other. On no account should you perceive them as pertaining to the same substance. If something is true, it is from Islam, and if it is false, it is from self-determination. The most important thing in which to exert effort is nothing but conquering self. Although conquering self and having self are the same in form and appearance, they are distant from each other in right and wrong. One is good and the other evil. How is it possible for you not to discriminate between the two?

---

38. Instead of "stillness" (*jing* 靜), the editions of 1873 and Yang-Yu have "cleanliness" (*jing* 淨).

2.10. Wakeful Reflection

The Classic says, "In your own body—why do you not have wakeful reflection?"[39]

The Sage said, "You should have wakeful reflection on the Real Lord's inward and outward merciful solicitude, but you cannot have wakeful reflection on the Real Lord's Root Suchness."[40] Why is this?

The Root Suchness has no relation to sound and color, nor does it fall under being and nonbeing. It is of the utmost mystery and the utmost subtlety, without beginning and end, not allowing for any thought or consideration. Human attentiveness, clarity, wisdom, intelligence, words, and speech can only be used within the high and the low, the four directions, beginnings and ends, sounds and colors. Even if you go beyond and outside all of these levels such that wakeful reflection reaches all, in the end you will be aware that it is vague and uncertain.

The Real Lord has compassion and pity for the people of the world, so He sent down the Classic specifically so that everyone might reach the final goal. Hence the Classic says, "In your own body—why do you not have wakeful reflection?" Distinctly and clearly this instruction arouses the people of the world from their drunken dreams so that they may begin to exert effort.

For example, spring has no form in itself, but red and green are its displays; red and green are not spring but rather signs that spring is becoming manifest. Even more so is the Real Lord, who created and transformed heaven and earth and whose power can command spring to be like this. If we can awaken completely to the outward and inward mercy, then we can come to apprehend thoroughly the Real Being. This is not what the Sage specifically prohibited and warned against.

What is called mercy has three meanings: outward mercy, inward mercy, and real mercy. Outward mercy is heaven, earth, and the myriad things, which are means for human use. Inward mercy is body, life, talent, and power, which are for deducing the principles of

---

39. "And in your selves—what, do you not see?" (Qur'an 51:21).

40. This is a well-known hadith: "Reflect upon God's blessings, but reflect not upon God;" or, in another version, "Reflect upon everything, but reflect not upon God's Essence."

affairs. Real mercy is the teachings and laws of the True Way, which are for guiding people away from the paths of delusion.

In order to talk about these mercies you must first know what profit and loss are. Often worldly people's profit is loss for sages and worthies, and loss for sages and worthies is profit for worldly people. You should know that loss may be profit and profit loss. Only then can you talk about real mercy.

The Real Lord has compassion and pity for the people of the world. He nurtures them with mercy and makes them fearful with severity. He makes them wakeful with suffering and hardship and does not let them stay heedless and act foolishly. He is like a compassionate mother who wants to cut her child off from milk and teach him eating and drinking. She smears something bitter on her breast so that he will not drink from it. Thus we see that when people suffer from things and affairs, there are surely deeper meanings. How can their loss not be profit?

When small people attain positions, they become cruel and harsh, not possessors of humaneness. They act recklessly and without restraint, carry out tasks without cease, and obtain countless sins. How can their profit not be loss?

When you awaken to profit and loss like this, you will surely reflect on why He established these three great mercies. In examining the meaning of their establishment, you will see that all are there to be entrusted to perfect human beings. If you can perceive them like this, then indeed you will be the complete human being who represents His governance.

You should think about the fact that were there no Real Lord, there would be neither the Creative and Receptive nor the myriad things; nor would there be the descent and transmission of the clear mandate in order to establish the Constant Bonds. Were there no complete human beings, there would be no one to embody the utmost humaneness of the Real Lord, nor would there be anyone to continue and maintain the utmost way of Islam.

At root heaven and earth are molds for casting shapes. The human body is a mirror, and nature and mandate are its light and brightness. The teaching and the way are the mirror's cleansing and polishing. How could any of these be lacking? Thus it is said that when a beautiful woman faces a mirror that does not have light, it is as if her graceful beauty is facing trees and stones. This is the great meaning of [the three mercies] entrusted [to perfect human beings].

The rules taught by the True Way have the utmost importance for perfecting human beings and for prescribing good medicine to cure illness. Illness may be in the root or on the surface, so the physician will have cures for some and not for others. Illness in the root is like a flaw in jade, and illness on the surface is like dirt on a mirror. If the symptoms are not recognized correctly, there will certainly be mistakes in using the medicine. This is related to life and death, so it is not a small matter.

Generally speaking, there are various symptoms of human peace and danger, and these do not go beyond two kinds, good and evil. It is easy to know evil in the midst of evil, but it is difficult to discern evil in the midst of good. The most important crossroads for man lies precisely in wakeful reflection on this issue. The most important matter is to know self as root, and then to know others. It is easy to praise the good of others and to hide their evil, but it is difficult to make manifest one's own evil and to hide one's own good.

Although there are many sorts of good and evil, each has one root. The root of good is born from knowing self, and the root of evil emerges from not knowing self. Knowing self is to become no-self, and becoming no-self is to demean self and be modest. Not knowing self is to have self, and having self is to honor self and be arrogant.

Here we are talking not simply about highness and nobility according to the world's rules, we are also discussing those who dwell with the way's virtue but are fond of reputation.[41] You should know that when virtue and modesty come together, self-respect dwells in lowness. When honor and nobility come together, arrogance accords with highness. If you do not open up to the fountainhead of modesty and lowness, you will not cut yourself off from the root of honor and highness. You may have the most meritorious virtue in the world, but if you are praised and admired ceaselessly and you consider yourself worthy of that, your glory will be manifest in name but you will be disgraced in reality.

Just as drums and bells sound when struck, so also the way's virtue prospers when praised. But bells and drums wear out by being struck, and the way's virtue is ruined by praise. Many meet calamities

---

41. Wang now turns to the issue of *kibr wa 'ujb*, pride and self-admiration, to which Ghazālī devotes the twenty-ninth book of the *Iḥyā'*. These are characteristics of people who observe the Shariah and think that they are thereby good and full of merit.

and difficulties without losing the truth, but few hold on to name and reputation without losing the truth. Thus the harm of praising others to their face is much more than that of criticizing them to their face. Criticizing others to their face will bring forth their evil; thereby they will know themselves and have humility. Praising others to their face will hide their evil and bring forth their good; thereby they will forget themselves and think highly of themselves.

Praising someone to the face is just like a mirror, similar but reversed. When you are on the left, your image is on the right, and when you are in the east, your image is in the west. Flattering words make right and wrong, joy and anger, agreeable to you, but the thought in the speaker's heart is otherwise. Even if a myriad mouths share in giving honor, that is not equal to one thought of self-disparagement.

Gold is the noblest of the myriad things, but its body is heavy and sinks by itself. A branch that has much fruit is heavy and hangs down. When someone has virtue in his body, his heart has more reverence and awe. In himself he sees only deficiencies and makes himself more lowly.

The virtue of the way is the most precious thing in man. If it is manifest and not concealed, those who admire it will praise and flatter him, so he will esteem himself. Jealous people will criticize and slander him, so he will demean himself. If the precious things of the world are not concealed, they will be lost. Much more so is the case with the way's virtue, which is the most precious thing.

There is no firmer container in which to gather virtues than the heart. Demons and spirits cannot peer into it, and thieves cannot steal it. A person who collects and lets go of virtues in himself can bring them out whenever he wants.

When you enjoy name and reputation, the approval is lodged in the mouths of others, so virtues decrease or increase only from the mouth. It is others who make you lose and gain, not yourself. When others praise and admire you, you gain, and when they criticize and slander you, you lose. How can this be your own possession?

Moreover, virtuous deeds can be real or false. The virtue of sages and worthies is at origin lively and vigorous. It does not wait for help but is born by itself. It does not increase or decrease with outside reputation. It acts by itself and stops by itself.

Someone with false virtue will look for praise and admiration before he starts moving. This is like a flute without sound. It makes noise only when someone blows into it. Sailing vessels have no feet. When wind fills the sails, they go, but when the air stops and the wind rests, they do not move at all.

This is why at root real virtue is living virtue. When praise comes, it is not deluded, and when criticism comes, it is not dismayed. It is weighty like metal and stone, so when it encounters gales, it does not move. False virtue is light like floating ashes, flying and dancing away with the tiniest breath.

You will never gain the most precious thing in the world at a low price. If that were to happen, it would be false or stolen. Anyone who engages in such trade is ignorant. And you must know that virtue is the most precious thing. If you engage in trade with it under a false name and at a low price, is this not falsehood, stealing, or ignorance? If you do not have discrimination and discernment, will you not be perplexed about self?

Those who want to be thankful for this mercy and the ability to receive this trust must first thoroughly understand the difference between real and false. They must clean and purify their bodies and hearts with the true teaching. When they rely on cultivating proofs, the subtle clarity will manifest and disclose itself. They will surpass themselves and become selfless, gaining the station that has nothing beyond it and actually receiving and carrying the One Real.

If you cannot discriminate right from wrong, you will follow your own desires in your deeds and not comply with the clear mandate. If you know only yourself, you may have great spiritual penetration, broad and wide, but unless you awaken to Him who granted it, you will have concealed the great mercy and betrayed this heavy trust.

If you do not repent of your mistakes beforehand, you will surely be more deluded than birds and beasts. Why? Birds and beasts have no relationship with the teaching and the way, but human beings are responsible for the clear mandate. You must turn away from dreaming so that your heart may come back, emerge from delusion, and enter into wakefulness. Moment by moment you need to arouse yourself, and instant by instant you should observe the details. Day by day this will increase your reverence and awe and you will come to know that there is only the Lord. Then you will be near to treading on the True Way and climbing up to the human level. Only then will you not betray the three mercies.

2.11. Name and Profit

Name and profit decorate appearances, but good and evil are the original face. Only in sages and worthies do the traces tally with the heart, there being no difference between inward and outward.

Worldly people are immersed in floating name and empty profit. They guard their words and actions, but these do not necessarily emerge from the root heart; rather, some are for name, some are for profit, and some are bait to fish for their desires.

Those who do good deeds without good intentions are like manikins, without nature and mandate. They are not human in reality, only in form.

Those who are fond of name do not set out to be prideful, but pride is born as a matter of course. Those who are fond of profit do not set out to be greedy, but greed is born as a matter of course. These two have a deep origin, for they began with the ancestors of men and spirits and issued forth at the beginning of the cleaving of heaven and earth. They are the taproots that nourish and give rise to all the faults that riddle the fruit[42] of the myriad sorts of good. You cannot but know about them.

Those who are fond of name are like gamblers who have the heart of loving preeminence, so pride is born as a matter of course. Pride is opposed to virtue, so real virtue does not enter a proud heart. The various sins have limits, but the sin of pride has no ultimate limit. Envy deprives only others, anger deprives oneself and others, but pride wants to deprive the Lord. The proud man treads in the steps of others trying to go up, but he does not tread in others' steps to come down. When he falls, it happens suddenly, as swift as lightning. How can anyone remain with pride?

Long ago the honorable Bāyazīd said that you should repent for mistakes and errors once in your life, but you should not stop repenting for merit and virtue even after a thousand times.[43]

---

42. The 1922 edition has "speech" (*yan* 言) instead of "fruit" (*guo* 果).

43. 'Aṭṭār gives the text like this: "Repentance for disobedience is once, and repentance for obedience one thousand times." He then comments: "He means that self-admiration in obedience is worse than disobedience" (*Tadhkira* 190; *Memorial* 220).

You should know that merit and virtue themselves may bring forth haughtiness, and this is much more serious than the sins of error and transgression. When you eat delicious food and become ill, this is not equal to treating a disease with poisonous medicine. When you become proud of good deeds, this is not equal to modesty and humility as a result of sin and error. When pride dwells together with virtue, the virtue will surely disperse; when it dwells together with sin, the sin will increase. When humility dwells together with sin, the sin will perish as a matter of course; when it dwells together with virtue, the virtue will increase.

The workman surely does not show imperfect workmanship to others. You should have shame so as to hide and conceal your imperfect good. Then it will still be possible to suppress yourself. Whenever a conceited person discloses something to others in order to make them praise him or be envious, that is like fruit growing by the wayside. Passersby pick it, whether ripe or not. When those who pick are many, there may be hundreds of thousands of fruits, but none will reach perfection. In this case, there will be neither the name nor the reality. This is indeed sad.

Greedy people take joy in their own profit, but profit has two sorts, like someone's two wives. If he makes one of them happy, he certainly will not make the other happy.[44] Birth is coming to lodge, death is going home. It is lamentable that worldly people forget their native place, the everlasting abode. Instead, they greedily fall in love with illusory scenes on the pathway of the lodging. They do not know that wealth and nobility before their eyes are the playthings of evil devils. Even if they gain wealth and nobility, this is like hunting for honey. They may obtain a bit of sweetness, but they cannot escape the stings of the bees. Others keep themselves busy all day, their mouths watering in desire for a taste, but they do not obtain a bit of it. They vainly suffer bitterness right up to death. When the way and the world both perish, that will be their ultimate suffering.

Sages and worthies see that worldly people keep themselves urgently busy with playthings. They see that their wisdom and cleverness are ignorance and stupidity. Those with clear eyes call those who fail to see the principles of reality blind. Worldly people usually take

---

44. Wang probably has in mind a well-known saying, ascribed sometimes to the Prophet and sometimes to others: "The likeness of this world and the next is a man's two wives: In the measure that he makes one happy, he makes the other angry."

as true all affairs that are not for the sake of the Lord, or the way, or life and death. Those with wisdom look at all of them as nothing but a company of actors and puppets.

When people reach the time of facing death, they will have many hindrances and obstacles, such as bodily sickness and suffering, love that attaches them to wife and children, casting away nobility and wealth, and fear because of wrongs and transgressions against others. Moreover, evil devils will attack them with intensity, stirring up turmoil in their hearts and breasts. At this moment, all the adornment they had put on during their lifetime will be dispersed, and their original face will be completely disclosed. In the end they will no longer be able to cheat by concealing good and evil, real and false.

The distinction between sages and ordinary men, wise and ignorant, can be seen in the difference between joyfulness and coercion. One who is joyful is like someone who dives into the sea in search of a pearl; finding it, he climbs out happily on the other shore. One who is coerced is like a runaway servant who has been captured and fears seeing the lord of the house. In his fear and grief at the moment, he is no different from a sacrificial animal taken by the butcher.

There are people in the world who are diligent in worldly affairs but lazy in the tasks of virtue. There are four reasons for this: One is that there is no Real Lord for them to serve. Second is that there is no True Way for them to walk upon. Third is that there is no Final Abode for them to lodge in. Fourth is that there is no examination of being called to account for them to fear. Wailing and wavering, they do not know which direction to take.

2.12. Living up to the Measure

The Classic says, "The noblest of you in nearness to the Lord are those who best live up to the measure."[45] Those who live up to the measure must be true and honest in affairs and not bring about injustice and meanness. The six roots of your body must comply with the original meaning of the creative transformation for the sake of which it was established. This means that you must be thankful for the Lord's mercy toward you, you must be true to His solicitude, and you must not dare to use these in the ground of disobeying the mandate.

---

45. "Surely the noblest of you before God is the most godwary" (Qur'an 49:13).

"Look not at what is contrary to propriety"—you must look correctly. "Listen not to what is contrary to propriety"—you must listen correctly. "Speak not of what is contrary to propriety"—you must speak correctly.[46] This is the meaning of being thankful for mercy.

Exerting effort in cultivating the way of the true teaching can never come to an end. For those who enter it for the first time, there are three levels and ten regulations, none of which should be lacking.

The three levels are sincere faith in the heart, firm remembrance on the tongue, and compliant activity in the corporeal body.[47]

These three are like the root and trunk, branches and leaves, and flowers and fruit. All are so by the self-so. Why? When there are root and trunk, there must be branches and leaves. When there are branches and leaves, there must be flowers and fruit.

Although there are three levels and six names, at root they go by way of one vein. There are not two affairs. Depraved and heterodox theories speak rather about cultivating inwardness and not cultivating outwardness. Is this not cheating and deception? If something has root and trunk without branches, leaves, flowers, and fruit, then its root is certainly withered. This is self-evident, without any need for argument.

Sincere faith means having sincere faith in the Real Lord, the Unique One, along with untainted purity and cleanliness without any doubt whatsoever. When remembrance issues forth in the midst of this, the heavenly immortals will not be able to assist you, and the spirits and demons will not be able to envy and harm you. This is called sincerity. If a bit of human desire is dragged into it, evil immediately seizes the opportunity and enters in. This is like a fruit with worms. Outside it is blue or green, but inside it is totally rotten. What does this have to do with humaneness?

Firm remembrance is the firm remembrance of Him who is not two. It is not merely to recite praise. It must come to the tongue from the heart, and it must have clarity and stem from sincerity.

Compliant activity means to govern and guide all the members and bones of the body while coming and going, sitting and sleeping,

---

46. The quotes are from the explanation of how to achieve humaneness in *Analects* 12:1.

47. Wang no doubt has in mind a well-known theological formula describing faith as "Assent in the heart, speech on the tongue, and activity with the limbs."

acting forcefully without rest and going through perfectly without defect. If the moment is not right, you must attend only to your own good. When you encounter the right moment, you must regulate the family and govern the country. This is what it means to say that when the fountainhead is pure, its outflow will also be pure.

The first of the ten regulations is moderation in eating and drinking. Moderation means to be pure and clean and to reduce the amount. Food and drink are the first place where you must exert effort to establish the body and cultivate the way. Moderation is of the utmost importance in becoming a perfect human being; without it you cannot establish your body or cultivate the way. The Classic says, "If you eat or drink a mouthful of the unclear and impure and it enters the breast and belly, the Real Lord will not grant you meritorious deeds for forty days."[48] Why? The Lord of the Pure and Clean enjoys only the pure and clean. If someone establishes his body with impure food and drink and cultivates the way, this is like washing a white cloth in muddy water. The more you wash it, the dirtier it becomes.

Reducing the amount means that someone who is cultivating the way should wear clothing to keep out the cold and cover his body and that he should eat to satisfy hunger and stay alive. If he eats too much, his spirit will become dark and he will sleep much. When yin prospers and yang declines, vitality and clarity cannot be stored up. If a lamp's wick absorbs too much oil, the lamp will go out. If there is too much water for the sprouts in the field, they will be ruined. This is the principle of the self-so.

The second regulation is moderation in speech and words. Moderation does not mean to stop speaking. Rather, one should look at the appropriateness and inappropriateness of speech, nothing else. When it is appropriate to speak but you do not speak, this is like seeing someone drowning but not trying to save him. When it is inappropriate to speak but you do speak, this is like meeting with someone drunk or dreaming and talking with him. Speaking words that should not be spoken may take away all the meritorious deeds of a lifetime. If you see something that is not real, it is fitting simply to shut your mouth and keep silent. The Classic says, "When ignorant people are cautious in speech, this curtains them. When wise

---

48. Ghazālī cites this hadith: "If someone eats a forbidden morsel, God will not accept his ritual prayer for forty days" (*Iḥyā'* 2:135).

scholars are cautious in speech, this adorns them." When someone is curtained, his ignorance and vileness are concealed. When someone is adorned, his highness and elegance increase. When you observe this carefully, can you make light of speech?

Third is moderation in sleep. Sleep is the image of pure yin and the sign of death. The various sorts of heavenly immortals are endowed with great purity and have no desires and lusts. Flying and walking things are endowed with great turbidity and have desires. Man dwells between the pure and the turbid, completely embodying the principle of the Great Ultimate. If you sleep less and reject desires and lusts, you will excel and surpass the heavenly immortals. If you enjoy sleep and are greedy in what you like, you will not be equal even to birds and beasts.[49] Moreover, time is priceless—one breath has the value of a myriad pieces of gold. How can you pass your time in emptiness and drunken dreams?

Fourth is repentance for mistakes. This shows your meritorious effort. It is like the affairs of farming. First you till the ground, pull out weeds, remove stones and bricks, and take away the bad water. Then you can plant good crops. Those who advance in the way must first put aside evil. Then they can start to reach the good. When they stop doing certain things, then they can really act. This is truly its meaning.

Fifth is stillness in seclusion. Those who cultivate the way avoid objects of desire. Those who attain the way forget their feelings about circumstances and dwell in the world without being tainted, but this cannot be achieved by beginners. Eyes and ears are the gate of sound and color, mouth and tongue are the keys of right and wrong. If you wish to cut off the myriad causes, you must live in the seclusion of stillness and silence. This has nothing to do with silent perishing or empty nonbeing, for it is to dedicate oneself to the Real Being, the Unique One. When you sweep away all evil, the Root Origin will be disclosed. This is truly the meaning of the saying, "If you wish for this level, you must restore stillness. If you aspire to become a perfect human being, you must cut off the myriad causes."

---

49. Wang may have in mind the saying, sometimes attributed to the Prophet, "God mounted intelligence without appetite in the angels, appetite without intelligence in the beasts, and both in human beings. When someone's intelligence dominates over his appetite, he is better than the angels, and when someone's appetite dominates over his intelligence, he is worse than the beasts."

Sixth is contentment with poverty. Poverty is the secret of the Practicing One and is essential to cultivating the way. The poor entrust their affairs to the Lord; the wealthy entrust their affairs to property. The Classic says that when a poor man guards himself, people throughout the country will guess that he has sufficient wealth. He will be wealthy in will and remembrance, for he has the Real Lord on whom to rely. Hence the people of the world will not fathom that he is poor.

The Sage said, "The poor are the kings of both worlds." Why? To be a king means to be unrestrained and honored. The world's poor are those who do not serve the government, do not pay taxes, do not act foolishly, are not proud, and are not insulted. Robbers and thieves do not attack them, nor does anyone envy them. Are they not unrestrained? When they go home to the Origin in the afterworld, they have no fright or fear, no dragging or binding, no enemies or rivals, no examination of being called to account. In the end they climb up to the Heavenly Country and enjoy ultimate happiness forever. Is this not the honor of a king?

Seventh is contentment with one's allotment. To be content with one's allotment is to be content with one's clothing and food, but not with the principle of the way, for the principle of the way is without measure. How can one be content with stopping and not moving?

Someone asked: If there is no firm stopping place, what is the expectation?

I said: To be firm is to comply with the clear mandate of the Real Lord and to embody the real transmission of the Utmost Sage. Being content with stopping outside of these two is not to be content with stopping within the true teaching. Worldly people stop short of the true teaching and do not practice it. They disobey the clear mandate and are not content with their allotment. They do not think about who had the ability to provide for them when they were in their mother's womb drinking her blood, or when they were born and suckling her milk, or when they were given spiritual clarity and the vigor of life. Those who grasp this are firmly content as a matter of course. Muddle-headed people are content when they should not be content and not content when they should be content.

Eighth is patience. Patience is the complete endeavor of surpassing the common people and witnessing sagehood. It is the essential method of cultivating the way and becoming a perfect human being. Ever since human beings were begotten, no one has ever become a sage or a worthy easily; first he experienced toil and suffering.

There are three levels of patience: patience in cultivating the way, patience in seeing the way, and patience in attaining the way.

Patience in cultivating the way is to listen to the mandate of the self-so in all cases of failure and success, gain and loss. The rules and procedures of advancing on the way do not rely on self-nature, nor do they aim to bring about contentment and ease. You must comply with the clear mandate while passing through toil and suffering.

Patience in seeing the way is to exert effort ceaselessly in the purification and cleanliness[50] of your body and heart. When you come to see your nature, you will enter and emerge as you please. You will have a body outside the body. You will not drown when you enter water, you will not burn when you enter fire, and you will not fall when you walk on air. Metal and stone will not hinder you, yin and yang will not restrain you, the ancient and the now will be one, near and far the same. All of these are realms and boundaries in the midst of the path. If you stop moving because of these obstacles, you will be deluded.

Patience in attaining the way surpasses heaven and earth. You will make the Creative turn and the Receptive revolve, you will raise the dead and bring them back to life, you will create and transform in accordance with self. At this very moment you will attain the knowledge and vision of the sage and be worthy of entering into the level of the complete human being. You will climb up to the forbidden realm of the Real Lord and see heaven and earth suspended without root, attached like tiny dust motes to the palace of the Honorable Majesty. Although the manifestation of subtle clarity illuminates all things in the myriad directions, it is like the light of a firefly next to the Real Lord.

Those who are outside the way are ignorant. They recognize their own nature as lord and think wrongly that free and easy spiritual penetration is within their power. This can be compared to the ability to see and differentiate the five colors, which depends on the light of the sun. Were there no light to help them, people's seeing would be like that of a blind man.

You must never take a likeness as real, nor should you take outside help[51] as the inside root. If a wooden kite flies or a wooden

---

50. Yang-Yu has "stillness" (*jing* 靜) in place of "cleanliness" (*jing* 淨).
51. Yang-Yu has "display" (*zhu* 著) for "help" (*zhu* 助).

horse runs, this is not rooted in the spiritual of that thing. There must be the ebb and flow of outside help. Those who have lost their way in such things will be sick all their lives. Unless someone attains the clear mandate and the real transmission, as a matter of course he will enter deeply into the realm of the devil. He will fall down to the ultimate lowness, never to rise up above. What a great pity!

Ninth is obedient submission. The principle of obedient submission is that the myriad affairs and the myriad things, gain and loss, peace and danger, all listen to the mandate of the self-so, without any choice whatsoever. Why? It is often the case that you encounter an affair that you take as the most beautiful based on your own opinion, but hidden within it are calamity and harm that you do not know. Or you may see its outside as extreme evil, but contained within it are happiness and profit that you cannot fathom. Thus you will come to know that the mysterious secret of the Real Lord is beyond human intention and vision. From then on you must empty your heart and entrust yourself totally to the Real Lord. When something happens suddenly, you will not be surprised, and when someone interferes without reason, you will not be angry. This is because you will have attained this mysterious secret.

Tenth is joyful following. Although joyful following is similar to obedient submission, there is a distinction to be drawn between the two, for each has a different meaning. Obedient submission is to be obedient without murmur, and joyful following is to be joyful and pleased in following. This cannot but be known.

You should keep your most essential efforts like this and never be apart from them for a moment.

2.13. Sacrificing Animals

The great assembly at the Heavenly Chamber is commonly called the Small Festival.[52] It continues the past tradition of the Sage and complies with the ancient propriety. For the great mass of people, sacrificing animals is essential. In reality, it is a cause of nearness to the Lord, helping people to cross the fiery ocean of evil causes.

---

52. Wang is referring to the Festival of Sacrifice (*'īd al-aḍḥā*) at the end of the hajj, which is typically called the Great Festival; the Small Festival is that of breaking the fast of Ramadan.

The sheep offered up at the announcing of a new moon [at the end of the Chinese year] is also called the ancient propriety, and it has still not been abandoned. Confucius said, "O Zi, you love the sheep, but I love the propriety!"[53] This lets us know that preserving the name while letting go of the reality is better than losing both the name and the reality.

Moreover, the true teaching is based entirely on the clear mandate. How could anyone abandon it lightly?

You must know that there are inward and outward animals and that affairs have fountainheads and flows. You sacrifice the outward animal so as not to discard the ancient code and to comply with the law of the Sage; thereby you are prevented from thinking you are intelligent. You sacrifice the inward animal so that self-nature will surrender; thereby you embody sagehood without a moment's interval.

Ordinary people reach the inward from the outward, for they obtain the meaning by hearing and seeing. The utmost person reaches the outward from the inward, for the ground of his nature is clear at root. If someone inclines only to the inward, this is a great mistake, for it cannot be a public action under heaven. If he is attached only to the outward, this is not enough, for he will not attain the utmost propriety in the midst. When plants display red and green, this is because they are grounded in the root's liveliness; when they show the purple and yellow of silent perishing, this is because empty nonbeing is inside the seeds. When both inward and outward are maintained and one does not lean toward either, one can act in the True Way.

There are three great obstacles between true people and the Real Lord: property, affection, and self. When the ox nature is subdued, the human way begins to display itself. A man of the ordinary class will give up what he loves and bestow his property. Someone who dwells in the utmost level will fully realize loyalty and give up himself. When the inward is sincere and it appears outwardly, a man will tread in the traces of the sages and worthies and enter into the chamber,[54] giving guidance and instruction to ignorant and untaught people.

---

53. This is from *Analects* 3:17. The verse begins, "Zi Gong wanted to abandon the sacrifice of the sheep on the first of the month."

54. This is probably an allusion to the words of Confucius concerning one of his disciples: "He has ascended the hall but has not yet entered the inner chamber" (*Analects* 11.15).

If you do not leap over the three obstacles, how can you attain to the world of Islam? If the four natures have not surrendered, in the end you will fall into the ocean of delirious suffering.

To sacrifice the spirit of the faultless domestic animal for the sake of redeeming the faults of the profound person is called bestowing for the poor and helping those who are in difficulty. In the principle it also embraces [the sacrifice of] property, desires, and the corporeal body. Ordinary people do not have this knowledge, so they rebel against the ancient way and do not comply. Unless someone is a man of wisdom, he will not awaken to the utmost principle of Islam.

Both Cheng Ying and Ji Xin let themselves be put to death for the sake of their lords, Zhao Wu and the King of Han.[55] From ancient times until now they have been praised and admired for this, their names handed down by historians. How could they have achieved this without loyalty and righteousness?

Even though animals do not know the principle of loyalty and righteousness, when people use them for the affairs of loyalty and righteousness, both will attain everlasting happiness, and this is best. Moreover, animals dwell in the bodily prison. They have the toil of cultivation, the suffering of cold and heat, and the pain of the whip. If they are used for true affairs, they escape from the imprisonment of being kept in custody and attain the ground of wandering about in leisure. There is no profit greater than this. A poet said,

> When you overcome the devil in the midst of your heart,
> roaring lions will follow you as fine servants.
> When you sacrifice the cow of your own house,
> everyone under heaven will submit and yield to you.

When you reach this state, the great assembly will be completed and all under heaven will be united.

---

55. Cheng Ying 程嬰 was a retainer of Duke Jing of Jin 晉景公 (r. 599–581 BCE) who became the guardian of the Duke's son, Zhao Wu 趙武, and eventually sacrificed his life for him (the story was made into the 2010 film, *Sacrifice*). Ji Xin 紀信 (d. 204 BCE) was a general serving Liu Bang 劉邦, who became the first emperor of the Western Han dynasty. Ji acted as a decoy and was killed so that Liu could escape a siege.

The secrets of letting live and slaughtering are extremely diverse. There are many cases in which [animals] should be benefited,[56] but they are harmed, or in which they should be exterminated, but they are released. This is only because taking and putting aside are not clear. Moreover, the imperial court renounces unnecessary officials, and society dismisses servants without abilities. All the more so should this be the case with animals.

The Buddha let go of his body to feed a tiger, and he cut off some of his flesh for an eagle to eat. This, however, is only small compassion and sympathy. He did not know that he was making the great mistake of increasing loose tigers and allowing eagles to make mischief. What difference is there between this and aiding thieves with food or putting oil on fire? If, however, the tiger was killed or the eagle shot, that would have saved a great many lives. That would have been great compassion and sympathy, but he did not know how to act. He fell short in the good work of abandoning the small and following the great. We can say that this is a case in which taking and putting aside were not clarified and the light and the heavy were not differentiated. Not only does this fail to educate people, it also further stirs up their delusions.

Moreover, between heaven above and earth below and within the eight directions, both animals and plants are nothing but things. Why then do they not pity the flourishing and fading of grass and trees and grieve only at the perishing of the fliers and runners? They also say that green bamboo and yellow flowers have nothing but the buddha-nature. When we look from this standpoint, how partial this is! Since compassion and sympathy should be given equally, people should have compassion and sympathy not only for father and mother, wife and children, but they should also have it for tigers and wolves, snakes and scorpions. Abandoning and putting aside should be equal, but they only make people abandon and put aside property for monks, and they do not make monks abandon and put aside their collected property to save the people. Why is this?

Heaven, earth, and the myriad things have come into being because they are rooted in the Human Ultimate. Were there no Human Ultimate, none of the myriad things would have been established. At

---

56. Yang-Yu has *li* 立, "established," rather than *li* 利, "benefited."

origin, the various beings are there for the sake of assisting the use of the human. For worldly people, this principle is not clear, so they all love life and hate killing. Many of those who love life, however, turn to the killing of life without knowing the harm of love for life. In contrast, many of those who love killing turn to sustaining life without knowing the benefit of love for killing. From this standpoint, lovers of life are partial toward life, and lovers of killing kill carelessly. Only when the shifting and changing of the creative transformation, the waxing and waning of the four seasons, and the sufficiency and insufficiency of the myriad things are clarified can one speak of the utmost principle of life and killing.

In ancient times Li Xie, an envoy from the north, arrived in the Liang Kingdom.[57] The emperor of Liang took him to see the sights. When they arrived at the place of letting animals go, the emperor asked him, "Do they also let animals go in your country?"

Xie said, "They neither seize nor let go."

The emperor was greatly ashamed when he understood Xie's ridicule. We can say that he came to know the harm of loving life.

At the time of Tai Zong of the Tang Dynasty, the western monk Guan Ding became ill.[58] People asked the emperor to release prisoners. He said, "I do not begrudge releasing prisoners for the sake of praying for the benefit of the master. But I think that if evil people are pardoned frequently, they will go on to harm genuinely good people. Where is the benefit? On the contrary, only when these people are removed will genuinely good people be at ease."

We can say from this that he knew the benefit of love for killing. As the poem says,

> The living travel the path of death and the dead go on to life.
> Life and death intertwine without ceasing for a breath.
> There are no more obstacles beyond these two gateways.
> Who understands that everlasting life begins at death?

---

57. The Liang 梁 Kingdom flourished in the 4th and 3rd centuries BCE.

58. Tai Zong 太宗, the second Tang emperor, ruled from 626–49 CE. Guan Ding 灌頂 (d. 632) compiled an important collection of lectures by Zhiyi 智顗 (d. 597), typically considered the founder of the Tiantai 天台 school of Buddhism.

2.14. Meat and Vegetables

The human is the spiritual of the myriad things, surpassing the subtleties of being and nonbeing. But how many people in the universe are able to know whence they came?

The Real Lord's creative transformation of heaven, earth, and the myriad things was established at root for the sake of the human. This is like the human heart, which is the ruler of the body. All the body's members and bones are functions of the heart. This is why nothing is useless in heaven and earth, and there is no extra aperture in the human body, as already clarified.

Generally speaking, there is no greater way of nourishing the body than drinking and eating. The revolving of sun and moon in heaven and the carrying of mountains and rivers in the great earth—all are for the granaries and treasuries of human food and clothing. The flyers and walkers in water and on the ground, the essences of the flowers, fruits, grass, and trees—all are for nourishing the human corporeal body. From this standpoint, our human level is indeed great.

Once you know the nobility of your body, you ought to think about proper nourishment. Small people have no fear and make no distinctions, but profound people are firm in suitable acting and stopping. When something is suitable for eating but is not eaten, this is to disobey the mercy of the Creator. When something is not suitable for eating but is eaten, this belongs to selfish use. Is it possible that there would be no measured rules to observe in food and drink?

In the true teachings about food and drink, nothing is stipulated concerning meat or vegetables. Concerning meat, however, the regulation is that it is permitted not to eat meat on days other than specific occasions such as serving one's parents, festivals, curing diseases, and hosting guests during weddings and funerals. Not providing meat when serving parents is called lack of filial piety. Not slaughtering on the days of festival is called heterodoxy. Not feeding with meat to cure disease is called lack of compassion. Not offering it to guests at weddings and funerals is called not having propriety.

The Real Lord created and transformed heaven, earth, and the myriad things for the sake of the human. Is it permissible for the human to abandon them? When the ruler or senior officials bestow something on courtiers, certainly they do not dare to decline. This is propriety.

Moreover, throughout the body the human root is blood and flesh. In the mother's womb, blood is drunk. After birth, milk is suckled. During all this time people are on a diet of meat. They are entirely reliant on the Creator, not on what belongs to human acts.

If it were proper to have a vegetarian diet, such a diet's foundation should be explained. Going halfway and altering the origin is the presumptuous and depraved path of the heretics. Which idea is correct? The origin, or altering the origin? Listening to the mandate, or acting by self?

From ancient times until now sages and worthies slaughtered animals and ate meat. They did not abstain from it, because they embodied the origin and were obedient to the mandate. Heaven and earth embody the form of the Great Ultimate. The human body embodies the principle of the Great Ultimate. Heaven and earth are the body, and the human form is the heart. If you gaze on heaven and earth, you will know the utmost principle of the human body, and if you gaze on the human body, you will know the refined subtlety of heaven and earth.

The Great Ultimate produced the two forces, and the two forces transformed and became heaven and earth. Heaven covers and earth carries, encompassing the myriad things. After there were grass and trees, there were flyers and walkers. After flyers and walkers came the Human Ultimate. Lacking any of them, the world would not have been perfected. After the Human Ultimate, there were man and woman. After man and woman, there were husband and wife. When husband and wife are intimately united, they give birth to the hundred bones of the body. After begetting and growth, there is turning and moving. After turning and moving, there is spiritual clarity. Lacking any of these, the human corporeal body would not be perfected.

Thus the world's grass and trees assist the begetting and growth of the human body, and the world's flyers and walkers assist the turning and moving of the human body. The sages and worthies of the world open up their intelligence to the principle and nature of the human body. When heaven and the human unite as each other's tally, principle and form are not different. How then could either be lacking?

The way of the true teaching is to be impartial, not to lean to one side, and to be settled in every situation. Having vegetables in hand and not thinking about meat is not the same as not eating meat. Having meat in hand without need to have vegetables is not the same as not eating vegetables. This is to comply with the mandate of the self-so and not to desire or yearn to act on one's own.

Long ago there was a worthy who visited the honorable Bāyazīd. When he welcomed him into his room, the room was transformed into a large sea, and the honorable one quickly entered into it. He invited his guest to come and swim with him, but the guest said he could not do so. The honorable one said, "You cannot do so because you have eaten food that was not refined and clean. Thus you cannot pass through this pure and clean sea." This indicates that he was partial because he ate only a diet of vegetables.[59]

There was another worthy who visited the honorable Rābi'a. He saw that birds and beasts were gathered around her, but all at once they ran away and hid. The guest said, "Why did they all hide from me?"

The honorable one asked what he had eaten that day, and he replied that he had eaten meat. She said, "You like to eat their meat. How could they not hide from you?" This indicates that he was partial because he ate only a diet of meat.[60]

Eating meat emerged from the self-so of the creative transformation, so those who abstain from it are mistaken. Moreover, a vegetarian diet depends on human excretions, so those who choose the partiality of a vegetarian diet are deluded.

There are various kinds of meat, however, and it is permitted to eat some but not others, so you should know this. Among those whose eating is permitted are the kinds of animals that you feed, such as cow, sheep, chicken, and geese; the kinds that are in the fields, such as river deer, rabbit, and deer; the kinds that hide away in water, such as fish and shrimp; and the kinds that fly and hover, such as wild geese and ducks.

It is not permitted to eat seven kinds of meat: animals that are habitually perverse and snatch food from other animals, like hawks and kites; those whose nature is cruel, like tigers and wolves; those whose forms are not normal, like fresh water turtles, mud eels, and hedgehogs; those that are disgustingly filthy, like pigs and dogs; those that are born from a disorder in the species, like mules and donkeys; those that are transformed only halfway, like cats and mice; and those

---

59. 'Aṭṭār provides the story in *Tadhkira* 177 (*Memorial* 205), but Wang has altered the details and moral to make his point.

60. 'Aṭṭār tells the story, identifying the visitor as Ḥasan Baṣrī (*Tadhkira* 78; *Memorial* 103); here also Wang has modified the details to suit his purposes.

that have great merit in the world, like a cow that cannot be slaughtered lightly. So, when people need to make choices in acting, is it proper to eat meat carelessly?

Someone asked: When a cow has merit, why would you want to slaughter it?

I answered: If you want to slaughter it so that your mouth and stomach will have a delicacy, that is not permissible. But if you use it in true propriety, that is ruled to be appropriate. This is like a deceitful and hypocritical person who shrinks in fear but meets a good ending, or a loyal and chaste person who puts himself forward to be killed in war. Who is right and who is wrong?

The classical law of the true teaching holds that when someone makes slaughtering cows his profession in order to cater to people's appetite to eat savory food, this should be more prohibited than slaughtering all other living creatures. There is no greater sin than this.

2.15. Gambling and Drinking

Gambling and wine-drinking are prohibited by the true teaching. Our conduct in the way of Islam is to be dedicated to the Lord with one heart, such that no other doctrines enter into the midst. Gambling and drinking do nothing but delude people's hearts. Once the heart becomes irresolute, it will be obscured and empty of the Lord, and then the devil will take advantage and seduce it.

The devil seduces man in more than one situation. He follows peoples' desires, subtly turning and revolving. If someone goes forth to the good, the devil takes advantage of the good, using it as bait that will surely bring him out of the good into the bad. Given that this is the case, it is much more so when people themselves go forth into evil and lowliness.

Gambling is the devil's clever device to seduce people. Any kind of gambling causes division of the heart and agitation of the lower soul. The ears hear confused noises, the eyes see many confusing things, the heart thinks about success and failure, and the spirit attends to gain and loss. When this situation does not leave him even for a moment, how can he preserve peaceful settledness and quiet consideration? When he does not hear and does not see, how can fear and awe be present? At hard-pressed, critical crossroads, he will be overcome by complete thoughtlessness and broken discernment. He will become like the mad flow of a falling torrent, ruining the dikes and breaking the barricades. Or he will be like a wild colt or a violent horse, throwing off the bridle and biting off the bit. Once it runs away in a rush, nothing can make it stop.

If someone has this situation, even if a thunderclap comes suddenly and heavy rain falls, he will not turn around and look. When the rain ends, he will not know the aftereffects. He will look but not see, listen but not hear. Even if calamity or good luck is as big as a mountain, he will not discern that he should avoid it or run toward it. He may have a body of a hundred years, but he will forget his hundred-year body. He may possess an estate worth a thousand ounces of gold, but he will waste the estate. He will forget himself and forget his parents. In one day he will abandon entirely the endeavor of rectifying the heart and cultivating the body. He will not know that time is priceless—difficult to obtain, and easy to lose. Today is already gone and will not come again tomorrow. This is like obtaining a precious container in which many beautiful things should be stored, but over the years he stores up stinking and rotten things. What a pity!

Sages and worthies make progress in cultivation. They esteem each moment because laziness and delusion for one breath would bring about the loss of extremely precious treasures. They stay anxiously alert without a moment of idleness.

Ignorant and dull people are totally confused and do not wake up. Dwelling in the wind and waves of the ocean of dust, standing on the perilous ground of life and death, they wander around scattered and boastful, considering this to be true and real comfort and forgetting the root origin of the eternal abode. Were they to know the eternal abode in true detail and see that this world becomes nonbeing in the twinkling of an eye, how could they wander around gambling and throwing away precious treasures by themselves?

Moreover, the negligence that wine brings in people is more serious than this. Hence the Classic says, "Wine is the key to all evils."[61] If they open this lock, there is no evil that will not reach them. This is why this strict prohibition has never been loosened from the beginning until now.

---

61. A saying of the Prophet: "Avoid wine, for it is the key to every evil."

Who will understand this? If someone admonishes people with words that they cannot understand, that is the mistake of the admonisher, not their transgression. But there are also people who do not admit or talk about it, so it does no harm to repeat it.

From ancient times until now those who ruined the country and destroyed the family by drinking wine are beyond reckoning. They destroyed the content of the laws and ruined the constant human relationships, all because of wine, which brought about calamity and violence. It can change people's will, make their spirits turbid, and delude men of wisdom. It can make the worthy ignorant, the modest greedy, the chaste licentious, men of faith wavering, and the obedient rebellious.

Thus we have "the meeting when tassels were plucked," "the throwing of jujubes and chestnuts," the killing of his father the emperor by Yang Guang, and the account of Lushan when he violated the mother of the country.[62] Prince and minister, father and son, propriety and righteousness, modesty and shame—all were wasted and easily transgressed. Without the madness caused by wine, none of these serious sins would have been committed. The most ignorant and ferocious people of the world could not have willingly committed these well-known crimes. If they were compelled to do them, surely it was because of wine.

A drunkard enters a lofty castle and considers it his own private, six-foot cubicle. He tries to ford vast and deep water, considering it an ordinary ditch, only because wine has darkened his knowledge and discernment. We see worldly people, addicted to wine, capering about with a bit of drunkenness, their mouths singing and cursing at the same time. When they are very drunk, they throw away all dignity and totally disregard propriety. Yet those who are on good terms with them regard them as exceptional, and those who talk about them consider them eminently wonderful.

---

62. The plucking of the tassels refers to a story in *The Romance of the Three Kingdom* 三國演義 involving the character Jiang Xiong 蔣雄. The throwing of the jujubes was an episode associated with Emperor Wu 武 (d. 549 CE) of the Liang 梁 dynasty and his general Xiao Chen 蕭琛. Emperor Yang Guang 楊廣 (d. 618 CE) of the Sui 隋 Dynasty is said to have killed his father to assume the throne. An Lushan 安祿山 (d. 757 CE) was a general who mounted a catastrophic rebellion against the Tang dynasty and was eventually killed by his own son.

Ah! Although there are accounts like the excellence of Yuan Ming and the talent of Taibai, both of whom felt enriched the whole day when drunk, what kind of aid can that offer in true affairs?[63]

Moreover, if someone is greedy and gluttonous and gives himself over to drinking, is it not that he has no shame in his heart? A person's food for a day is not more than one *sheng* of rice, but those with appetite for drink consume many times more than that, so people under heaven become impoverished. If nearly half the inhabitants in a village of one hundred *mu*[64] plant sweet rice, this will surely cause hunger under heaven.

If people can stop drinking, there will not be the calamities of hunger and cold under heaven, or the grief of the dying and perishing of one's own body. Propriety between prince and minister and friendship between friends will be completed outwardly, and intimacy between father and son and chastity between husband and wife will be completed inwardly. When the propriety[65] of human relationships is kept bright and the whole code of the teaching has been adopted, everything will be complete. Those who destroy the constants and become muddled by drinking have no awe toward the mandate of the Lord or compliance with the sayings of the Sage. We can only say that those who desire greedily to become drunk and freed from a thousand anxieties have not considered that they will be going home to the Real. They will repent when it is too late.

2.16. Interest and Hoarding

Taking monthly interest to produce wealth, and purchasing grain to hoard it while waiting for the price to rise, are two affairs strictly prohibited by Islam. Those who do these things will surely not be able to attain the mercy and compassion of the Real Lord, for this is to disobey the clear mandate and betray and conceal His great mercy.

---

63. Yuan Ming 淵明 (365–427) is considered the greatest poet in the Six Dynasties era. Taibai 太白 (705–62), also known as Li Bai 李白, was a prominent poet of the Tang dynasty.

64. One *mu* 亩 is about 1/16th of a hectare. One *sheng* 升 is about a pint of dry rice.

65. Yang-Yu has "principle" (*li* 理) instead of "propriety" (*li* 禮).

Such people consider money and things as their own possessions and think that they can strip people to make themselves prosperous. They do not awaken to the fact that interest is born from the root, nor do they see whence comes the root and whence they themselves come. They are severely lacking in humaneness. They firmly guard their wealth so that there is increase but no decrease. They look for interest on the fixed date and never change the fixed rules, choosing only to benefit themselves and never reflecting on the harm they do to others. They are harsh and without compassion. Is there any difference between them and the birds and beasts?

Right here is found the distinction between people and things. Those who collect without knowing how to distribute while being endlessly greedy and stingy are birds and beasts. The human way is moderation in taking and putting aside, assistance to those in distress, and aid to those in peril.

At root body and life, money and things, are not human possessions. All are the merciful solicitude of the Real Lord. This is why the humane human loves the people. If you do not love the people, how can you show gratitude for His mercy?

There are two ways of extending humaneness and righteousness. The humane human puts himself in place of others and examines the difference between himself and others. If you speak of humaneness and righteousness but do not differentiate between yourself and others, this is a mistake. If all people and things are one body with the I, the I will know only to love itself and serve itself. He who does not put himself in place of others is a small person. Why? Because small people know only that there is an I; they do not know that there are others. How can such a person be called a humane and righteous human? When someone's virtue is genuine, it reaches those who are far away and do not live nearby. If your love reaches only those nearby—self and those whom you love intimately—that can also be done by animals, not to speak of small people.

Only the wise and profound can love those far away, enwrapping and enclosing the universe, such that love reaches everywhere. Since all the people of the world emerged from the Real Lord's creative transformation and began together from the same fountainhead, in fact you should love everyone; much more so your ruler, parents, siblings, and weighty people who have shown you kindness and benevolence. Just as the Classic decrees, you should not deal with these in the same manner as with others.

Moreover, love is not empty love. If people are hungry, you should feed them. If they are thirsty, you should provide them with drink. If they have no clothing, you should clothe them. If they have no dwelling, you should give them a lodging place. If they are ignorant and untaught, you should teach them. If they are suffering from illness, you should look after them. If they make mistakes, you should admonish them. If they are lonely and neglected, you should nurture them. If they have disputes with one another, you should help them find solutions. If they insult and ridicule you, you should forgive them. If they die, you should bury them. If they have nothing, you should assist them. Comparing them with those who injure others to profit themselves and who are harsh and have no compassion, what can one say?

If some people are poverty-stricken and have no means of livelihood but strongly desire[66] wealth and happily follow those who collect interest, their punishment is the same as those who collect it. Why? Just think about this. Ever since you were given life inside your mother's belly, who reared you? When you were born and there was milk, whose solicitude was that? When you gained the ability to eat, who guided you? When day-by-day you grew stronger, who made you grow? When your knowledge and discernment gradually increased, who taught you? When you compare human affairs with covering by heaven, carrying by earth, and invigorating and nourishing by the myriad things, which is greater?

Once someone is deluded and perplexed, he will treat the clear mandate lightly. He will become unmindful of the Real Lord who transformed him and gave him life. Hoping for wealth and things, he will rely on those mean fellows who succeeded by luck. Is there any transgression, disobedience, and betrayal more serious than this?

You must know that there is the great way of producing wealth as a matter of course when business transactions are fair and honest. You should embody the alteration and transformation of yin and yang and follow the waxing and waning of the seasons. Benefit and harm should be considered equal, gain and loss accepted together. Thus should you listen to what is so by the self-so.

The proverb says, "Whether you travel fast or slow, the path ahead is the same road. Whether you take obediently or rebelliously,

---

66. Yang-Yu has *yuan* 愿 in place of the *yuan* 願 with the same meaning.

there is only so much wealth in the midst of the allotment." It cannot be increased or decreased even a bit. The enumeration of wealth was arranged by predetermination. You invite it, but it will not come. You scatter it, but it will not go away. How can you rely on people's oppressive stripping of others?

Moreover, the span of a human life between heaven and earth is as ephemeral as that of a mayfly. Life and death, failure and success—in no way do these rely on self.

Once there were two people, one whose occupation was trading fish and another who caught them. The trader came back and saw his companion happy as if he had something in hand. He asked, "Did you catch many fish today?"

He replied, "I happened to get a huge fish, but it escaped from the net and damaged my fishing gear."

He said, "Then why are you happy?"

He answered, "Because I saw a millipede that was running so fast that it seemed to be flying, but a blind man stepped on it and killed it. That touched me and I composed a poem:

> The life of the fish was not yet exhausted,
> so I did not gain the means.
> How can I look forward to a great delicacy
> when its time has not yet come?
> Life reaches its end like a millipede
> going beneath a blind man's foot.

When you grasp this, you can see that if something does not pertain to your allotment—whether it is longevity or young death, failure or success, peace or danger, gain or loss—you cannot yourself increase it or decrease it by a single mote.

Worldly people are greatly deluded in two affairs, and in the end they will have a pitiable state. One affair is collecting excessive money and things, whether obediently or rebelliously; once the body dies, these are left for others. The other affair is that they will arrive at the day of fair reckoning in the latter world. The suitability and unsuitability of each instance when money and things came and went will be investigated to their detriment. The toil and suffering that they faced here will turn into further trouble in the latter world. How ignorant they are!

I wish that the people of the world would destroy the barrier of name and undo the lock of profit. Once they know that these are vain and absurd, as a matter of course they will not take them seriously. At this moment how then could they dare to strip people for the sake of their own abundance and firmly regulate the monthly interest?

When people purchase grain to hoard it and produce wealth, this is even more evil and poisonous. Here, however, there are three different intentions: to relieve and aid the people, to provide against famine, and to produce interest. Those who do this to relieve and aid the people are worthies. Those who provide against famine are ordinary people. Those who produce profit are evil people.

When people relieve and aid the people, sometimes they do it with the heart, sometimes with the body, and sometimes with things. For example, in the silence of stillness the sage roars thunderously. His intention is so sincere that he can transform and influence the people. He has pity on those in difficulty and distress, as if he himself has fallen in a ditch. He has sympathy for the masses and certainly desires to put them in a peaceful place of rest. This is aiding with the heart.

When people are struck by severe calamities like an epidemic and are starving throughout the country, when infants are sobbing miserably because of hunger, and when people do not have anything with which to live, a worthy bears their keen pain personally and he prays that he may take the place of the people. This is aiding with the body.

When a righteous man takes out all that he possesses and empties what he has stored, giving nourishment to the aged and showing pity to orphans and all those who are in danger and difficulty, this is aiding with things; even if he cannot reach everyone far and near, he surely thinks with fairness about everyone in the villages and neighborhoods of his area.

In ancient times there was a worthy who made it his own affair to aid the people every day. Someone asked him if he had a teacher in this. He replied, "When I was young, I retired to a mountain. One day I saw a lion rush out and kill a camel. Then it retreated to hide in the valley and waited until a group of beasts came, ate their fill, and left. Then the lion came out and ate what was left. I was utterly surprised, so I told the story to a woodcutter. He said, 'This is not strange at all. It is simply the righteousness that is specific to certain animals.'"

All people should aid others with their bodies and lives, not yielding simply to the desires of mouth and belly. To provide against famine means to make an effort to store up enough grain for one-half year or one year so that you will always be prepared for sudden changes. If you serve parents without lack, this is filial piety. If you rear those in front of your knees without deficiency, this is compassion. If you provide your relatives and the villagers with kindness, this is righteousness. How could humaneness be protecting only your own body?

Life for humans is such that if you have the life of one day, you have the body of one day. If you have the body of one day, you have the nourishment of one day. There is a well-established saying: "There is no such thing as young death or longevity. Once your wages have been exhausted, you will die." When you are prepared, you will not suffer waiting for the final blow. We can say that this is the meaning of providing against famine.

When people receive interest, their hearts are deluded by wealth and interest. The intention of compassion and happiness is destroyed. They hope to cut off the lives of tens of thousands of people while they fill up sacks in their houses. They rebel against the mandate of the Real Lord and go against the humaneness of the Utmost Sage.

As for those who fill their warehouses with boxes seeking profit and who pile high their stores waiting for the right time, their deepest anxiety is that there will be peaceful times. They think happily about drought and famine. When they hear that young plants have shriveled and the harvest is deficient, their pleasure increases. When they see that the wind is gentle and the rain sweet, they become anxious. Only when everyone under heaven is suffering from poverty, when the markets are filled with people starving to death, and when one peck has risen to the price of pearl and jade, selling for a hundred gold pieces, is their intention fulfilled.

Compared with the ones who produce wealth by fixed interest, these are many times more evil. Those who charge interest want others to be prosperous, but those who buy grain and hoard it detest the year of a good harvest. The intentions of the two are far apart.

I earnestly think that intention is the root of the myriad deeds. It is this that distinguishes the sages and the ordinary. If someone's intention is good, he is a sage and a worthy, and if his intention is evil, he is the same as the animals.

Intention is to the heart as speech is to the tongue. When there is a tongue, there will be speech; he who has no speech is dumb. When there is a heart, there will be intention; he who has no intention is wood and stone. If a high tower does not have a firm foundation, it will not rise. Meritorious deeds without sincere intentions will not be established. People will be judged as worthy or ignorant by their good and evil intentions.[67]

In ancient times two people were hunting together in the mountains. One of them saw something concealed in the woods that looked like a beast. He thought it might harm people, so he shot it. When he came to look, it was a person. The other saw something like a person that was moving around in the woods, so he shot it. When he came to look, it was a river deer. The former injured someone by mistake; his intention was to save people, so he should be rewarded. The latter took a river deer; his intention was to kill someone, so he should be punished. Why? Both shooting the river deer and shooting the person were by mistake, but in one case the intention was good, and in the other it was evil. The principle will not allow anyone to escape.

This means that if someone sets aside money and things in order to aid those who are suffering from poverty, but his intention is to acquire name, that is good along with evil, for the selfish intention destroys the true deed. This is like a pool of pure water. If some filth accidentally falls into it, it can no longer be used. All the more so when someone does evil with an evil intention.

How sad it is! Someone buys and hoards grain, which looks good in name, but the intention is to produce profit, so it becomes harsh and cruel. He does not know that time flies quickly and that everything alters and shifts in the blink of an eye, so he will possess nothing. Mistakenly he takes emptiness and falsehood as real, and he keeps on stripping and depriving. He creates inexhaustible bad actions and will receive immeasurable punishment. What benefit is there?

You must know that wealth and nobility before the eyes are like flowing water. From the start it goes many places, reaching this ground now, then, in the blink of an eye, it shifts and flows to other places, never stopping. When it has not yet reached you, it is not your water. When it reaches you, you can irrigate your field, or clean your filth, or quench your thirst. In reality it is your water, but if you do not use it, it flows on, so it does not belong to you either.

This is like two people who are traveling together with one servant following behind. At this point no one knows which is the

---

67. Wang probably has in mind the sound hadith, "Deeds follow upon intentions, and surely every man shall have what he intends."

master. Only when they part does this become known. When worldly people are dwelling here, wealth and nobility follow them, and foolish people mistakenly recognize these as their possessions. When they leave the world, the wealth and nobility stay with the world and do not follow the people. How could they possess them personally? At root, they are public things of this world.

Oh, those greedy for wealth become slaves of the wealth, not masters of the wealth! People have servants so that they can share their grief and replace their toil, but they cannot send their wealth outside for their sake. Wealth can make people go far away, taking great pains and great risks, such that they obediently follow in anything. If they are not slaves of the wealth, whose slaves are they? How sad it is!

2.17. Wind and Water [*fengshui*]

Those who use human strength in choosing auspicious ground to bury the dead and benefit the living are superficial. Certainly they do not know that good and evil are the roots of yin and yang, and the heart-ground is the fountainhead of Wind and Water.

Good thoughts provide moisture like gentle winds and seasonal rains, nourishing and bringing forth the myriad kinds. Evil thoughts issue forth like hail and dust storms, destroying everything they encounter. If this is the way you discern yin and yang, your fragrant reputation will remain for a thousand ages and your station will be elevated when you go home to the Origin. Those who act contrary to this will leave behind foulness for a myriad years. How could they reach a high place after death?

When you finally shut your eyes, body and life will be separate from each other and good and evil will have already been fixed. At that point officials will no longer have people to tend, and people will no longer have officials to govern them. Even if they want to do good, it will be impossible.

Those with foolish hearts choose the ground, indulging in the vain hope that their progeny will display glory. How will it benefit them? It makes no difference to those who are greedy and desirous whether something is green or red. Those who are pure and true, without selfish desires, immediately differentiate between black and white. Who can cheat and deceive the Real Lord, who is utmost in justice?

In short, the teaching of Islam takes the method of yin and yang as incoherent[68] and regards the clarity of foreknowledge as shallow. This is because, though its name is seeking [advantage] and avoiding [disadvantage], it loses the reality of seeking and avoiding. Rather, it brings about transgression for those who use it, so true people do not adopt it.

When Kongming[69] had not yet left Nanyang, he knew beforehand that all under heaven would be divided into three kingdoms. He led six expeditions over Mount Qi. But before obtaining an inch of land, he died. What benefit did he have from his foreknowledge?

Moreover the first emperor of the Han Dynasty and the first emperor of our Ming dynasty, who were excellent among all people, were commoners in origin. No one has ever heard that their grandfathers or fathers had chosen what was said by yin and yang or had obtained the signs of good omens. Yet their progeny had wealth in the myriad directions and their thrones were sustained for several hundred years. When favor is cut off and influence decreases, where are yin and yang?

The foolish people of the world talk happily about [the method of yin and yang] and have great faith in it. If what they say is correct, then why do those who have taken the name of [experts in] yin and yang fail to choose for themselves the best luck? Why do they not receive everlasting glory and prosperity? Why do they labor throughout their lives to be of service to others? There is an ancient saying, "Before you move the soil from a mountain top, first look to see who will be inside the house." It is also said, "A person of good fortune will not be buried in a ground without good fortune." These sayings sweep away yin and yang completely and thoroughly. How often we see people choosing good ground, but once calamity has been incited, the ground does not have the effect of good fortune for them. Why are they still deluded?

Know that yin and yang are the creative transformation of the Real Lord, and Wind and Water are also governed by the Real Lord. Moreover, small knowledge does not reach great knowledge—a sum-

---

68. The 1857 edition and Yang-Yu have what appears to be a typographical error (*jiexiao* 戒小 instead of *xianxiao* 咸小).
69. Kongming 孔明, the honorific of Zhuge Liang 諸葛亮 (d. 234), was a famous military strategist.

mer insect knows nothing of ice and snow.[70] How much more is this true of the ignorant and stupid small person, who presumptuously wants to steal the secret of the creative transformation with his own narrow viewpoint. His foolishness is extreme.

The heart-ground of wise people is refined and clear. They carry in their breasts the utmost way, neither relying on the myriad things nor borrowing the actions of others. Life is life, without depending on people; death is death, without depending on people; nobility is nobility, without depending on people; and meanness is meanness, without depending on people. Success and failure, gain and loss, all are like this. In the business of choosing the ground, they presumptuously try to change the prearrangement. How could it depend on people? When people cast away the Real Lord, who created and transformed heaven and earth and who clothed and fed everyone, and when they turn to the heresy of others, relying on and trusting in one piece of turbid soil, they are betraying the root and forgetting the fountainhead, so their perplexity and shallowness are extreme.

Know that people are buried because they will be returning to the root and going back to the origin. This is the principle of the mutual transferal of yin and yang. Why? Because the Great Ultimate produces the two forces, and the two forces are transformed, making heaven and earth. The light and pure ascend up high, and the heavy and turbid descend down low. People's nature and mandate dwell in heaven as the taproot of heaven, but their corporeal body emerges in the midst of earth as the essence and ornament of earth. When form and spirit are united as a pair, they receive the mandate and become a human being, standing between heaven and earth. This is the ultimate great cause and effect, which cannot be explained completely in a few words.

When people are born into the world, they cannot choose the location, but when they leave the world, they must go home to the original soil. Islam inters people because they should return to the midst of the great earth, the root from which they originally came. No other action is needed.

When someone attains the True Way, his spiritual returns and goes home to heaven in an ascended station because of his meri-

---

70. The 1873, 1904, and 1922 editions have "frost" (*shuang* 霜) instead of "snow" (*xue* 雪).

torious virtue. When someone attains a crooked way, his spiritual is placed down in the earth in a descended station because of his heterodoxy. The bodies of both the true and the crooked, however, take up lodging in the soil and stay there forever. This is like water that is thrown into water—it goes home to its fountainhead. Although the body becomes separate from life, the spiritual clarity is not interrupted, because once the myriad things have gone home together, form and spirit will be reunited. Is this not blessing? Then the diverse affairs will no longer have any benefit.

This is not equal to provision before the eyes, for this provision has nothing to do with being buried in the earth or with inner and outer caskets, but with the companions that go along with the body. When living in the world, human beings have three companions: money and things, wife and children, good and evil. At root neither money and things nor wife and children will always be there, for when someone encounters the affliction of death, he will be separated from them. But good and evil in the heart will follow along like faithful friends. When someone meets calamity and harm, good and evil will guard him forever. It is only these companions that can be with him in both life and death, sharing in both his suffering and his happiness. What then is the benefit of all the others?

Someone said: The law of the true teaching of Islam is refined and strict. But in the matter of burial, inner and outer caskets are not used. This means that the teaching does not take human feelings into account.

I said: The utmost principle of not using inner and outer caskets has two reasons. One is the self-so, the other is purity and cleanliness. The self-so is that man's origin is from soil, so he returns to the root and circles back to the origin. Coming back to soil again is called the self-so.

As for purity and cleanliness, when human flesh and blood are buried in the great earth, in the end they will be transformed and become soil. This is like impure water that is thrown into the ocean—it no longer tastes of impurity. If it is poured into a container, its filth will go to the extreme. In comparison with that principle, is this not pure and clean?

At root man emerged from earth and soil. If in the end he is preserved in an inner and outer casket, this is like ice and charcoal put together in a fireplace; the two will never unite. This is called forgetting the root. Forgetting the root is to fail to accord with the self-so.

If a deceased person has no knowledge, how will a gold inner casket and a jade outer casket benefit him? If he knows that his body has been placed in the midst of pus and blood and there is no place where he can escape the extreme filth sticking to his body, how can he be pure and clean? Filial piety in life has a limited period, but filial piety after death has no end. If the deceased parents fall into this suffering and difficulty, how can this be filial piety?

From this standpoint, which one is pure and clean, and which one is impure and unclean? Which one accords with the self-so, and which one does not accord with the self-so? Someone expressed this in a poem:

> When a seed encounters a covered basket,
> red and yellow stay silent and alone forever.[71]
> If it circles back and enters the soil,
> it casts off its shell and wanders freely.

Wind and Water are not in mountains and rivers, but in your own body. Burial is not in the binding, but in the self-so. Who is right and who is wrong? A man of discernment will discriminate.

2.18. The True Mandate

When one receives the mandate to go home to the Real, this is to leave and not come back. Gain and loss lie in this one event. This is not what is called the going and coming of transmigration, nor is it the theory of the consequences of actions.

The way of Islam takes death as the true mandate and it takes grief and sadness as human feelings. It takes the root origin as most important, followed by ritual propriety. One should not only be sad and grieving, one should also combine this with harmony and obedience. One who grasps this will attain both the side of the true mandate and the side of human feelings.

The customs of Tianfang esteem black for the propriety of mourning. Death belongs to the form of earth, so the suitable color is dark and black. In this land, however, the regulation is to use plain

---

71. Yang-Yu has "seeking" (*qiu* 求) in place of "forever" (*yong* 永).

white cloth. Although this accords with the time, it loses the root intention. Hence I say that it is customary.

The form of heaven and earth is the guise of yin and yang. Yin and yang become water and fire. Dust is contained inside water, and air is stored inside fire. In the principles there is no before and after, but forms have slight differences. At root the four agents are one body, and then they intermix. The light and pure ascend, and the heavy and turbid descend. Thus heaven is high and clear. It rotates and revolves and is called yang. Earth is low and beneath. It does not move and is called yin.

The root of yang is spiritual and subtle, and the root of yin is heavy and turbid. When we talk about them as differentiated, they are yin and yang and the four agents. When we talk about them as united, they are the one corporeal body of the human. This is different from the five-agent theory, in which metal belongs firmly to water and wood belongs firmly to fire, and both are produced by intermixing. How is it possible to compare this with the storing up of air inside fire and the containing of dust inside water, all in one body? After all, this neglects the original being of the root suchness and instead adopts metal and wood, which are produced later. The mistakes of this theory are clear, without need for argument.[72]

You should know that when a human being is born in the world, thereby entering the drunken dream of the floating life, this is called a descent. When a human being departs from the world, thereby actually going beyond the perplexity and delusion of empty death, this is called an ascent. This is like planting seeds in the ground. The form will gradually be completed. Even when the branches and trunk wither, the fruit on the tips of the branches will not itself decay.

Just as a tree comes to bear fruit, so also the body makes a person perfect. Just as the essence of grass and trees, flowers and leaves, is entirely embedded inside the fruit, so also all the subtleties of the body's one hundred members and bones go home in the midst of the nature of the spiritual. What is left over after death is nothing but dregs. At the time of coming, good and evil are not yet divided. At the time of leaving, high and low can at once be distinguished.

---

72. Liu Zhi provides an explanation of the differing rationales for the four- and five-element theories under diagram 2.8.

The various [Confucian] authorities say that regardless of whether the deceased person is worthy or ignorant, death is a great and inauspicious change. The propriety of mourning is to dress in plain white cloth. When they hear about death, they are all afraid. Moreover, things used in mourning are shunned and avoided. These are all customs and habits in China. How can these be the universal way?

Man's life and death are two crossroads in the path of a traveler. They have been public affairs from ancient times until now. Neither sages nor ordinary people can escape returning to the mandate and going home to the Real. Why do they call it inauspicious? Moreover, plain white cloth has the true color of the Root Suchness. Why do they call it the cloth of inauspiciousness? Among the five colors, white is the most auspicious, for at origin it is pure and clean and is not caused by human making. Other colors can certainly not come up to it.

At the time of mourning in the way of Islam, the garment is changed. This will do for the outward ritual, but not for the root intention. Why? If you do not change the garment from what is ordinary for the living, you will not attend to human feelings. But if your heart grieves excessively, you may disobey the true mandate.

When someone good passes away, this is like a good trader who gains profit and goes home in triumph. How can you say it is inauspicious? When someone not good passes away, another story is suitable. The people of the world who do not know the root and branch grieve and become sorrowful in all situations. This is because they are seeing only partially without what is conveyed by the way.

Death will follow in continuity, whether early or late. But in their drunken dream people do not wake up, as if they take their body as existing forever. They should think about the relationship between fruit and plants, deep sleep and wakefulness, ascending above and descending below, the everlasting abode and the lodging place, the heavenly and the worldly, the true mandate and human feelings. Which should be taken as lightweight, which heavy? Which is joy, which grief? If you observe these in detail, you will not delude yourself.

To talk about affairs of mourning is to talk about customs and human feelings. Investigating the utmost way, however, is about going home to the Origin, which is the proof of the fruit. In respect of human feelings, you must grieve, but in respect of the true mandate, you must obey. If someone grieves and complains too much in the way of being a subject or a son, he has no sincerity in loyalty or filial piety. So much more so is this the case with the Real Lord's true mandate.

What is called transmigration is the way of the Buddhists, which began from the time of the Han dynasty. During that dynasty some Chinese people followed this way, founded this theory, and established the teachings. They made statements about the consequences of actions in terms of profit and loss. Using metaphors for the empty theory of transmigration, they seduced the people of the world to hurry and adhere to this way so that they might have a livelihood.

When people asked about the evidence for the theory of transmigration, they said that if you want to know the causes of the previous world, it is what you receive in this life, and if you want to know the causes of the later world, it is what you do in this life. Throughout the country people submitted to this theory, like those who are hungry and will eat any food and those who are cold and will wear any clothing.

The people do not know that before the Jin and Han dynasties, the Confucians and the Mohists were like ice and fire, and afterwards in the Tang and Song dynasties, the Three Teachings were established as equal, though they contradicted each other.

Loyalty and filial piety are the pivot of Confucianism. The Buddhists, however, do not have the propriety[73] of ruler and parents. Instead they receive prostrations from their father and mother. Moreover, they teach that progeny should be cut off and cease, whereas Confucians esteem continuity. The Buddhists say, "I alone am uniquely honored," but the Confucians openly serve the supreme ruler. The Buddhists say that the creative transformation is inside oneself, and the Confucians say that the mandate is in heaven.

The root intentions of the three schools are different from each other, but in later times people wanted to unite them by force. Is this not false?

As for the Three Teachings, one says nonbeing, one says emptiness, and one says being. No affairs under heaven contradict each other more than emptiness and fullness, being and nonbeing. If they can be united and made one, then water and fire, or squares and circles, can be combined together without difficulty. Is there any principle like this? Recently there have been some true persons who were deluded by this theory, but this is only because they lost the learning and became corrupted.

---

73. Yang-Yu has "principle" (*li* 理) instead of "propriety" (*li* 禮).

Let me try to call your attention to the errors in transmigration. They say that the essence of the human soul will be reborn repeatedly in the human world, either to be another person or an animal. This, however, will not make them lose the spiritual of the root nature. They will be able to remember entirely the affairs of the previous body. On the one hand they themselves will repent, and on the other they will exhort others. Is this not to gain a double advantage?

None of them, however, have self-knowledge concerning who they were before they were born, and their bodily activity is confused by the law of reward and punishment. The work of the previous person causes the praise or punishment of the later person. On what does this principle depend? This is not fair in terms of law.

When we look at the books of these two schools [Buddhism and Daoism], some texts say that there are people who can remember the affairs of the previous body. This, however, is the deception of evil spirits, who make people follow their teachings and partake of sacrificial offerings. They lie about past affairs in order to substantiate falseness. Sometimes they use deception or wild rumors to delude ignorant people, but they are often exposed by failure, so they lose their influence and everyone around the country knows about it.

They also explain the prohibition of killing by saying that people should fear slaughtering cows, sheep, and other kinds because they might be their parents in later bodies. Thus they cannot bear to kill or harm them. How then can they bear to spare a cow to cultivate the land or be harnessed to a vehicle or to ride a horse and make it carry heavy burdens for great distances? Killing them is one time and is not as hard as a lifetime of suffering and pain because of cultivating the land, being harnessed to a vehicle, or bearing the disgrace of being whipped. It is certainly impossible to abolish agriculture and military expeditions, so it is impossible to avoid rearing and feeding them, whipping and spurring them. Why then should only killing them be prohibited?

If we suppose that the deceased transmigrate and again become human, affairs like contracting a marriage and commanding servants become impossible. Why? When a man marries, he would fear that in a previous life his spouse was his mother or his elder or younger sister. When a young servant is in his service, the master would fear that in a previous life he was his father, elder brother, senior relative, teacher, or friend. All of these are transgressions of the constant human bonds. Now that the argument has reached this point, what more can I say about the falsity?

Ever since mankind came to be born, people and things increased daily, ceaselessly overflowing. This is like the imperial family of the Ming dynasty, which originated with the first emperor himself. Now, however, the clan has branched off into more than a hundred thousand people. The situation of other people is similar to this, as well as all things. Transmigration is like a windlass following a circle, going and coming back, so there is nothing but old things. From which clan come those who are newly born? Now that our explication has reached here, their shallowness and perversity can be decided with one word.

According to our true teaching, in the chaos at the beginning, the human ancestor Adam first descended to Tianfang. There were only two people, husband and wife, and they gave birth to and nurtured seventy-some pregnancies. From each pregnancy came forth two persons, a male and a female. They interchanged and they all became husbands and wives. At that moment, poverty and wealth, ignorance and wisdom, longevity and young death, beauty and ugliness, good and evil, all belonged to the beginning of human birth and had nothing whatsoever to do with the causes of a previous world. High and low were already embedded.

The hidden purport of the secret of transformation is deep and subtle and cannot be fathomed. The people of the world, recklessly grasping the partiality of their selves, want to regulate and encompass the broadness and greatness of the creative transformation. This is like fathoming the sea with a bamboo pole. When the pole goes all the way down, they regard it as the depth of the sea. Their delusion is extreme.

In ancient times the evil deeds of Gusou were worthy of recompense by a great punishment; on the contrary, his recompense was his sage son Shun. The virtues of Xun [Emperor Yao] and Hua [Emperor Shun] were worthy of recompense by wise sons to carry on their virtues for generations and preserve them under heaven, but their recompense was degenerate heirs. When we look at this, there is no reward and recompense as such.

In the same way, pearls are taken from water, mirrors from fire. Sunflowers face the sun, and crabs walk sideways. Clear wisdom can still not discriminate the principles of things before the eyes. Wanting to peep into the mysterious secret of the creative transformation, they presumptuously show off their own partial and narrow views. When they fell into deep perplexity one day, they transmitted their illusions and foolishness and wrongly established the "three currents" and falsely proclaimed the "six domains."⁷⁴ Is this not a dream told by a foolish person? The poet says,

> The people of old were few and gradually prospered,
> both spiritual and doltish, moving but staying the same.
> If the windlass keeps on turning as before,
> how did the old things become so many?

When you know this, it is not necessary to explain the falsity of transmigration.

They also say that originally everyone is good, but gradually people make mistakes that day-by-day become more serious. In the end they become pure evil. When the root good becomes pure evil, is it possible for pure evil to become good again? If mankind is transformed to become animals, what kind of outcome will there be in the end?

Having reached here, you will see that their theories are not at all like going home to the Real according to the true teaching. Life and death rely only on the mandate of the Lord. They do not go away only to come back and return. Everyone has the root origin of his own everlasting abode, and everyone will have the judgment of reward and punishment with utmost justice.

2.19. This World

The Classic says, "Living in the earthly world is one act of a drama."⁷⁵ It also says, "There may not be one true person left, but if there is, he will have four enemies: self-nature, the chief devil, deluded people, and the earthly world."⁷⁶

---

74. Reference to a Buddhist teaching that people's karma determines which of three currents they will meet in the river of death (slow, medium, and fast) before they end up in one of the six domains (heaven, man, demons, beasts, hungry ghosts, and hell).

75. Qur'an 6:32.

76. This is perhaps based on a saying of Shiblī given by 'Attār (*Tadhkira* 419): "I have been tried by four trials, and they are the four enemies: the soul, this world, Satan, and caprice."

The earthly world has been one great theater from ancient times until now. Merit and name, wealth and nobility, the myriad affairs and the myriad things—all are puppets in the theater. The chief devil is an actor in costume, and the deluded people are the ones entertained by the drama. Self-nature sits together with you. The true person is but a passing guest in the theater.

The Classic says, "The earthly world is a bridge from ancient times to now, a path everyone must surely travel. You will pass over it, but you cannot repair it."

It also says, "Inside the theater with its singing and dancing, those who sit with you are helpers, those entertained are sinners, and the true person passes through but never looks at the drama."

Among the four enemies, self-nature is the greatest. Why? It can be the theater, it can be a costumed actor, it can be the entertainment of the play, it can sit together with you, and it can be a traveler. Compared to the other enemies, its connection with you is uniquely intimate. Hence those who can suppress self-nature have the great courage of sages and worthies.

Although self-nature and true nature can be differentiated as subject and lord, it is difficult to distinguish them as two substances. This is like one water in the midst of another water. Someone with a good sense of taste will be able to discriminate them. Or, it is like a scent in the midst of the wind. Someone with a good sense of smell will be able to know it. Unless one is an utmost person, certainly it will be impossible to discern the root substance of oneself. Even if you read numerous books and sayings, you will not be able to comprehend the subtlety of this principle.

When a true person finds himself in this place, he will be as if holding a precious jewel in his hand when suddenly he enters into the midst of danger; he will want to guard the jewel. How many precautions he needs to take and how much he should be fearful and alarmed! If he makes any mistakes or becomes negligent, what happens will not be something small. How can he go back to the play? Much more so in the case of a play within a play!

If people knew that they are acting in a play, they would not take it seriously. If they do not know that they are acting in a play, they will become part of the play. They will be unwilling to leave by themselves until it is time for the gathering to break up.

Whenever there is a gathering, it will break up in the end. Whenever there is a life, there will be death in the end. Whenever there is happiness, there will be suffering in the end. Whenever there is an inn for travelers, there will be a home in the end.

When there is anxiety without happiness, the wise man is he who seeks happiness without anxiety. Those who attain this happiness have nothing to do with the joy and grief of the drama. Hence the Classic says that people in the world are traveling merchants who have nothing but borrowed and rented things. In the end a traveling merchant will certainly return home, and the borrowed things will surely go back to their original owners. How could this be the real being of the everlasting dwelling?

How sad it is! Worldly people regard the traveler's inn as their native place and the borrowed things as their own possessions. They are tainted by selfish desire for name and profit, so the clear substance of their root hearts is deluded and reckless. They are fully preoccupied all day long and forget life and death altogether. How lamentable and pitiful they are!

The Classic says, "O people, in the floating life before your eyes you must prepare for immeasurable happiness after you shed your body in death, whose moment is like the twinkling of an eye. Indeed, you do not know if you will be alive or dead tomorrow."

You should know that there is no calamity greater than the death of the heart. The death of the body follows after that. If body and heart die together, what will grant them the provisions to go home? The proverb says, "From ancient times, who has been born without dying? Let us look to see who has passed by without death."

Since you will certainly meet death, you must have correct and proper faith in it. You must put it before your eyes at every moment and consider who will be your companion at the time of death. Wealth and nobility cannot be carried, but good and evil will stick to your body and go along with it. When the talk reaches this point, wise people will be alarmed and will reflect upon themselves. They will look back upon their past actions. Should their hearts not be ashamed of them? Crying in regret will be of no use at that time, not to speak of happiness.

A worthy said, "Worldly people are like cows and horses, eating and drinking at the manger of the earthly world."

Someone asked him, "Where do you eat?"

He said, "I also eat there, but when they eat, they are pleased and happy. When I eat, I only become sad and sorrowful."

Those who are pleased and happy are still not equal to cows and horses. Why? Because when cows and horses are satisfied with food, they sleep peacefully, knowing that it was enough. Greedy people are never peaceful by day or night, because they have forgotten that they will die.

The way of abiding in the world must consist of five affairs: eating to satisfy hunger, drinking to allay thirst, putting on clothing to cover the body, having a house to contain the body, and learning for the sake of use. Anything more than this is surplus. A wise person will not neglect true affairs because of surplus affairs. The time before your eyes has immeasurable value, so you must investigate it thoroughly and with delicate care. You must not carelessly let it pass by.

If you want to go beyond the earthly world, you must have genuine friends. A worthy said, "If you want to have friendship with a genuine friend, the conduct of the Sage is enough. If you want to choose a fellow traveler, the heavenly immortal recording your good and evil is enough. If you want someone with whom to grieve, the changing and shifting affairs of the world are enough. If you want to do a deed that is not good, the punishment of hellfire is enough. If you want a companion, the subtle purport of the Honorable Classic is enough. If you want to act for one affair, acting for the sake of the Lord is enough. If you want to receive one serious admonition, death is enough."

If your actions are illuminated by this advice, perhaps you will not fall into mistakes.

Worldly people are tainted by the tiny and vague things before their eyes, so they are blind to the large view that they have not yet seen. If a jailed woman is pregnant, she will give birth to a child in a dark prison. When the child grows to manhood, he will not know the light and brightness of the sun and moon, the elegant beauty of rivers and mountains, the prosperous display of human affairs, or the ornaments of the myriad things. He will take a large lamp as the sun, a small lamp as the moon, and the people and things of the prison as the most beautiful. He will have nothing with which to compare them, nor will he be aware of the prison's filth, so he will consider it the happiest place. He will be strongly attached to the prison, and it will never occur to him that he should leave. But as soon as someone comes and tells him that heaven is high and earth deep, the sun is brilliant and the moon bright, people are eminent and things splendorous, rivers are flowing and mountains beautiful, rare delicacies please the mouth and silk brocade makes a display on the body, he will awaken for the first time to the light coming from the cracks in the wall, the misery of the rows of cangues, the strictness of the restraints and prohibitions, the coarseness of the food and drink, and the meanness of the clothing and blankets. He will of course not want to live there forever. At this moment he will be like a dreamer who wakes up from sleep for the first time. Only then will he plan to escape from this dirty and impure place.

If there were no examinations, how would people's talents and abilities be discriminated? If there were no explanations and expositions, how would they awaken to the subtle principles? This is why, when a great responsibility should be sent down on someone, first the will of his heart is made to suffer, then his flesh and skin are made to starve, his muscles and bones are given toil, and he is made to experience dangers and difficulties. How can you spend your whole life in the theater? The poet says,

> A broad and endless drama envelops the ancient and the new,
> the actors hidden by their costumes.
> The dream of man's world is a dream within a dream—
> after death this dream will be known as unreal.

Oh, am I looking at the great drama, ancient and new, or at the small drama before my eyes? Am I a traveler or am I a dweller in the eternal abode? Is my suffering being drawn out or am I being entertained? Will I have eternal life or will I go the way of death? My tale has reached here and I can only sigh. How many people will leap off this stage?

2.20. The Afterworld

The Classic says, "Do you indeed guess that the Real Lord's creative transformation is only for your amusement and that you will not have to return home to the Real Lord's honorable threshold?"[77] Based on

---

77. Reference to the verse, "What, did you think that We created you only for sport, and that you would not be returned to Us?" (23:115).

this clear proclamation, we can judge that people have three worlds: the original beginning, the present time, and returning home. These are similar to the three stages that are the original seed, its issuing forth to disclose, and the perfecting of the fruit. If any of these is lacking, there will be incompleteness from beginning to end. Thus the earthly world is the floating life, a lodging place for man.

This is like searching in the ocean for pearls. Those who obtain them will then climb up to the shore. Or it is like a loyal minister who receives a mandate, or a filial child sent out by his parents. Once the instructions are delivered, how can one venture to delay for a moment? If one does not return to the mandate, how can one be loyal and filial?

You must know that if you gain when you return home to the afterworld, you will gain forever, but if you lose, you will lose forever. Certainly no one will be both honored and disgraced. No one will stand on the ground of equal fortune in gain and loss. It will not be like this world, where good and evil abide together and happiness and calamity are accepted equally; where an evil person may finish with worldly honor and glory, and a good person may be poor and distressed for his whole life.

Hence those in the drunken dream say that life and death are vague and obscure, so longevity and young death are inexplicable. Right and wrong are upside down as if no one is managing them, so there is no benefit in cultivating the good and no harm in doing evil. People's nobility and baseness are accidents of time, so good is not necessarily rewarded and evil is not necessarily punished. Thoughts of "silent perishing" and "empty nonbeing" came to be because of these sorts of doubt.

Oh, if a state has no officials, everything in the state will be in disorder! If a country has no ruler, everything in the country will be in disorder! If there were a ruler but no trustworthy reward and punishment, no one would act on his commands. Observe carefully: Everything in heaven, earth, and the myriad things is short and long, diverse in color, big and small, high and low. The sun and the moon revolve, day and night are bright and dark, the four seasons never miss the mark. All have been the same for a myriad ages. Such is the evidence that there must be one Real Lord of utmost honor acting with utmost justice in reward and punishment. There is no room for doubt, not even a hair's breadth.

Hence the Real Lord appointed a time for a great assembly in the afterworld, when the myriad things will return together for judgment and calling to account. The people of this world will return to life in their original bodies, and He will display the utmost justice to the great mass of people from ancient to modern. At that moment it will be known for the first time that He did not bestow worldly happiness on evil people because He was pleased with them. Rather He rewarded them for their accidental deeds of minute good with the trifling value of the blink of an eye. After death He will punish them with unlimited suffering for their evil deeds side by side with the evil spirits in the dark prison. Nor did He increase the worldly suffering of good people because He hated them. Rather He did so to redeem their small sins and transgressions and to purify and cleanse them of the taints and flaws of the affairs of this world. After death He will reward them for their real sincerity and meritorious virtue with complete happiness side by side with the heavenly immortals in the boundless Heavenly Country.

Someone said: When the people of the world die, some are burned by fire, some are drowned in water, some are buried in the earth. The bodies of those who are burned by fire become floating dust, the bodies of those drowned in water rot, and the bodies of those buried in the earth decay. How can they return to the original body? Moreover, the Real Lord is without likeness or form. How can He confront people face to face or back to back? And people from ancient to modern cannot be merely a few thousands of millions. How can they be examined and judged one by one? His honorable speech is not of a kind that can be heard in sound or in the patterns of letters. How is it possible for Him to question and answer with the local languages of the myriad countries?

I answered: Fire can make man into dust, water can make him rot, and soil can make him decay, but these are not the self-abilities of fire, water, and soil. All accord with the Real Lord's mandate. All of them—dust, rot, and decay—will return to become the original human body by His mandate. This is not strange at all.

Moreover, there was no human body before, and later He created and transformed the body from nothing. Now He will perfect the body's existence with His existence. Do you still doubt this?

The Real Lord's being has no color or guise, but it is absolute being, so there is nothing that is not His being. His clarity does not come from the three lights, but it is absolute clarity, so there is nothing that He does not make clear. His speech does not come from mouth and tongue, for it is absolute speech, so there is nothing He does not speak. For Him affairs have no difficult or easy, no many or few, no big or small. He created heaven and earth like a pellet and regulates the myriad things as if He were regulating one thing. This is like the sun when it illuminates one thing with its complete light—it also illuminates the myriad things with its complete light. Mount Tai and a mustard seed both receive the same one illumination. When things' light increases, His light does not increase, and when things' light decreases, His light does not decrease. Comparing the trifling and tiny clarity of a firefly's fire with the immeasurable, mysterious subtlety of the Real Lord is extremely absurd and ludicrous.

After people of good and evil return to life together in their original bodies, the judgment and calling to account will be completed. Good people will climb up to the Heavenly Country and, along with the original nature of their spiritual, will receive complete happiness. Both form and spirit will be filled with joy, and the calamities of the bodily form will be taken away completely. They will have the clarity of light, both inside and out, and there will be no difference between young and old. All will have the likeness of the human ancestor in his outward form at the prime of life, and there will be no difference of tall and short, big and small.

His solicitude will give them whatever they wish and whatever is agreeable with their bodies. The greatest of these are four affairs:

First is lack of perishing and ruin. None of the calamities and harms of water, fire, weapons, and injurious things will be able to encroach upon them. They will not be violated by the seven feelings and six desires. Hence they will never die again.

Second is thorough penetration. Nothing that is hard or solid will be able to hinder them. They will thread through metal and enter into iron as they will.

Third is clarity of light. An illumination and brightness will issue forth from them that cannot be reached even by the sun's light.

Fourth is marvelous quickness. The bodies that have returned to life will not have the turbidity of the present. They will fly without wings and feathers, they will reach the goal without walking and moving, they will come and go according to their willful intentions, and they will reach anything, far or near, high or low, in the twinkling of an eye. Thus has it been said,

> Pure autumn dew,
> wine in crystal cup,
> Cup and wine together
> not discerned as two.
> You see the cup but not
> the wine inside the cup.
> You see the wine but not
> the cup outside the wine.[78]

This points to the meaning of the clarity of light, both inside and outside. The complete happiness in its midst is "what no eye has ever seen, what no ear has ever heard, and what has never been thought by any heart."[79] There will be nothing with which you are discontented, nothing that is not fulfilled. Were this not so, it could not be called complete happiness.

Know that the human form and spirit will have been united together and become as one body, but their joy will not be the same. A body functions with form, so the body's happiness is received by form and cannot be conveyed entirely to the spirit; such are the pleasures of rare jewels, excellent castles in precious space, clothing and garments of silk brocade, and the refined tastes of food and drink. All these are the pleasures of form. A spirit functions with spirit, so its joy is received by spirit and cannot be conveyed entirely to the body; such are the clear grasp of the principles of heaven, earth, and the myriad things and the recognition and discernment of the Real Lord's subtlety. These are the ultimate joy of the spirit.

An emperor of today may have the wealth of everything surrounded by the four seas, but that is nothing but the twinkling of an eye compared to the Heavenly Country. How could it be similar even to one of a myriad?

---

78. Translation of a famous Arabic poem by Ṣāḥib ibn 'Abbād (d. 995). Wang probably took it from Fakhr al-Dīn 'Irāqī's *Lama'āt* (Flash 5), a book whose commentary by Jāmī was translated into Chinese by She Yunshan 舍蘊善 not too long after Wang's book was published. On She see Benite, *Tao of Muhammad*, pp. 52–54. For 'Irāqī's *Lama'āt*, see Chittick and Wilson, *Fakhruddin 'Iraqi*.

79. Part of a *ḥadīth qudsī* about paradise found in the standard sources (with echoes of Isaiah 64.4 and I Corinthians 2.9).

Deluded people will not be like this. Although they will return to life at the same time, in reality it will be as if they are neither dead nor alive. Although they themselves will want to die everlastingly, they cannot by themselves die. They will not be like those who dwell in the Heavenly Country, whose state is called everlasting life. Life means that you move as you wish without restraint. This is like a spring's fountainhead, overflowing ceaselessly day and night, so it is called living water. Deluded people will be imprisoned and unable to turn around or shift at all. This is like digging a hole in the earth and pouring water into it. It will not flow and move, so it is dead water.

Once someone enters the Earthly Dungeon, he will be bound in the midst of a myriad sufferings. Every day he will have pain and distress without cease for one moment. Although he begs that his breath be stopped, his request will not be fulfilled. Moreover, his disgrace will increase even further. He will be like this forever and not perish again. In the prisons of this world suffering for heavy sin has a limit—one death, and that is all. This is unlike that, for that will be the utmost distress and cruelty, without final limit or end.

Someone said: Humans live in this world either obediently or disobediently, and long life is no more than one hundred years. Why is there no end to reward and punishment?

I said: The Real Lord rewards good and punishes evil on the basis of gauging the will of people's hearts, no matter how many or few the years and months. Why? When an obedient person lives one hundred years, he has been obedient for one hundred years. If he lives one thousand years, he will be obedient for one thousand years. If he lives an immeasurably long time, he will be obedient for an immeasurably long time. Someone who disobeys the mandate is the same way. Since there is no final end to the thought of good or evil, there will be no utmost end for recompense, whether reward or punishment.

This is the utmost justice. It is not comparable with worldly law, which judges people and calls them to account in keeping with outward appearances. Here those who set down the law sometimes make it crooked, and those under the law sometimes happily escape. The Classic says, "This world is the field of the afterworld."[80] He who

---

80. Commonly said to be a hadith of the Prophet.

plants flowers gains flowers, and he who plants thorns reaps thorns. Thus it is said that you yourself have gathered the thorns you carry on your back, and you yourself have woven the silk on your body.

You should never negligently reject everlasting glory for the tiny profit of the floating life. If you lose it with carelessness, the suffering will be endless. How sad indeed would that be!

Cited Works

Abū Nu'aym al-Iṣfahānī. *Ḥilyat al-awliyā'*. 10 volumes. Cairo: Maṭba'at al-Sa'āda, 1971–74.
'Aṭṭār, Farīd al-Dīn. *Tadhkirat al-awliyā'*. Edited by Muḥammad Isti'lāmī. Tehran: Zuwwār, 1346/1967.
———. *Farid ul-Din 'Attār's Memorial of God's Friends*. Translated by Paul Losensky. New York: Paulist Press, 2009.
Benite, Zvi Ben-Dor. *The Dao of Muhammad: A Cultural History of Muslims in Late Imperial China*. Cambridge, MA: Harvard University Asia Center, 2005.
———. "The Marrano Emperor: The Mysterious, Intimate, Bond between Zhu Yuanzhang and his Muslims." In Sarah Schneewind, *Long Live the Emperor! Uses of the Ming Founder Across Six Centuries of East Asian History*, Ming studies research series, no. 4, 2008, pp. 275–308.
Chan, Wing-Tsit. *A Source Book in Chinese Philosophy*. Princeton, NJ: Princeton University Press, 1963.
Chittick, William C. *Divine Love: Islamic Literature and the Path to God*. New Haven, CT: Yale University Press, 2013.
———. "Qūnawī, Neoplatonism, and the Circle of Ascent." *In Search of the Lost Heart*. Albany: State University of New York Press, 2012, pp. 113–32.
———. *The Sufi Path of Knowledge: Ibn al-'Arabī's Metaphysics of Imagination*. Albany: State University of New York Press, 1989.
———. *Sufism: A Beginner's Guide*. Oxford: Oneworld, 2008.
Chittick, William C., and Peter Lamborn Wilson. *Fakhruddin 'Iraqi: Divine Flashes*. New York: Paulist Press, 1982.
Ernst, Carl. *The Shambhala Guide to Sufism*. Boston: Shambhala Publications, 1997.
Ghazālī, Abū Ḥāmid al-. *Iḥyā' 'ulūm al-dīn*. Beirut: Dār al-Hādī, 1992.
Horiike, Nobuo 堀池信夫. *Chūgoku Isurāmu tetsugaku no keisei: Ō Tai-Yo kenkyū* 中国イスラーム哲学の形成―王岱輿研究. Kyoto 2012.
Huizu diancang quanshu 回族典藏全書. 235 vols. Gansu/Ningxia 2008.
Jaschok, Maria, and Jingjun Shui. *The History of Women's Mosques in Chinese Islam: A Mosque of Their Own*. Surrey: Curzon Press, 2000.

Ji Fangtong 季芳桐. *Yiru huitong yanju* 伊儒会通研究. Ningxia 2015.
Jin Yijiu 金宜久. *Wang Daiyu sixiang yanjiu* 王岱與思想研究. Beijing 2008.
Kuwata, Rokurō 桑田六郎. "Minmatsu Shinsho no kaiju" 明末清初の回儒. In *Shiratori hakushi kanreki kinen tōyōshi ronsō* 白鳥博士還曆記念東洋史論叢. Tokyo: Iwanami Shoten, 1925, pp. 377–86.
Laozi. *Daodejing.* http://ctext.org/dao-de-jing.
Legge, James. *The Chinese Classics.* 7 vols. Oxford, 1892.
Leslie, Donald D. *Islamic Literature in Chinese.* Canberra, Australia: Canberra College of Advanced Education, 1981.
———, Yang Daye, and Ahmed Youssef. *Islam in Traditional China: A Bibliographical Guide.* Sankt Augustin: Institut Monumenta Serica, 2006.
Mencius. In Legge, *Chinese Classics* 1.
Murata, Sachiko. *Chinese Gleams of Sufi Light: Wang Tai-yü's "Great Learning of the Pure and Real" and Liu Chih's "Displaying the Concealment of the Real Realm."* Albany: State University of New York Press, 2000.
———. "Lan Zixi's 'Epitaphs of the Real Humans.'" *Tales of God's Friends: Islamic Hagiography in Translation.* Edited by John Renard. Berkeley: University of California Press, 2009, pp. 359–70.
———. *The Tao of Islam: A Sourcebook on Gender Relationships in Islamic Thought.* Albany: State University of New York Press, 1992.
Murata, Sachiko, and William C. Chittick. *The Vision of Islam.* New York: Paragon, 1994.
———. "The Implicit Dialogue of Confucian Muslims." *The Wiley-Blackwell Companion to Inter-Religious Dialogue,* edited by Catherine Cornille (Malden, MA: John Wiley & Sons, 2013), pp. 438–49.
Murata, Sachiko, William C. Chittick, and Tu Weiming. *The Sage Learning of Liu Zhi: Islamic Thought in Confucian Terms.* Cambridge, MA: Harvard University Asia Center, 2009.
Nasafī, ʿAzīz. *Maqṣad-i aqṣā.* English translation by Lloyd Ridgeon in *Persian Metaphysics and Mysticism: Selected Treatises of ʿAzīz Nasafī.* Richmond, Surrey: Curzon, 2002.
Nasr, S. H., et al. *The Study Quran.* New York: HarperCollins, 2015.
Petersen, Kristian. "The Heart of Wang Daiyu's Philosophy: The Seven Subtleties of Islamic Spiritual Physiology." *Journal of Sufi Studies* 2 (2013) 177–201.
Qinzhen dadian 清真大典, 25 vols. Beijing 2005.
Rāzī, Najm al-Dīn. *Mirṣād al-ʿibād min al-mabdaʾ ilaʾl-maʿād.* Ed. M. A. Riyāḥī. Tehran: Bungāh-i Tarjama wa Nashr-i Kitāb, 1352/1973.
———. *The Path of God's Bondsmen from Origin to Return.* Translated by Hamid Algar. Delmar, NY: Caravan Books, 1982.
Rūmī. *The Discourses of Rumi (Fīhi mā fīh).* Translated by A. J. Arberry. London: John Murray, 1961.
Ṭabarī, al-. *The History of Ṭabarī.* Edited by Ehsan Yarshater. 40 vols. Albany: State University of New York Press, 2007.

Tahānawī. *Kashshāf iṣṭilāḥāt al-funūn.* http://shamela.ws/browse.php/book-2573.

Tazaka, Kōdō 田坂興道. *Chūgoku ni okeru Kaikyō no denrai to sono gutsū* 中国における回教の傳來とその弘通. Tokyo: Tōyō bunko, 1964.

Wang Daiyu 王岱輿. *Zhengjiao zhenquan* 正教真詮. Edited by Yang Huaizhong 楊懷中 and Yu Zhengui 余振貴. Yinchuan: Ningxia Renmin Chuban She, 1987.

Yang Xiaochun 楊曉春. *Zaoqi hanwen yisilanjiao dianji yanjiu.* 早期汉文伊斯兰教典籍研究. Shanghai: Gujiu Chuban She, 2011.

Yang-Yu. *See* Wang Daiyu.

Index

abode (*zhu* 住), everlasting (eternal), 85, 153, 178, 194, 195, 210, 225, 229, 233
Abraham, 68–69
abstaining (*jie* 戒), 129, 145, 150 52, 207, 208
action, activity (*wei* 為, *xing* 行), 3, 25, 37, 48–50, 60, 61, 91, 94, 105, 106, 108, 121, 126, 134, 139, 144, 151, 167, 170, 172, 178, 182, 186, 187, 196–98, 202, 206, 209, 221, 227, 231, 232; creative, 50, 53; human, 120, 207; myriad, 145, 152; results of, 64, 66, 218, 223, 226; and speech, 90, 193
Adam (Adan 阿丹), 6, 7, 55–58, 127, 130–31, 153, 228
'*adam*, 106
Adham, Ibrāhīm, 165
'*adl*, 61
admonition, 73, 175, 232
advancing, in the way, 99, 141, 198, 200
advantage, 57, 184, 227; and disadvantage, 62, 140; taking, 63, 102, 209
afterworld (*houshi* 後世), 17, 67, 150, 165, 199, 215, 233–39. *See also* world
agents (*xing* 行). *See* elements
aḥadiyya, 13

aḥwāl, 25
aid, assistance, 75, 77, 126, 138, 160, 162–63, 165, 184, 187, 204, 205, 207, 213–14, 216
air (*qi* 氣), and fire, 53, 224. *See* elements
akhlāq, 25
'*ālam*, 13
'Alī (ibn Abī Ṭālib), 29, 44, 59, 73, 136
allotment (*fen* 分), 61, 128, 147, 199, 215
alteration (*bian* 變, *geng* 更), 54, 63, 83, 142, 207; and change (shift), 42, 60, 66, 71, 115, 116, 134, 178, 179, 185, 218; and transformation, 47, 79, 137, 214
amr, 15
An Lushan 安祿山, 211
Analects. *See* Confucius
ancestor, 35, 37, 80, 87, 133, 134, 142, 143, 160; buddha-, 157; human, 50, 55–58, 130–31, 153, 193, 228, 236; original, 50, 171–72
ancient (*gu* 古), 85, 220; document of the body, 116, 120, 142, 144; and modern, 144, 146, 233, 235; people, 35, 92, 131, 132, 138, 144, 171; propriety, 201–3; times (antiquity until now), 8, 55, 58, 61, 63, 69–71, 81, 82, 92, 96, 109,

245

ancient *(continued)*
  111, 115, 117, 120, 124, 133, 134, 142, 146, 153, 164, 172, 174, 175, 180, 182, 200, 203, 205, 207, 211, 216, 218, 225, 228, 230, 231
angels, 13, 50, 57, 59, 125, 198
anger (*nu* 怒), 170–71, 193, 201; and greed, 110, 140, 165; and joy, 168, 191; of the Lord, 170
animals, 13, 14, 75, 108–9, 111, 121, 151, 156, 168, 195, 198, 201–5, 207, 208, 213, 216, 217, 227, 229; bees, 194; camel, 88, 168, 216; cat, 61, 208; cattle, 165; chicken, 208; cicada, 59; cow, 71, 91, 139, 165, 168, 185, 203, 208–9, 227, 231, 232; crabs, 228; crane, 55; deer (river), 208, 218; dog, 159, 165, 208; donkey, 208; duck, 208; eagle, 204; eels, 208; firefly, 138, 200, 236; fish, 59, 63, 91, 100, 109, 118, 130, 142, 208, 215; flies, 137; flood dragon, 99; geese, 208; hawks, 208; horse, 91, 107, 119, 139, 159, 165, 168, 185, 201, 210, 227, 231, 232; insects (and worms), 64, 67, 84, 121, 125, 196, 221; kite, 208; leopard, 43; lion, 203, 216; loach, 179; magpie, 61; mayfly, 56, 215; mice, 208; millipede, 215; mosquitoes, 137; mule, 168, 208; ox, 119, 202; phoenix, 77, 99; pig, 185, 208; rabbit, 208; scorpion, 125, 204; sheep, 19, 164, 185, 202, 208, 227; shellfish, 64, 100; shrimp, 208; snakes, 125, 204; tiger, 139, 204, 208; turtle, 208; unicorn, 99; wolf, 139, 204, 208. *See also* birds and beasts
anthropocosmism, 29–30
antiquity (*gu* 古). *See* ancient
anxiety, anxious, 66, 164, 169, 179, 210, 217, 231
apertures (*qiao* 竅), bodily, 56, 62, 142, 206
appetite, 109, 111, 209, 212
'aql, 14, 105
Arabic and Persian, 4, 30–31
arc (*qaws*), two, 10, 147
argument, 36–39, 49, 80, 84, 95, 99, 112, 161–62, 196, 225, 227
Aristotelianism, 14
arousing (*xing* 醒), 105, 147, 185, 188, 192; and awakening, 108, 181; Sign of Arousing (*zhen* 震), 80
arrangement, 52, 62, 82, 97, 125, 127, 130, 180, 215, 221; subtle, 69, 127, 128, 143
arrogance (*gaoao* 高傲), 127, 136, 157, 177, 187, 190
'arsh, 75
ascent (*sheng* 升), 12, 56, 89, 126; and descent, 10, 13, 17–18, 47, 49, 53, 57–58, 69, 100, 103, 115, 125, 147–48, 221, 224, 225; to heaven, 25, 57, 71, 127, 128, 169, 221, 224
Ash'arite theology, 42
Ashike 阿世喀, 85
aspiration (*zhi* 志), 37, 135, 138, 198
assembly (*ju* 聚), 145, 152–53; great, 201, 203, 235
astronomy, 35
attainment (*de* 得), 61, 65–67, 73, 77, 112, 129, 134, 179, 181, 185, 189, 202, 203, 212, 231; of the clear mandate, 112, 201, 223; real, 66, 76; of recognition (truth, the Real), 41, 42, 44–45, 60, 70, 71, 79, 84, 101, 105, 116, 144, 152, 178; of the Non-Ultimate, 141, 148; of the way, 67, 99, 139, 140, 198, 200, 221–22
'Aṭṭār, 28; *Tadhkira*, 110, 141, 164, 165, 173, 178, 193, 208, 229
attributes (*ṣifa*), of the Real, 12–13, 21, 29, 42, 45–47, 50–51, 57, 64, 75, 86–87, 116, 126, 150, 235–36

authorities (*zhujia* 諸家), 96, 97, 99, 160, 225
awakening, wakefulness (*wu* 悟), 41, 58, 63, 68–69, 77, 89, 104, 108, 116, 124, 130, 138, 140, 142, 149, 153, 165, 167, 178, 181, 188–90, 203, 210, 213; and dreaming, 70, 73, 116, 142, 179, 192, 225, 233; to the Real, 79, 143, 177, 192
awareness (*jue* 覺), 56, 73, 98, 112, 135, 140, 166, 185, 188, 232; of animals, 75, 105, 113; knowledge and, 47, 49, 74–75, 105, 109, 113, 114; mandate of, 76–77; nature of, 15–16, 42–43, 93, 109–11, 113–15; perfect, 92–94; spiritual, 51–54; true, 64, 79, 93, 133
āyāt, 69

Babel, 131–32
baseness, 130, 135, 150, 234
Baṣrī, Ḥasan, 164, 208
Bāyazīd Basṭāmī (d. ca. 875), 178, 193, 208
beautiful-doing (*iḥsān*), 21, 158
beauty, 28, 107, 112, 114, 118, 127, 152, 170, 172, 177, 185, 189, 201, 232–33; and ugliness, 60, 106, 228
becoming (*cheng* 成), the One, 16, 72
begetting (*sheng* 生), 41, 73, 75, 87, 88, 97, 121, 124, 126, 131, 142, 180; and growth, 75, 104–5, 113, 149, 207; lowly gate of (*chanmen* 產門), 177; nature of, 15–16, 104–5, 113–14. *See also* transformation
beginning (*shi* 始, *chu* 初), 93, 98; of creation, 11, 41, 51–52, 57–59, 91, 101, 117, 121, 130, 144, 153, 154, 193, 228; and end, 11, 52, 66, 105, 107, 113, 120, 130–31, 152, 172, 188, 234; of myriad things, 50, 75, 87, 96; original, 49, 57–59, 77, 131, 140, 143, 145, 148, 149, 172, 234;

without beginning (and end), 41, 50, 57, 79, 110, 113, 116, 178, 188
being (*you* 有), beginningless (and endless), 41, 50, 79, 110, 113, 116, 178; levels of, 14–15, 17, 51–52, 65, 74, 113, 147; myriad, 42, 71, 75, 87, 88, 117, 120, 141, 148, 154; and nonbeing, 47, 48, 50, 52, 76, 79–80, 90, 113, 115–16, 140, 153, 176, 187, 188, 206, 226; Original, 41, 42, 44, 50–52, 96, 110, 115, 116, 133, 139, 157, 176, 178, 224; Powerful, 51; real, 60, 152, 187, 188, 198, 231, 235
bells and drums, 94, 190
benefit, 64, 73, 97, 122, 127, 133, 144, 152, 170, 176, 185, 218–20, 222, 223; and harm, 69, 181–82, 154, 171, 173, 180–81, 204–5, 213, 214, 234; real, 181
Benite, Zvi Bendor, 2, 5, 7, 34, 35, 84, 85, 237
Bian Que 扁鵲, 174
birds and beasts, 15–17, 84, 99, 208; awareness of, 115; killing of, 121, 155–56, 205; nature of, 15–16, 106, 113–15; flyers (and walkers), 47, 52, 55, 113, 148–49, 198, 204, 206, 207. *See also* animals, human
birth (*sheng* 生), 52, 69, 78, 174, 206, 207, 228, 232; and death, 46, 48, 194; three, 111
blind, 48, 123, 125, 138, 183, 194, 200, 215, 232
bliss, 99, 155; complete, 57, 58, 150
blood, 180, 222–23; of mother 69, 139, 142, 177, 199, 206; and vital-energy, 151, 168, 170
Bo Yi 伯夷, 61
body (*ti* 體, *shen* 身), 42–44, 49, 188, 195, 235; ancient document of, 116, 120, 142, 144; apertures of, 56, 62, 142, 206; as basis, 47,

body (continued)
49, 67, 116, 166; corporeal, 42, 48, 56, 69, 107, 117, 139, 157, 162, 163, 179, 182, 196, 203, 206, 207, 221; and mandate, 88–89; one, 42–43, 56, 58, 84–85, 87, 90–91, 96, 118–19, 167, 213, 224, 237; original, 235–36; principle of, 44, 207; reliance on, 113–14, 166; root, 49, 91, 96, 113, 120, 124, 126, 144; and spirit, 25, 54, 110, 113, 114, 119, 197, 221, 237. *See also* form, substance

bonds (*gang* 綱), constant, 92, 121, 130, 150, 172, 175, 189, 227; five human, 158; Three, 117, 124, 130, 150, 156

bones, 119, 148, 151, 196, 206, 233; one hundred, 62, 167, 186, 207, 224

bright. *See* dark

Buddha, 68, 71, 87, 89, 92, 94, 155, 204; buddha, 89, 92, 94, 96, 99, 133, 148, 157, 204; Buddhism, 2, 22–24, 30, 34, 38–39, 41, 48, 84–85, 87, 112, 133, 140, 143, 205, 226; criticism of, 5, 10, 49, 86–99, 143, 155–58, 196, 204, 226–29. *See also* nonbeing, perishing

Bukhārī, *Ṣaḥīḥ* of, 19

burial, 80, 214, 219–23, 235

calamity, 42, 55, 61, 98, 102, 127, 142, 159, 172, 190, 201, 210–12, 216, 220, 222, 231, 234, 236

canon (*dian* 典), 131; classical, 36, 39, 64; of Shun, 180

caprice (*hawā*), 22, 88, 229

carrying (*zai* 載), by earth (and sages), 55, 65, 69, 79, 108, 146, 174, 192, 206, 214

cause (*yin* 因), 38, 57, 76, 94, 97, 98, 137, 139, 151–53, 169, 176–77, 198, 201, 225, 226, 228; and effect, 62, 107, 120, 142, 144, 221; myriad, 153, 198

celibacy, 121–22

chamber (*shi* 室), 86, 124, 202; Heavenly Chamber (*tianfang* 天房), 153, 201

Chan, Wing-tsit, 34, 81, 100, 155

change (*yi* 易, *bian* 變, *geng* 更), 106, 132, 211, 217, 221, 225; lack of, 70, 96, 128, 149, 180; of the Real, 83. *See also* alteration

chaos (*hundun* 混沌), 54, 101, 131, 228

character, 83, 132, 161; heavenly, 144; character traits (*akhlāq*), 21, 25

chastity (*jie* 節, *zhen* 貞), 64, 67, 107, 122, 212

cheating, 120, 173, 195, 196, 219

Cheng Hao 程顥, 101

Cheng Yi 程頤, 101

Cheng Ying 程嬰, 203

Chengzi 程子, 101–2

chief (*shou* 首), devil, 57, 133, 229–30; leader, 166; original, 51, 78; ruler, 68, 81

children (*zi* 子), 19, 77, 82, 88, 90, 109, 129, 159–61, 183, 189, 195, 204, 222, 232, 234

China (eastern land), 33, 35, 77, 80, 132, 162, 225

cinnabar (*dansha* 丹砂), 38, 129

circle, 226, 228; of existence, 9–11, 16, 148; of the Great Ultimate, 141; circling back, 25, 116, 139, 222, 223

clarity, clear, clarifying (*ming* 明), 17, 20, 37, 39, 50, 54, 58, 64, 67, 84, 97–98, 112, 116, 120, 138, 150, 157, 160, 175, 178, 188, 196, 197, 204, 205, 220, 236; and heart, 80, 111, 135, 144, 151; and light, 120, 236–37; mandate of, 76–77; and principles, 36, 44, 105, 113, 115; of the Real, 180, 235–36; spiritual, 56,

142, 199, 207, 222; subtle, 50, 51, 53, 94, 109, 144, 192, 200; three, 92, 156, 236. *See also* mandate, virtue

classic (*jing* 經), 78, 81, 84, 135, 136; Buddhist, 86, 92; (Confucian), 80, 83, 130, 180; Heavenly/ Honorable, 36, 76, 134, 136, 144, 147, 171, 177, 232; (Islamic), 8–9, 36, 50, 53, 83–85, 104, 131, 164; three great, 69–70; Root, 69–70; the Classic cited, 44, 58–59, 71, 73, 74, 85, 88, 104, 108, 111, 118, 122, 123, 129, 136, 147, 150, 152, 156, 158, 159, 165, 168, 170, 172, 176, 179, 188, 195, 197, 199, 210, 213, 229, 230, 231, 233, 238

clean, cleanliness, 97, 98, 122, 139, 140, 187, 189, 218; of the heart, 73, 120, 166, 192, 200. *See also* pure

clothing, 48, 56. *See* food

clouds, 84, 125, 147, 179; floating, 107, 116, 120

cold, 130; and heat, 45, 47, 114, 121, 168, 203. *See also* hunger

color (*se* 色), 63, 96, 223, 234, 235; five, 62, 93, 102, 118, 200, 225; and form, 67, 82, 86, 110, 170; and subtlety, 54, 110, 145. *See also* sounds

command (*ling* 令, *ming* 命), 88, 102, 104, 123, 127, 141, 161–62, 165, 188, 227, 234; (*amr*), 11; creative and religious, 15–16, 50, 76, 139

companions, 232; in death, 222, 231

compass (*zhinan* 指南), 72, 134

compassion (*ci* 慈), 204, 206, 213, 214, 217; of the Real Lord, 52, 53, 58, 61, 64–65, 70, 177, 188–89, 212; universal, 64–65, 166

completion, 43, 51–53, 56, 58, 62, 73, 75, 122, 125, 153, 156, 159, 162, 172, 189, 212, 224, 236–37; of the Real, 126; of the way, 163

compliance (*zun* 遵), 64, 71, 73, 124, 160, 164, 170, 195, 196, 201–3, 212. *See* mandate

conclusions, drawing (*panduan* 判斷), 45–48

conduct, 48, 71, 135, 164, 184, 209, 232

conforming, 100, 109, 110

Confucius, 6, 38, 39, 71, 80, 81, 98; *Analects*, 22, 25, 62, 63, 77, 101, 123, 202; *Kongzi jiaoyu*, 123; Confucianism, 8–9, 22, 30; critique of, 5, 10, 37–38, 49, 80–83, 96–102, 108–12, 130–31, 136–38, 144, 161–62, 180, 182–84, 225–26. *See also* Nature and Principle, scholar

confusion, 49, 57, 72, 82, 85, 87, 96, 109, 112, 116, 119, 128, 129, 132, 137, 138, 158, 177, 179, 185, 186, 209, 210, 227

conquering (*ke* 克), self (nature), 22–23, 25, 58, 109, 111, 130, 162–64, 176, 187

Constants (*chang* 常), 212; Five, 20, 25, 117, 124, 130, 156; of Islam, 145–53, 172. *See also* bonds

contentment, 187, 199–200, 237

corporeal body (*shenti* 身體). *See* body

cosmos (*'ālam*), 13, 29, 47, 72, 74, 147

country. *See* governance

courage (*yong* 勇), 109, 136, 170, 187, 230

covenant (*yue* 約), 129, 152–53

covering (*fu* 覆), by heaven (and sages), 69, 79, 146, 174, 207, 214

creation (*zao* 造, *khalq*), by the Lord, 11–14, 47, 48, 50, 53–57, 60, 74, 82, 83, 96, 117, 124, 126, 127, 129, 133, 138, 142, 143, 157, 236; by humans, 50, 52, 85, 90–91, 119, 131, 218; levels of, 51–53; secret of, 59, 70, 121, 142, 155, 221, 228. *See also* transformation

Creative (*qian* 乾), 80; and Receptive, 43, 49, 50, 91, 99, 120, 124, 136, 184, 189, 200. *See also* command
Creator (*zaohua* 造化, *zaowu* 造物), 84, 89–91, 110, 157, 158, 167, 206, 207
crossroads (*guantou* 関頭), 66, 148, 207; of life and death, 60, 142, 153, 225; most important, 177, 190
cruelty, 61, 63, 100, 187, 189, 208, 218, 238
cultivation (*xiu* 修), 9, 128, 192, 234; of the body, 6, 20, 22, 38, 48, 77, 83, 135, 144, 155, 160, 178, 210; of virtue, 130, 180; of the way, 70, 96, 109, 196–200; of fields (*geng* 耕), 91, 165, 168, 185, 203, 227
customs (*xi* 習, *fengsu* 風俗), 35, 174, 223–25

dā'irat al-wujūd, 9
Dan Zhu 丹朱, 98
danger, 60, 106, 146, 173, 174, 179, 216, 230, 233. *See also* peace
dao 道, 24–25; of heaven and earth, 18. *See* way
Dao Zhi 盜跖, 61–62, 98, 119
Daodejing. *See* Laozi
Daoism, 1, 2, 23, 30, 34, 38–39, 61, 76, 84, 226; critique of, 5, 10, 49, 87–89, 97, 99, 129, 133, 196, 227. *See also* nonbeing (empty), perishing (silent)
dark, darkness, 49, 55, 58, 86, 91, 104, 127, 128, 138, 151, 197, 211, 232, 235; and brightness, 44, 52, 73, 87, 102, 136, 234; of heart, 43, 47, 68, 173, 176
darkening (*mei* 昧), 88, 171
day, divisions of, 186; and night, 47, 55, 62, 69, 116, 232, 234, 238; days (*ri* 朕), of creation, 54–55

death (*si* 死), 77, 90, 98, 145, 159, 169, 174, 179, 194, 198, 203, 222–25, 231, 232, 238; after, 124–25, 128, 180, 182, 219, 223, 224, 233, 235; and birth, 46, 48, 194; of the body, 66, 115, 231; preparation for, 179–80, 185, 217, 231. *See also* life, longevity
decay, 47, 107, 113, 115, 182, 224, 235; of all things, 85, 176
deceiving, deception, 43, 58, 94, 196, 219, 227; self, 128, 138, 173, 186
deducing (*tui* 推), 49; principles 16, 105, 113, 131, 188
delusion (*huo* 惑, *mi* 迷), 83, 85, 88, 89, 95, 111, 153, 165, 177, 178, 189, 192, 204, 210, 224, 228; deluded, 37, 60, 68, 69, 75, 87, 120, 123, 127–29, 136, 146, 148, 192, 200, 208–11, 214, 215, 217, 220, 225–31, 238
demon (*gui* 鬼), 124–25, 127, 128; and spirits, 50, 51, 78, 105, 121, 124–25, 129, 133, 191, 196
dependence, 41, 49, 59, 92, 107, 113, 131, 137, 146, 184, 185, 200, 208, 221, 227; on self, 142, 166; on willful nature, 71, 73
depravity (*xie* 邪), 97, 98, 121–24, 196, 207; vs. true, 93, 122, 126, 128, 146, 175
descendants, cutting off (*juehou* 絕後), 160–62
descent (*jiang* 降), 87; of Adam, 50, 58, 153, 228; of the mandate, 76, 104, 125, 130, 164, 189. *See* ascent
designation (*cheng* 稱), 119; of the Lord, 46, 82–83, 88
desire (*yu* 欲), 57, 83, 108–9, 121, 124, 126, 128, 140, 148, 151, 152, 163, 178–79, 185, 192, 193, 196, 198, 203, 207, 209, 216, 236; selfish, 91, 219, 231; six, 246; desire (*irâda*), God's 11, 13, 46, 50

Index

devil (*mo* 魔), 57–58, 110, 124, 128, 133, 194, 195, 201, 203, 209, 229–30
dew, 65, 120, 129, 138, 184, 237
dharma (*fa* 法), 41, 87, 92, 94, 155, 157
dhāt, 46
di 地, 43
difference (*yi* 異), 36, 38, 52, 62, 86–87, 96–101, 119, 128, 133, 146, 192, 193, 213, 224
differentiation (*fen* 分), 17, 18, 43, 46, 50–54, 58, 60, 63, 65, 69, 70, 74, 79, 82–85, 87, 95–97, 101–2, 104, 107, 117, 126, 131, 132, 137, 144, 147, 152, 184, 187, 200, 204, 213, 219, 224, 230; between Lord and servant, 20, 80, 82, 87, 95–96, 118, 157. *See also* undifferentiated
dil-i ḥaqīqī, 23
dīn, 6, 129
Ding Yan 丁彥, 32
directions (*fang* 方), 93; four, 83, 95, 132, 188; eight, 204; five, 55; myriad, 200, 220; six (*liuhe* 六合), 134; without, 86, 147
discernment (*shi* 識), 36, 60, 72, 80, 89, 106, 108, 120, 121, 126, 135, 141, 144, 157, 167, 177, 178, 190, 192, 210, 211, 214, 219, 223, 230, 237; of the Lord, 70, 87, 167
disclosing (*lu* 露), 109, 144, 171, 192, 194, 195, 198, 234. *See also* issuing forth
discrimination (*bian* 辨), 37, 43, 63, 88, 91, 92, 105, 114, 122, 125, 126, 128, 134, 137, 157, 175, 177, 186, 187, 192, 223, 228, 230, 233
disease, illness, sickness, 36, 38, 55, 64, 68, 77, 87, 88, 95, 122, 123, 135–37, 151–52, 159, 168, 169, 172–74, 178, 185, 190, 194, 195, 201, 205, 206, 214

disgrace (*ru* 辱), 227, 238. *See also* honor
disobedience (*wei* 違). *See also* obedience
disorder (*luan* 亂), 42–43, 48, 72, 81, 92, 102, 158, 163, 167, 176, 108, 234
display, 46, 60, 69, 79, 92, 101, 131, 133, 188, 202, 219, 232–35
distinction, distinguishing, 42, 47, 53, 67, 82, 84, 88, 102, 103, 105, 112, 114–16, 119, 120, 128, 133, 157, 160, 171, 176, 195, 201, 206, 213, 217, 224, 230
document (*ce* 冊, *shu* 書), of body, 116, 120, 142, 144
dong 動, 45; *dongjing*, 45
drama, 71, 182, 229–30, 233
dreaming (*meng* 夢), 60, 66, 71, 73, 76, 90, 116, 124, 140, 153, 179, 185, 192, 197, 198, 229, 233; drunken, 57, 70, 73, 85, 93, 127, 142, 145, 148, 188, 224, 225, 234
drinking (*yin* 飲). *See* wine
drunkenness, 211–12. *See* dreaming
Dungeon, Earthly, 71, 86, 100, 128, 184, 238
dunyā, 71
dust (*chen* 塵), 48, 63, 86, 91, 160, 219, 235; mote, 120, 137, 153, 200; ocean of, 180, 210; inside water, 53, 224; world of, 71

earth (*di* 地), 43. *See* heaven
eastern land (China), 33, 132, 162
effect (*yuan* 緣). *See* cause
elder, 38, 158, 171; and younger, 21, 123, 168, 172, 227
elements (agents, greats), five, 49, 224; four, 17, 43–44, 47, 53, 57, 74, 91, 107, 139, 224
elixir, 129, 144
embedding (*ju* 具), 70, 78, 111; at the beginning, 70, 97, 125, 228; in the body (heart), 90, 112, 120, 224

embodiment (*ti* 體), 104, 110, 147, 151, 214; of the Real (the Ultimate), 12, 24, 117, 121, 141, 189, 198, 207; by sages, 104, 207; of sagehood, 99, 160, 199, 202

emperor (*huangdi* 皇帝, *jun* 君), 19, 51, 66, 80–81, 112, 181, 182, 205, 220, 228, 237; Five, 60, 131

empty, emptiness (*kong* 空, *xu* 虛), 10, 58, 65, 66, 83, 93, 95, 99, 110, 142, 143, 176, 193, 202, 209, 214, 198, 218, 224, 226; of heart (self), 116, 137, 176, 178, 201; king of, 92; Real, 86, 87. *See also* nonbeing

endeavor (*gong* 功), 91, 106, 115, 126, 128, 149, 150, 183, 185, 199, 210

endowment (*bing* 稟), diversity of (the human), 57, 71, 97, 198; endowed nature, 107, 114

enemy, 37, 73, 92, 107, 171, 199, 229–30

entrusting, 127, 155, 189, 192, 199, 201

envy, 127, 138, 193, 194, 196, 199

enwrapping (*bao* 包), 44, 58; heaven and earth, 111, 136, 146, 213; the myriad images, 50, 96, 116

equality (*jun* 均), 61–62, 65, 67, 85, 157, 166, 168, 169, 171, 172, 191, 194, 198, 204, 222, 226, 232, 234

error, 61, 68, 73, 108, 130, 140, 143, 149, 177, 186, 193, 194, 227

essence (*jing* 精), 9, 18, 36, 76–78, 82, 99, 122, 131, 137, 167, 199, 201, 206, 221, 224; of body, 110; of father, 139, 142; pure, 113; of soul, 227; Essence (*dhāt*) of God, 12–13, 188; and attributes, 12–13, 45–46

establishing (*li* 立), the Bonds, 124, 130, 189; good, 106, 130, 218; self, 134, 146, 197; teachings (the way), 58, 70, 82–83, 96, 109, 127, 130, 133, 146, 154, 182, 195, 226, 228; the universe, 43, 59, 81, 86, 97, 120, 204, 206

eternal, eternity, 42, 71, 130, 181, 185; abode, 153, 178, 210, 233

ethics, 6, 18–26, 29, 77

Eve, 56

everlasting (*chang* 長, *yong* 永), 44, 55, 65, 86, 99, 113, 115, 124, 129, 142, 147, 151, 182; glory, 220, 239; happiness, 57, 203; punishment, 99, 167. *See also* abode, life

evidence (*zheng* 證, *ju* 據), 60, 67–68, 70, 73, 78, 94, 108, 109, 113, 115–16, 120, 137, 153, 156, 178, 226, 234; clear, 44, 49, 67–68, 76, 86, 175

evil (*e* 惡; *sharr*), 71, 91, 103, 106. *See also* good

evolution, 17

examination, of officials, 60, 180, 233; after death, 195, 199, 235

existence (*zai* 在; *wujūd*), circle of, 9–13, 16; constant, 60, 176–77, 182; levels of, 14–17, 44; of the Real, 42, 92, 126, 176–77, 235; of things, 44, 92, 110, 118, 143, 164

eyes, 186; clear, 133, 194; and ears (and nose and tongue), 45, 46, 56, 70, 86, 113–14, 137, 145, 151, 186, 198, 209

face, original (*mianmu* 面目), 141, 193, 195

faḍā'il, 25

faith, faithfulness (*xin* 信), 21, 39, 42, 101, 127, 130, 138, 152, 153, 155, 156, 163, 173, 186, 196, 211, 220, 222, 231; (*īmān*), 16, 59, 70, 196

false, falsehood, 68, 112, 128, 130, 140, 144, 148, 226. *See* real, truth

family. *See* regulation

farming. *See* planting
father (*fu* 父), and mother, 48, 68, 96, 123, 139, 142, 159, 160, 204, 226; original, 88; and son, 21, 65, 90, 117, 121, 155–57, 211, 212. *See also* parent
Fāṭima, 123
fear (*kong* 恐), 67, 70, 73, 137, 170, 175, 176, 189, 195, 199, 206, 209, 227, 230
feelings (*qing* 情), 63, 91, 95, 111, 115, 122, 185, 198, 222, 223, 225; and desire, 140, 152, 236; and nature, 91, 105–6, 123; seven, 236
Feng Yangwu 馮養吾, 7
Fenghou 風後, 76
fengshui 風水, 219
festival (*jie* 節), 206; Small, 77, 201
fiʾl, 46
filial piety (*xiao* 孝), 48, 64, 67, 92, 110, 114, 129, 133, 155, 156, 158–63, 206, 217, 223, 225, 226, 234
fiqh, 3
fire (*huo* 火), 44, 93, 97, 128, 151, 204, 236; and ice, 121, 222, 226; and soil, 127–29; and wood, 224. *See also* elements, water
fishing, for desires, 193; for praise, 138, 176
floating (*fu* 浮), 66, 192, 193, 235; clouds, 107, 116, 120. *See also* life
flow (*liu* 流), 17, 94, 114, 138, 153–54, 160, 170, 202; of heaven, 144; of nature, 102; of water, 63, 91, 104, 137, 166, 197, 201, 210, 218, 233, 238
flowers (*hua* 花), 171, 178, 204, 239; and fruit, 43, 63, 127, 134, 206, 224; in the sky, 60, 73, 92–93, 143. *See also* seed
flyers (*fei* 飛). *See* birds
following, 72, 97, 114, 124, 127, 185, 201, 203, 218–19, 222; nature, 15, 101–3, 107, 109; self-nature, 96, 134, 137, 162, 192; the right way, 73, 93, 130, 134, 136, 144, 153, 154, 181, 204, 214; the wrong way, 88, 94, 142, 151, 178, 214, 226, 227
food, 63, 114, 129, 154, 165, 194, 208, 209, 232; and clothing, 61, 65, 135, 146, 150, 151, 197, 199, 206, 214, 226, 232, 233; and drink, 151–52, 197, 206, 212, 214, 232, 233, 237
foolishness, folly (*wang* 妄), 61, 83, 84, 86, 87, 89, 94, 103, 107, 119, 121, 133, 138, 140, 156, 176, 178, 187, 189, 199, 219, 220, 221, 228, 229; arising of, 91, 93
Footstool (*kursī*), 86
forces, two, 207, 221
forgetting (*wang* 忘), 122; the myriad things, 71, 198; the fountainhead (the Real), 95, 102, 128, 129, 136, 140, 145–50, 153, 173, 181, 194, 210, 221, 222, 231; self, 191, 210
forgiving (*shu* 恕), 171, 187; by Lord, 128, 167–68, 214; others vs. self, 163, 169
form (*xing* 形), 10, 12, 13, 63, 76, 81, 90, 91, 103, 111–13, 115, 125, 139, 148, 188, 193, 208; bodily, 43, 53, 55, 79, 110, 113–15, 146, 150, 237; and color, 67, 82, 86, 110; and formlessness, 10, 12–14, 53, 54, 76, 125, 147, 235; of earth, 53, 54, 81, 117, 223; of heaven, 53, 54, 81, 117, 224; of humans, 148, 207; of the myriad things, 99, 118; outward, 115, 182, 236, 238; and principle, 81, 90, 99, 117, 148–49, 207, 224; and spirit, 13, 91, 221, 222, 236, 237
fortune, good, 78, 79, 92, 220; and misfortune, 55, 107

fountainhead (*yuan* 源), 52, 80, 94, 106, 114, 121, 138, 146, 202, 219, 238; of clear virtue, 20, 70; forgetting, 95, 102, 147, 178, 181, 221; of mandate, 51, 56, 136, 141; of myriad things, 75, 91, 176, 213; of purity, 153, 155, 197; six (roots), 67, 70, 113–14, 151, 195; stopping up, 80, 121
free will (*ziyou* 自由), 15, 95, 133; and predetermination, 59, 63, 67, 97, 108
friend, friendship, 77, 155, 156, 164, 168, 171–76, 212, 227, 232
fruit (*guo* 果), 194, 196, 225. *See also* flowers, seed
fu 覆, 69
Fu Xi 伏羲, 7, 131, 132
fuming (復命), 48
function (*yong* 用), 11, 45, 65, 113, 121, 126, 137, 139, 237; of heart (spirit), 112–14, 206; root (and working), 103–4, 114; subtle, 127, 149. *See also* substance
Fuyue 傅說, 76

gain (*de* 得) and loss (*shi* 失), 49, 65, 69, 71, 107, 133, 163, 177, 179, 181, 191, 200, 201, 209, 214, 215, 221, 223, 234
gambling (*bo* 博), 193, 209–10
gangchang 綱常, 130
Gao 高, Emperor, 35
Gate of All Subtleties. *See* subtlety
generations, 37, 86, 87, 100–1, 123, 130, 161, 182, 228
Ghazālī, Abū Ḥāmid (d. 1111), 21, 28–31, 167; *Iḥyā' 'ulūm al-dīn*, 3, 31, 173, 190, 197
giving (*shi* 施), self and things, 145–46
God, 42, 75. *See also* Lord, Real
gold, 65, 71, 90, 128, 140, 156, 172, 191, 198, 210, 217, 223

good (*shan* 善), 73, 77, 128, 134, 160, 175, 194, 197; and evil, 22–23, 52, 59, 61–63, 66, 85, 91–94, 97–106, 109, 115–16, 122–24, 125, 127, 128, 136, 140, 164, 169, 172–74, 176, 180, 183–85, 187, 190, 191, 193, 195, 198, 209, 217–18, 219, 222, 224, 228, 229, 231, 232, 234–36, 238; practiced, 77, 106, 109; root, 106, 229; sorts of, 106, 190. *See also* people
governance (*zheng* 政, *zhi* 治), 42, 80, 125, 135, 180, 186, 196, 219; of the country, 6, 20, 38, 48, 76–78, 110, 114, 126, 135, 155, 160, 197; by the Real, 184, 189, 220; by the Sage, 76–78, 146; of the world, 58, 87, 133, 169, 184, 187
grass (*cao* 草). *See* plants
gratitude (*gan* 感), 97, 133, 146, 148–50, 162–65, 192, 195–96, 213
great (*da* 大). *See* element
greed (*tan* 貪), 63, 67, 98, 110, 116, 120, 140, 165, 169, 178, 193, 194, 198, 211–13, 219, 232
grief, 77, 169, 185, 195, 204, 212, 219, 223, 225, 232; and joy, 225, 231
growth (*zhang* 長), 17, 75, 122, 214, 232. *See also* begetting
Guan Ding 灌頂, 205
Guangcheng 廣成, 61–62
guidance, 67, 69, 70, 75, 104, 130, 165, 173, 175, 177, 181, 189, 202, 214
guise (*xiang* 相), 85–87, 92, 96, 119, 120, 149, 224; without, 147, 152, 185, 235
guizhen 歸眞, 48
Gusou 瞽叟, 161–62, 228

hadith (saying of Muhammad). *See* Muhammad
ḥadīth qudsī, 108, 237
Ḥāfiẓ, 28

hajj, 201
Han 漢 dynasty, 203, 220, 226
Han Feizi 韓非子, 101
Han Kitab 漢克塔補, 2, 33; *han qituobu* 漢启佗補, 33
happiness, 61, 70–71, 92, 158, 159, 169, 179, 184, 194, 201, 215, 217, 232, 234, 235; of afterlife, 58, 166, 185, 199, 203, 231, 235–37; complete, 183, 235–37; of moment, 158, 169; real, 70–71; and suffering, 60, 64, 159, 222, 231
Haqiqah (*ḥaqīqa*), 25, 78; *al-ḥaqīqat al-muḥammadiyya*, 11
ḥaqq, 1, 25
harmony (*he* 和), 75, 77, 99, 122, 124, 151, 164, 170, 176, 181, 187, 223
hawā, 22
hearing (*ting* 聽), 59, 83; of the Real, 46; hearing sounds (*shengwen* 聲聞), 94–95. *See also* seeing
heart (*xin* 心, *dil*, *qalb*), 19–20, 23–24, 45, 46, 59, 64, 81, 84, 86, 89–95, 99, 100, 105, 108–14, 121, 123, 125, 130, 131, 132, 137–39, 149, 151, 152, 154, 159, 162–64, 169, 170, 174–76, 179, 191, 195, 203, 212, 217, 222, 215, 233, 237, 238; animal, 108–9, 111, 113, 114; awakening of, 77; body and, 25, 42, 62, 67, 93, 146, 153, 154, 166, 167, 187, 192, 200, 206, 207, 210, 216, 231; clarification (emptying) of, 73, 80, 116, 120, 133, 135, 137, 144, 151–52, 165, 166, 176, 200, 201; darkness of, 43, 68, 87, 173; death of, 231; ground of, 136, 219, 221; human, 108–11, 114, 121, 145; intention of, 67, 133, 148, 161, 217; loss of, 145; no-heart, 24, 141; nobility of, 62; one, 107, 110, 153, 155, 162, 209; private, 164; real 92–94, 108–12; of the Real, 67; return of, 139–41; of right and wrong, 88; root, 77, 95, 111, 193, 231; as ruler, 153, 167, 186, 206; of the sage, 93, 174, 193; sincere, 97, 175–76, 183, 196; sorts of, 108–12, 114, 174; true, 23, 108, 140, 156, 160, 167, 177, 186
heaven (*tian* 天), and earth, 44, 47, 53–55, 71; and the human, 62, 96, 221; levels of, 54, 147, 149; principle of, 56, 76–77, 81, 155; and earth and myriad things, 13, 18, 42, 48, 50, 53, 55, 65, 70–72, 74–75, 81, 85, 87, 89–91, 97, 100, 110, 115, 117, 118, 125, 126, 129, 135, 143, 144, 149, 166, 183, 188, 204, 206, 234, 237; Former (and Latter), 10, 16–18, 43, 53–54, 60, 63, 72, 76, 77, 82, 103, 107, 108, 140, 142, 146, 148, 153; son of, 156; Heavenly Country, 57–58, 71, 86, 100, 106, 128, 152, 180, 199, 235–38
hell, 86, 99, 151, 229, 232. *See also* Dungeon
heresy, heterodoxy (*yiduan* 異端, *xieduan* 邪端), 48, 66, 68, 83–88, 120, 128, 130, 133, 155, 163, 167, 171, 206, 207, 221, 222
high(ness), 156–57, 164, 198, 219; and low(ness), 13, 47, 50, 52, 57, 58, 60–62, 65, 74, 86, 97, 99, 113, 119, 127, 135, 139, 149, 175, 179, 188, 190, 221, 224, 228, 232, 234, 236
history, 50, 53, 130, 131, 203; Classic of, 80, 180
hoarding (*gugu* 穀谷), 212, 216–18
home, going (*gui* 歸), 41, 85, 128, 138, 145, 194, 221; to emptiness (the void), 85, 99–100; to the Latter Heaven, 77, 221–22, 234; to the Real (the Origin) 9, 48, 64, 75, 80, 104, 108, 117, 129, 130, 135,

home, going *(continued)*
146, 153, 162, 177, 179, 185, 199, 212, 219, 223–25, 229; to return, 99, 115, 120, 139–40, 148–49, 153, 233–34
honesty (*zhi* 直), 64, 67, 195; (*gongping* 公平), 214
Hongwu Emperor 洪武帝, 35
honor, honoring, honorable (*zun* 尊), 65, 75, 86, 88, 96–97, 118, 136, 157, 158, 163, 178, 181, 190, 191, 199; of the (human) body, 72, 117; of the Lord, 50, 68, 86, 90, 126, 147, 150, 156, 157, 200, 234; Classic, 134, 147, 177, 232; designations, 46, 82–83; and disgrace (*rongru* 榮辱), 65–67, 183, 234
hope (*xi* 希, *wang* 望), 70–71, 158; of the Real, 147, 150, 157
houtian 後天, 10
Hu Dengzhou 胡登洲, 2, 7
Hua 華 (Emperor Shun), 228
Huangdi 黃帝, 76
Huihui 回回, 23–24, 139, 141; Huiru 回儒, 2, 4, 30
human (*ren* 人, *insān*), 48; vs. animals, 88, 105–6, 113–15, 119–21, 150–51, 164–65, 192, 198, 213; becoming, 20, 22, 128–30, 192, 197–99, 221, 227; complete, 21, 189, 200; creation of, 55–59, 235; as embodiment of Real (the Ultimate), 12, 24, 117, 121, 141, 189, 198, 207; as goal of creation, 10, 12, 18, 20, 55, 72, 75, 96, 97, 117–20, 127, 149, 189, 205–7; humane, 100, 213; level of, 50, 58, 71, 116–21, 125–26, 148–49, 152, 160, 192, 200, 202, 206; as origin of the myriad, 117, 121, 144; perfect, 4, 10–12, 21–25, 29, 50, 55–56, 75, 98, 111, 120, 140, 148, 189–90, 197–99, 207, 224, 235; principle of, 120; real, 7, 12, 154;

root, 154, 159, 182, 206; sorts of, 51, 74, 96, 97, 104, 109, 182, 202, 216; as spiritual of the myriad, 53, 88, 117–18, 121, 139, 142, 146, 149, 164, 204, 206; uniqueness of, 88, 105–6, 113–20, 124–25, 149–50, 192. *See also* nature, nobility, origin, people, Ultimate
humaneness (*ren* 仁), 20–22, 25, 64, 67, 100, 101, 108–10, 117, 119, 145–46, 150, 167, 171, 173, 183–84, 185, 187, 189, 196; of the Real, 21, 53, 58, 101, 104, 184, 189; and righteousness, 110, 135, 159, 180, 213, 217
humility (xun 遜, rang 讓), 58, 127, 136, 172, 176, 187, 191, 194
hunger, 216, 226; and cold, 64, 77, 146, 147, 168, 180, 197, 212, 226; and thirst, 114, 151, 166, 168, 214, 232
Huntington, Samuel, 26
husband (*fu* 夫) and wife, 21, 56, 58, 65, 117, 121–24, 155, 168, 194, 207, 212, 228

I (*wo* 我), 42, 53, 79, 86, 87, 152, 154, 168, 186, 213
Iblis, 126–28; as chief demon (devil, spirit), 57, 124, 133, 229–30
Ibn al-ʿArabī, 5, 10–11, 24, 29, 42, 85, 106
Ibn Taymiyya, 85
ice, and fire, 121, 222, 226; melting of, 85, 96; and snow, 67, 221
ʿīd al-aḍḥā, 201
idols (*xiang* 像), 69, 154, 155, 157
ignorance (*yu* 愚, *wuzhi* 無知), 62, 92–94, 99, 120, 138, 163, 176–77, 192, 194, 197–98, 228; ignorant people, 44, 60, 94, 96, 98, 104, 109, 120, 121, 127, 129, 132, 137, 138, 144, 146, 155, 156, 172, 173, 175, 176, 182, 183, 185, 195, 200, 202,

210, 211, 214, 215, 218, 221, 225, 227
iḥsān, 21
illness. *See* disease
illumination (*zhao* 照), 44, 51, 53, 120, 125, 136, 138, 175, 200, 232, 236
illusion (*huan* 幻), 60, 93, 107, 120, 153, 194, 228
image (*xiang* 象), 41, 49, 63, 90, 106, 127, 133, 147, 148, 180, 198; illusory, 60, 107; myriad, 50, 75, 90, 96, 116, 121, 140, 154
īmān, 16, 70
immortal (*xian* 仙), (Daoist), 23, 55, 61, 76, 89, 99, 129, 133; heavenly, 50, 51, 54–58, 76, 78, 113, 124–30, 132, 151, 196, 198, 232, 235
insān kāmil, 10
inch, square (*fangcun* 方寸), 89, 114
injustice, unjust, 62, 93, 100, 105, 109, 120, 163, 167–69, 171, 195
intellect (*'aql*), 14, 198; intelligence (*hui* 慧), 20, 41, 67, 84, 108, 134, 136, 139, 146, 150, 151, 162, 180, 184, 188, 198, 202, 207; mandate of, 16, 113, 114
intention (*yi* 意), 8, 20, 37, 52, 60, 67, 93, 108, 121, 122, 127, 133, 135, 145, 148, 161, 164, 167, 172, 175, 176, 181, 193, 201, 216–18; of the heart, 133, 148, 161, 217; of the Real, 67; root, 101, 135, 161, 171, 224–26; sincerity of, 20, 73, 101, 160, 172, 216, 218; and thought, 100, 162, 163; willful, 85, 95, 114, 126, 142, 149, 236
interest (*li* 利), 212–14, 216–17
intimacy, 123, 142, 172, 212, 213, 230; of marriage, 56, 207; with worthies, 152, 160
investigation, 35, 80, 89, 94, 102–3, 115, 116, 129, 144, 161, 176, 215, 225, 232

inward/inside (*li* 裡, *nei* 內), and outward/outside, 18, 43, 44, 83, 98, 105, 107, 109, 111, 112, 115, 118, 122, 125, 127, 134, 137, 141, 144, 145, 150, 153, 162, 177, 186–88, 193, 196, 200, 202, 212, 236, 237
'Irāqī, Fakhr al-Dīn, 237
Islam (*qingzhen* 清真), 36, 78, 124, 138–40, 145, 148, 187, 212; books of, 36, 37; distortion of, 84–87; principle (root) of, 69, 79, 203; teaching (way) of, 37, 76, 83, 84, 87, 88, 95, 102, 104, 109, 123, 133, 134, 141, 146, 147, 152, 177, 189, 209, 220–23, 225; (*islām*), 129
isrā', 25
issuing forth (*fa* 發), 17, 43, 51, 53, 60, 72, 101, 103, 105, 108, 114, 124, 128, 136, 145, 149, 156, 162, 193, 196, 219, 234, 236; and disclosing, 45–46, 60, 107, 111, 140, 171, 172, 177, 224

jade, 71, 73, 90, 190, 217, 223; vs. stone, 65, 99, 102, 133, 140
Jāmī, 'Abd al-Raḥmān, 237
Jesuits, 132
Jesus, 7, 68, 111
jewel, 93, 144, 156, 230, 237
Ji Xin 紀信, 203
Jiang Xiong 蔣雄, 211
Jie 桀, King, 98
Jin 晉 dynasty, 203, 226
Jin Yijiu 金宜久, 34
jing 靜, 45
Jing of Jin 晉景公, 203
jinn, 13, 50
Job, 68
John, Gospel of, 111
Joseph, 68
joy (*le* 樂, *xi* 喜, *huan* 歡), 108–10, 159, 168, 194, 195, 201, 236, 237; and anger, 168, 191; and grief,

joy *(continued)*
179, 226, 231; of virtue, 151–52, 183, 185
judgment after death, 67, 85, 129, 165, 168, 215, 229, 235–36
Junayd, 22
jurisprudence *(fiqh)*, 3–4, 30
justice *(gong* 公*)*, 13, 21, 165, 167–70; utmost (of the Real), 60–62, 67, 70, 100, 101, 180, 184, 219, 229, 234, 235, 238. *See also* injustice

Kaabah, 35
Kalam (dialectical theology), 27, 30
kalima, 84
karma, 229
kawn, 15
Kelimo Jie 克理默解, 84
khalq, 47
kibr, 190
kinds, diversity of, 52, 56, 58, 93, 104–5, 107, 118–20, 124, 143; myriad, 43, 46, 96, 99, 107, 132, 149, 164, 179, 219
kindness, 133, 175, 213, 217; of the Lord, 64, 153, 162; of parents, 90, 159
king *(wang* 王*)*, 66, 68, 184, 199; sovereign, 105, 166–67
knowledge *(zhi* 知*)*, 48, 59, 67, 68, 83, 89, 112, 120, 126, 137–38, 144, 176–77; and awareness, 47, 49, 74–75, 105, 109, 113, 114; great and small, 67, 220; innate vs. learned, 104; limitations of, 59, 67; real, 20, 38, 56, 67, 71, 83, 95, 103, 111, 136, 178, 179, 186; the Lord's knowledge, 11, 46, 74, 126; of the sage, 200; of self, 20, 23, 29, 79, 89, 103, 120, 136, 138, 164, 173, 176, 190–91, 227; vain, 135, 178. *See also* recognition
kong 空, 10
Kongming 孔明, 220

Kubrawī Order, 4, 5
Kullabite formula, 42, 45
kun 坤, 43
kun, 15
Kuwata Rokuro, 34

lā maqām, 24
lamp *(deng* 燈*)*, 43, 120, 232; and oil, 109, 197
Lan Zixi 籃子羲, 7–9; *Tianfang zhenxue* 天方正學, 33
language, 50; diversity of, 131–32, 235
Laozi 老子, 71, 87; *Daodejing*, 41, 74, 89, 154
laws *(fa* 法*)*, 76, 89, 115, 117, 123, 160, 167, 169, 170, 187, 211, 227; of the king (the world), 100, 180, 184, 238; of Islam, 78, 130, 134, 189, 202, 209, 222
laziness, 124, 152, 163, 185, 195, 210
learning *(xue* 學*)*, 8, 38, 104, 160, 163, 232; classical, 67–70; Confucian, 35; constant, 135; great, 48, 67–70, 135; heretical, 84, 178; loss of, 160, 226; middle, 135; other, 101, 136; root, 69–70; true, 35, 37, 38, 64, 87, 133–39, 172; way of, 134–35
Lee Cheuk Yin, 26
levels *(pin* 品*)*, 44, 46–47, 53, 55, 77, 92, 97, 99, 101, 158, 159, 170, 181, 188, 196, 200; of heart, 108–10; of immortals, 125–27; of mandate (nature), 17, 76–77, 113; myriad, 47, 117, 129, 149; of sage, 88, 160. *See also* being, human
li 里, 43, 44, 132, 138, 171
li 理, 14, 43, 53
li 禮, 21, 24, 25
Li Bai 李白, 212
Li Xie 李諧, 205
Liang 梁 Kingdom, 205, 211
Liang Yijun 梁以浚, 32, 33

life (*sheng* 生, *huo* 活), 46, 57, 71, 72, 156, 170, 176, 182, 184, 199, 205, 214, 226, 227; and body, 89, 146, 152, 159, 188, 213, 217, 219, 222; and death, 49, 60, 62, 66, 69, 71, 73, 88, 92, 95, 99, 112–13, 116, 125, 126, 129, 133, 142, 143, 153, 155, 157, 164, 176, 177, 185, 190, 195, 200, 205, 210, 215, 221–25, 229, 231, 233, 234; everlasting, 62, 178, 185, 233, 238; floating, 85, 112, 184, 224, 231, 234, 239; return to, 235, 236, 238. *See also* dream

light (*guang* 光), 13, 43, 44, 91, 92, 109, 126, 129, 200, 233; of Being (the Real), 51–52, 92, 236; clear (pure), 43, 52, 120, 124, 137, 139, 144, 169, 236–37; of mirror, 72, 112, 136, 139, 160, 185, 189; of sun, 43, 84, 120, 136, 138, 183, 200, 232, 236; surplus, 50–52, 74; three, 92, 156

light (*qing* 輕), and heavy, 49, 53, 122, 156, 157, 192, 204, 221, 224, 225

lightning, 120, 184, 185, 193; and thunder, 178, 179

Limu 力牧, 76

ling 靈, 14; *lingjue* 靈覺, 53; *lingming* 靈明, 56

Ling Wei 令威, 55

lingzhi (靈芝) mushrooms, 99

listening (*ting* 聽), 25, 46, 82, 85–87, 94, 103, 104, 123, 137, 196, 210, 214; to the mandate, 105, 157, 162–64, 200, 201, 207

literature, 80–81, 136, 144

Liu Bang 劉邦, 203

Liu Zhi 劉智, 1, 4–7, 12–14, 23, 27, 30, 31; *Nature and Principle in Islam (Tianfang xingli* 天方性理), 1, 9, 14; *Sage Learning*, 17–18, 23, 25, 41, 42, 52–54, 56, 59, 63, 72, 74, 75, 85, 89, 103, 104, 109, 111, 112, 117, 125, 147, 224

lodging (*ji* 寄, *yu* 寓), 162, 164, 194, 195, 222; place, 60, 64, 159, 178, 182, 214, 225, 231, 234

Logos, 11

longevity and young death, 60, 65, 155, 181, 215, 217, 228, 234

Lord (*zhu* 主), 46, 81–83; lord ruler, 82, 87–92, 111, 142, 167; Real, 10, 21, 41, 43–60, passim; and servant, 20, 82–83, 87, 95, 96, 116, 118, 144, 157; and subject, 65, 144. *See* Real

love (*ai* 愛), 21, 56, 105, 106, 114, 140, 176, 185, 194, 195, 202, 205, 213–14; the Lord's, 100, 146, 150

loyalty (*zhong* 忠), 58, 64, 67, 92, 93, 96, 102, 107, 110, 114, 129–30, 133, 138, 154–59, 185, 202, 203, 209, 225, 226, 234; real, 154–59; to the ruler, 48, 81, 154–55, 162–63

Lu 魯, 123

Lu Shang 呂尚, 76

luck, 182, 210, 214, 220

lust, 121, 136, 151, 198

Ma Chengyin 馬承蔭, 34

Ma Junshi 馬君實, 7, 34

Ma Minglong 馬明龍, 8

Ma Zhenwu 馬真吾, 7

Ma Zhu 馬注, 34

mabda' wa ma'ād, 9

macrocosm and microcosm, 13, 18, 29, 69, 167

majesty (*yan* 嚴), 52, 53, 179, 200

makeup, 107, 117, 182

male and female, 124, 126, 142, 228

ma'nā, 13

man. *See* human, woman

managing, 68, 126, 155, 234

mandate (*ming* 命), 5, 15–17, 54, 55, 88, 113, 115, 123, 159; of awareness, 76–77, 113; clear, 16, 48, 49, 58, 75–79, 82, 83, 95, 96, 99, 109, 110, 112, 120, 121, 125,

mandate (continued)
130, 133, 144, 145, 149, 150, 153, 167, 189, 192, 199–202, 212, 214; compliance with, 16–17, 48, 56, 58, 72, 79, 96, 99, 102, 109, 110, 112, 136, 144, 153, 192, 199, 200, 207, 212; creation of, 88–90, 100; fountainhead of, 51, 56, 141; of heaven, 5, 15, 76–77, 100–3, 109, 226; levels of, 15–16, 76–77, 113; listening to, 105, 157, 162–64, 200, 201, 207; of the Lord, 48, 49, 54–57, 76, 125, 132, 149–50, 157, 229, 235; (dis)obeying of, 121, 150, 164–67, 174, 177, 195, 199, 212, 217, 225, 238; reception of, 16–17, 41, 49, 70, 72, 76, 78, 89, 102, 107, 115, 116, 127, 170, 221, 223, 234; returning to, 16–17, 48, 72, 79, 146, 154, 225, 234; of signs, 76–77; of spiritual, 16, 113; true, 223, 225; and wisdom, 56–57. *See also* nature

mansions (*gong* 宮), twelve, 147

maqāmāt, 25

marriage, 121–23, 155, 161–62, 227

Mary, 7

master (*zhu* 主, *shi* 師), 43, 52, 72, 87, 92, 101, 134, 135, 138, 175–76, 205; and servant, 82, 168, 218–19, 227

Mean, Doctrine of (*Zhongyong* 中庸), 15, 101, 109

meaning (*ma'nā*), 13

meanness, 60–66, 92, 140, 195, 221, 233; ultimate, 64, 66. *See also* nobility

measure, 36, 55, 100, 109, 128, 137, 152, 159, 174, 183, 199; living up to, 195

meat-eating, 206–9

medicine, 36, 38, 135, 169, 178, 190, 194

members (*hai* 骸), 47, 49, 56, 119, 196, 206, 224; five (*wuti* 五體), 147

memory (*ji* 記), 136, 145, 167

Mencius (Mengzi 孟子), 6, 23, 38, 39, 77, 88, 101, 106, 180

merchant, 89, 183, 231

mercy (*en* 恩), 60, 64, 97, 133, 146, 149–50, 163–65, 188–89, 192, 195–96, 206, 212–13; real, 188–89; and severity, 52, 57, 189; (*raḥma*), 64

merit (*gong* 功), 128, 146, 155, 163, 184, 193–94, 209, 230; meritorious deeds, 106, 152, 166, 172, 176, 178, 180, 197, 198, 218; name, 71, 120; virtue, 190, 235

metal (*jin* 金), 17, 47, 49, 85, 139, 236; and stone, 53, 105, 113, 145–46, 192, 200; and water, 224; and wood, 24

metaphysics, 7, 30, 74

ming 命, 15; *mingming* 明命, 16

Ming 明 dynasty, 8, 35, 220, 228

minister, 100, 112, 143, 167, 211, 212, 234

mi'rāj, 25

mirror, 90, 117–18, 143, 175, 190, 191, 228; and light (and polishing), 72, 112, 120, 136, 139, 160, 185, 189

mistake, 43, 53, 58, 61, 73, 93, 108, 119, 134, 149–51, 158, 161, 164, 173, 175, 180, 186, 190, 192, 193, 198, 202, 204, 208, 211, 213, 214, 218, 219, 224, 229, 230, 232

moderation (*jie* 節), 187, 197–98, 213

modesty (*qian* 謙, *lian* 廉), 37, 56, 58, 67, 98, 114, 122, 151, 163, 164, 175, 176, 178, 190, 194, 211

Mohists 墨, 226

moment (*shi* 時), 66, 78; losing, 173–74, 178; observing, 186, 192, 197, 210, 231; right, 75, 180, 197

money, 146, 183; and things, 146, 162, 163, 168, 182, 185, 213, 215, 218, 222
monk, 48, 89, 143, 204, 205
moon, in water, 90, 112, 121. *See also* sun
morality. *See* ethics
Moses, 61
mother (*mu* 母), 111, 227; and child, 106, 189, 199, 206–7, 214; of the myriad things, 41, 144, 154. *See* father, womb
mourning, 223, 225
mouth (*kou* 口), 45, 59, 119, 191, 194, 197, 209, 211, 233; and stomach, 173, 209, 216; tongue, 162, 163, 175, 198, 236
movement (*dong* 動), 56, 72, 93, 108, 109, 114, 175, 224, 238; and stillness, 45–46, 52, 54, 65, 70, 99, 104, 143; movement-stillness, 45–47, 52
mu 畝, 212
Muhammad (the Prophet), cosmic role of, 10–11, 25, 51–52, 74–79, 88; as one with the Non-Ultimate, 51, 78; Reality of, 11, 12; sayings of, 19, 22, 30, 44–45, 55, 73, 74, 78, 101, 108, 113, 123, 124, 133, 134, 137, 141, 152, 166–69, 170, 171, 175, 179, 188, 197, 199, 218, 237, 238; Spirit of, 74, 78. *See also* Sage, Ultimate
muḥsin, 21
mu'min, 175
multitudes, 68, 106, 126, 127, 132, 153
myriad. *See* things
mystery (*xuan* 玄), 79, 108–10, 188; (=Daoism), 39, 83, 95; mysterious secret (subtlety), 44, 45, 48, 58, 82, 101, 110, 127, 139, 142, 143, 144, 149, 201, 228, 236

nabī, 6
nafs, 22, 103, 105; *nafs ammāra*, 103; *nafs nāṭiqa*, 14, 105
name (*ming* 名), 56, 112; and guise, 85–87, 96; of the Lord, 46, 82–83; meritorious, 120, 138, 155, 181, 187, 190–91, 218, 230; and profit, 71, 73, 120, 140, 172, 181, 193–94, 216, 219, 231; vs. reality, 57, 58, 66, 83, 141, 156, 178, 190, 194, 202, 219; seeking, 73, 120, 138, 187, 191, 193, 218, 231; named (*youming* 有名), 41, 87, 154; nameless (*wuming* 無名), 41, 87, 89, 154. *See also* attribute
Nanyang 南陽, 220
Nasafī, 'Azīz, 5, 75, 125; *Maqṣad-i aqṣā*, 5, 78; *Insān-i kāmil*, 69
Nasr, Seyyed Hossein, 26
native place, 107, 145, 147, 182, 194, 231
nature (*xing* 性), 14–17, 23, 25, 43, 53, 75, 79, 84, 88, 91, 94, 101–15, 123; of animals, 17, 19, 44, 75, 106, 113–15, 148, 202, 208; of awareness, 15–16, 42–43, 93, 109–11, 113–15; of begetting, 113–14; diversity of, 56, 71–72, 75, 102–4, 109, 112, 119; endowed, 107, 114; following, 15, 101, 103, 109; four, 139, 203; goodness of 77, 92, 101–4, 106, 109; great, 111, 144; of the heart, 111, 112, 144; of the human, 14, 49, 56, 71–72, 74–75, 103, 104–6, 110, 113, 117, 119–20, 221; and mandate, 7, 15–18, 79, 86, 95, 97, 101–8, 113, 120, 121, 135, 136, 139, 144, 160, 189, 193, 221; original, 56, 111, 236; ox, 202; and Principle (Neo-Confucianism), 14, 36, 38, 97, 98, 100–2; and principle, 9, 52, 76, 92, 97, 98, 102, 108, 112, 117, 207; purification of, 80, 135, 139,

nature *(continued)*
  144; of the real, 91–92; real, 9, 56, 107, 114; root, 43, 49, 92, 95, 98, 101, 111, 227; of the sage, 75, 111; secret of, 110; self-, 22, 89, 96, 134, 137, 144, 150–51, 162, 163, 170, 176, 177, 192, 200, 202, 229–30; Subtle, 86, 87; true, 108, 230; and vital-energy, 102–3; willful, 71, 73, 82, 162, 169. *See also* spiritual
Neo-Confucianism, 1, 5–6, 10, 14, 15, 23, 29, 30, 49, 101, 105, 155
newly born *(xinsheng* 新生*)*, 228; and Original Being, 42, 44, 52, 96, 115
night, 65, 70, 73, 91. *See also* day
nirvana *(niepan* 涅槃*)*, 48, 94
no-self *(wuji* 無己*, wuwo* 無我*)*, 22–23, 109, 142, 178, 190
nobility *(gui* 貴*)*, 164, 174, 190, 234; of the human (body), 62, 72, 96, 106, 117, 125, 126, 128, 149, 157, 206; and meanness, 46, 48, 49, 60, 62, 65, 221. *See also* wealth
nonbeing *(wu* 無*)*, 10, 47, 166, 183, 210; empty, 49, 80, 85, 86, 95, 99, 130, 140, 148, 177, 184, 187, 198, 202, 234. *See also* being
nourishing *(yang* 養*)*, 51, 73, 75, 97, 113, 128, 129, 151, 159, 175, 193, 206, 214, 216, 217, 219; by the Lord, 51, 75, 97
nubuwwa, 6
numerical *(shu* 數*)*. *See* One
nurturing *(yu* 育*)*, 124, 159, 189, 214, 228; *(peiyang* 培養*)*, 72

obedience *(shun* 順*)*, and/or disobedience, 57, 58, 65, 67, 71, 72, 121, 124, 126–27, 145, 149–51, 156, 158, 159, 161–67, 174, 177, 193, 195, 199, 201, 206, 207, 211, 212, 214, 215, 219, 223, 225, 238; obeying the One, 16, 72. *See also* mandate

observing *(cha* 察*)*, the moments, 186, 192, 197, 210, 231
obstacle, 44, 59, 167, 177, 178, 195, 200, 202–3, 205
ocean, 36, 48, 54, 59, 72, 97, 104, 112, 134, 137, 144, 201, 222, 234; of dust, 180, 210; of suffering, 140, 203; and streams, 74, 96, 177, 178
officials, 126, 164, 168, 180, 204, 206, 219, 234; offices of angels, 125
One *(yi* 一*)*, becoming, 16, 72; Numerical, 12–13, 20, 23, 41–42, 87, 96, 113, 116, 118, 154, 186; obeying, 16, 72; Only, 41, 50, 52; practicing, 12–13, 72, 154–55, 199; Real, 7, 10, 12, 16, 20–21, 41–43, 117–18, 144, 186; recognizing, 16, 72; Self-Single, 41, 44, 50, 75, 79, 81, 96; three, 12, 154; Unique, 12, 41–42, 50, 69–70, 79, 81, 87, 96, 97, 110, 113, 116, 130, 147, 154, 156, 196, 198
Only One *(zhiyi* 止一*)*, 41, 50, 52
oppression, 62, 100, 139, 163, 168, 215
origin, original *(yuan* 元*, yuan* 原*, benlai* 本來*)*, 9–10, 17, 46, 51–53, 56, 80, 85, 104, 109, 111, 113, 131, 140, 142, 142, 149, 153, 193, 207, 235–36; ancestor, 50, 88, 171; going home to, 146, 221–22; great, 53, 97, 101, 112; of the human, 56, 104, 117, 121, 150, 222; of the mandate, 107, 144; of the myriad things, 51–53, 76, 79, 81, 96, 107, 110, 117, 121, 129, 148; root, 8, 12, 51, 63, 76, 83, 87, 88, 99, 104, 117, 129, 132, 149, 172, 198, 210, 223, 229; seed, 81, 234; of the teaching, 130; 155 of the Utmost Sage, 52, 74–75. *See also* beginning, being
outward, outside *(biao* 表*, wai* 外*)*, 186, 225; form, 115, 236, 238. *See also* inward

painting, 92, 106
Pangu 盤古, 82
paradise, 86, 237. *See* Heavenly Country
parents, 69, 82, 107, 114, 133, 146–47, 155–63, 168, 174, 210, 213, 223, 226, 227, 234; serving, 155, 158–59, 206, 217
partiality (*pian* 偏), 125, 162, 163, 172, 204, 205, 208, 228
patience (*ren*[*nai*] 忍[耐]), 165, 187, 199–200
peace (*an* 安), 232; and danger, 49, 64, 65, 131, 157, 177, 179, 190, 201, 215
pearl, 91, 97, 217, 228; and diving, 138, 195, 234
Pen (*qalam*), Supreme, 74, 86
penetration (*tong* 通, *che* 徹), 8–9, 36, 44, 47, 56, 58, 63, 74, 76, 82, 83, 89, 101, 102, 105, 115, 136, 145, 151, 160, 236; of the heart, 70, 112; spiritual, 8, 79, 126, 127, 166, 192, 200
people, sorts of, 51, 182, 195, 216; common (ordinary), 51, 67, 72, 98, 104, 146, 157, 165, 172, 174–76, 182, 195, 199, 202, 203, 216, 217, 220, 225; evil, 58, 91, 100, 174, 205, 216, 235; good, 51, 58, 85, 100, 164, 174, 205, 235, 236; true, 23, 82, 84, 85, 95, 108–11, 126, 128, 137, 139, 170, 171, 175, 182, 202, 220, 226, 229, 230; utmost, 175, 202, 230
perfection (*cheng* 成), 43, 52, 81, 126, 152, 159, 172, 194; of awareness, 92–94; of the fruit, 72, 111, 120, 234; of the Great Ultimate, 111, 140; of things, 55, 98, 99, 139, 154, 207; of virtue, 107, 183. *See also* human
perishing, silent (*jimie* 寂滅), 49, 80, 85, 95, 130, 148, 184, 187, 198, 202, 234

perplexity, 42, 48, 51, 90, 104, 110, 112, 114, 127–29, 136, 138, 154, 156, 165, 167, 179, 192, 214, 221, 228
Persian, 3–5, 28–29, 31
Petersen, Kristian, 33, 109
philosophy, Islamic, 5, 15, 22, 27, 29, 31, 77, 106
physician, 38, 135, 169, 173, 190
pillars, five, 117, 141, 145
pity, 70, 77, 204, 216; of Real Lord, 153, 177, 188, 189
pivot (*shu* 樞 [*ji* 機]), 226; mysterious, 116, 118; ultimate, 110
planting (farming), 48, 72, 136, 140, 144, 179–80, 184, 197, 198, 212, 218, 224, 227, 238–39
plants, 13–14, 139, 148, 202, 204, 217, 225; apricot, 102; bamboo, 43, 90, 119, 204, 228; cypress, 99, 156, 172; grass, 53; grass and trees, 15, 17, 55, 65, 75, 99, 105, 113, 117, 119, 121–22, 125, 148, 149, 204, 206, 207, 224; mushrooms, 63, 99; mustard, 236; peach, 107, 172; pine, 99, 156, 172; plum, 102, 107, 172; thorns, 156, 180, 239. *See also* flower, seed
Poetry (*shi* 詩), Classic of, 48, 122
poison, 123, 151, 194, 216
Portent (*zhen* 朕), days of, 54, 55
position (*wei* 位), 54, 61, 65, 75, 83, 86, 87, 99, 110, 115, 127, 129, 148, 158, 167, 169, 179, 186, 189
possessions, 66, 71, 136, 140, 182, 191, 213, 219, 231
poverty (*pin* 貧), 68, 146, 163, 172, 178, 187, 199, 214, 217; and meanness, 60–66, 140; and wealth, 60–66, 140, 199, 228
power (*neng* 能), of creatures, 89, 137, 142, 143, 166, 168, 179, 188, 200; of heavenly immortals, 125, 126; of the Real, 13, 45–48, 50–51, 53, 83, 88–91, 107, 118, 126, 188

practice, 51, 64, 80, 86, 112, 134, 137, 152, 160, 187, 199; of evil, 66, 109, 137; of good, 66, 77, 106, 109; of virtue, 67, 106–7; Practicing One (*xiyi* 習一), 12, 154–54, 199

praise, 37, 162–63, 181, 183, 190–92, 194, 227; and criticism, 191–92; fishing for, 138, 176; remembrance of, 146, 196

prayer (*qi* 祈, *bai* 拜), 61, 70, 77, 147, 197, 205, 216; for parents, 159; to spirits, 96, 155. *See also* worship

predetermination (*qianding* 前定), 16, 59–63, 155, 215; (*taqdîr*), 59. *See also* free will

preparation (*yubei* [預]備), 138, 217; for death, 179–80, 185, 231

pride (*ao* 傲), 56, 131, 151, 176–77, 190–94, 199

principle (*li* 理), 14, 31, 37, 38, 42–44, 46, 55, 75, 78, 80–83, 89, 91, 96–105, 107, 112, 121, 122, 124, 126, 128, 130, 141, 148, 152, 175, 178, 194, 201, 203, 205, 218, 221, 222, 226, 227, 230, 233; of the body, 144, 207; clarification of, 113, 115, 138; deduction of, 16, 105, 113, 131, 188; examination (investigation) of, 80, 96, 103, 116, 129, 144, 186, 228; firm, 71, 80, 117, 119, 146; and forms, 81, 90, 99, 113, 117, 148–49, 207, 224; of the Great Ultimate, 81, 198, 297; of the heart, 186; of heaven (and earth), 56, 70, 76–77, 81, 140, 147, 155, 237; of the human, 120; Real, 130; of the self-so, 63, 65, 97, 197; utmost, 36, 49, 53, 59, 85, 107, 116, 130, 138, 144, 203, 205, 207, 222; and vital-energy, 17, 38, 49, 97–102; of the way, 36, 146, 172, 199. *See also* nature

prison, 64, 115, 128, 169, 203, 205, 232–33, 235, 238

private (*si* 私), 37, 164, 211; and public, 37, 105; self, 105, 109

proclamation, 53, 57, 77, 152, 234

profit (*li* 利), 63, 173, 203, 214, 217, 218, 225, 239; and harm (loss), 95, 110, 135, 181, 189, 201, 226. *See also* name

profound person (*junzi* 君子), 37, 48, 122, 123, 128, 133, 154, 203, 213; vs. small person, 61, 65, 137, 172, 206

prohibition (*jin* 禁), 54, 130, 155, 180, 188, 209, 210, 212, 227, 233

proof, 69, 70, 73, 116, 143, 157, 165, 192, 225

property, 150, 157, 199, 202–4

prophecy (*nubuwwa*), 6, 11

Prophet. *See* Muhammad

propriety (*li* 禮), 21–22, 24–26, 96, 114, 123, 147–51, 156–58, 162, 163, 196, 206, 209, 211, 212, 223, 225; ancient, 201–2; propriety-worship, 147, 149–50, 157; ritual, 156, 158, 159, 223

protecting, 51, 68, 73, 88, 90, 118, 122, 125, 128, 165, 217

psychology, 7, 30, 103

public (*gong* 公), 37, 70, 105, 126, 134, 202, 219, 225

punishment (*fa* 罰, *xing* 刑), 70, 100, 150, 155, 166, 167–71, 183–85, 187, 214, 218, 228, 232, 235; everlasting, 99, 167. *See also* reward

puppets, 195, 230

pure, purity (*qing* 清), 67, 75, 98, 109, 125, 139, 154, 175, 184, 187, 196, 198, 222; and clean, 43, 45, 56, 91–94, 109, 126, 130, 137, 139, 147, 148, 152, 154, 165, 166, 175, 177, 192, 196, 197, 200, 208, 222–23, 225, 235; of heavenly immortals, 125, 198; of the Real, 43, 50, 148, 152, 157; and turbid,

43, 44, 49, 53, 97, 98, 104, 114, 123, 124, 126, 198, 221, 224; Three Purities, 87. *See also* Islam
putting aside (*she* 舍), 73, 97, 107, 120, 133, 142, 176, 178–79, 181, 198, 204

qadar, 59
qi 氣, 41
Qi 齊, 61–62
Qi 祁, Mount, 220
qian 乾, 43
Qin dynasty, 6, 80
Qin Yueren 秦越人, 174
qing 情, 105
qing 頃, 127
Qur'an (*see also* classic). References to: 2:30 (57), 2:216 (172), 3:19 (129), 6:32 (71, 229), 21:35 (59), 21:55 (69), 27:80 (104), 28:50 (22), 28:88 (86), 30:21 (122), 30:41 (63), 32:5 (54), 36:82 (50), 41:53 (69), 49:13 (195), 51:21 (188), 55:26 (176), 67:2 (60), 70:4 (54), 95:4–5 (50)

Rābi'a, 110, 208
raḥmān, 64; *raḥīm*, 64
Ramadan, 201
rasūl, 6
Rāzī, Najm al-Dīn, 4–5; *Mirṣād al-'ibād*, 4, 25–26, 52, 55, 74, 108, 109, 125, 145, 149, 152
real (*zhen* 真, *ḥaqq*), 1, 24–25, 73, 91, 106, 130, 139, 144, 146, 182, 185, 197, 200, passim; and false, 66, 88, 93, 111, 120, 128, 137, 182–83, 187, 191–92, 195, 218; True, 141, 144. *See* attributes, being, existence, home, knowledge, Lord, One
reality (*shi* 實), 116, 127, 137, 151, 173, 177, 178, 182, 194, 218, 238; vs. name, 57, 58, 66, 112, 141, 156, 190, 193, 194, 202, 220; (*ḥaqīqa*),

vs. Shariah, 25; Muhammadan, 11–12
realizing fully (*jin* 盡), 44, 103, 128, 164, 166; the heart, 23, 112; loyalty, 102, 202; realized practice (*xiuzheng* 修證), 144
rebellion (*ni* 逆), 67, 100, 102, 121, 128–29, 158, 177; vs. obedience, 159, 211, 214, 215
receiving. *See* mandate
Receptive (*kun* 坤). *See* Creative
recognition (*ren* 認), 90, 111, 128, 151, 178, 190, 200, 219; of the Lord, 29, 44–45, 48, 69–70, 72, 75–77, 79, 82, 96, 101, 108, 110, 114, 116, 120, 135, 141–44, 156, 160, 167, 176, 177, 181, 186, 237; of self, 29, 44, 48, 79–80, 101, 116, 135, 142, 144, 155, 164, 176, 186
recompense (*bao* 報), 100, 152, 159, 183, 228, 238
rectifying (*zheng* 正), 104, 148, 210
redeeming, 149, 151, 203, 235
refinement (*jing* 精), 8, 9, 38, 44, 53, 59, 92, 98, 112, 117, 129, 138, 185, 207, 208, 221, 222, 237
reflection, 56, 58, 66, 71, 115, 150, 213, 231; wakeful (*canwu* 參悟), 188–90
regulation, 26, 67, 76, 100, 167, 170, 175, 180, 196, 216, 223, 228; of the body, 144, 167, 197; of the family, 6, 20, 38, 48, 110, 114, 155, 160, 197, 206; of the myriad things, 78, 90, 125, 236
relationships (*lun* 倫), 124, 150, 156, 212; constant, 211–12; five human, 16, 19, 21, 48, 121
relatives, family, 77, 123–24, 172, 173, 217, 227
release (*shi* 釋), 71, 167–68, 205; (*zong* 縱), 204
reliance, 41, 46, 85, 98, 100, 113, 126, 128, 143, 174; on body, 113–14,

reliance *(continued)*
166; on Buddha, 155; on Lord, 49, 78, 133, 199, 229; on people, 214–15; on principles, 49; on self, 59, 142, 200, 215; on teaching, 130, 131, 151, 192; on things, 221

remembrance *(nian* 念*)*, 145–46, 148, 160, 196, 199

ren 仁, 20–21

renji 人極, 10

renunciation *(zuhd)*, 178

repentance *(hui* 悔*)*, 8, 58, 151, 166, 168, 169, 180, 192, 193, 198, 212, 227

representative *(dai*[*li*] 代[理]), of the Real, 49, 57, 126, 130, 189

reputation, 136, 160, 176, 181, 187, 190, 191, 219

respect, 48, 56, 67, 80, 127, 133, 147–49, 153, 156–58, 163; self-respect, 190

responsibility *(ze* 責, *ren* 任*)*, 18–20, 126, 149, 150, 160–62, 166–67, 192, 233

resurrection *(fusheng* 復生*)*, 124

retribution *(bao* 報*)*, 167–69, 180

Return *(ma'ād)*, 6, 9–10, 12, 17, 23, 139–40, 148; compulsory and voluntary, 139, 140; return *(fu* 復, *fan* 返*)*, 24, 85, 104, 107, 120, 139–41, 229; to life, 235–36, 238; to the mandate, 48, 72, 80, 141, 146, 153, 225, 234, 235; to the origin, 148, 153, 221–22; sorts of, 139–40; utmost, 24, 141; returners *(hui* 回*)*, 23–24, 139–41. *See also* home

reverence, 68, 150, 156, 191, 192

revolving, 69, 73, 124, 143, 200, 209, 234; of heaven, 54, 125, 147, 206, 224, 234

reward *(shang* 賞*)*, and punishment, 67, 85, 91, 95, 100, 115, 119, 180, 183–84, 218, 227, 229, 234–35, 238

rice, 63, 212

right *(shi* 是*)*, and wrong, 38, 65, 66, 72, 81, 84, 97, 119, 122, 137, 174, 177, 187, 191, 198, 209, 234; discrimination between, 88, 114, 120, 192, 223

righteousness *(yi* 義*)*, 21, 67, 81, 106, 110, 119, 121, 130, 135, 156, 159, 163, 171, 173, 180, 181, 184, 185, 187, 203, 211, 213, 216–17

rite, ritual *(yi* 儀 [*li* 禮])*, 68, 70, 77, 144, 149–50, 156–59, 223, 225

Romance of the Three Kingdoms, 211

Rong Jing 鎔敬, 33

root *(ben* 本, *gen* 根*)*, 79, 98, 124, 147, 153, 156, 190, 221, 222; of all, 48, 73, 94, 95, 102, 120, 148; and body, 113, 139, 166–67; and branches, 89, 117, 176, 196, 202, 225; destroying, 80, 121; and fruit, 88, 89; of good and evil, 176–77, 190; great, 97, 112, 154–55; of human, 117, 146, 147, 154, 159, 182, 206; inward, 127, 200; of myriad, 76, 88, 97, 145, 217; one, 41, 71, 88, 95, 190; original, 83, 88, 129; of returning to, 221, 222; self as, 151, 177; six *(see* fountainheads*)*; and sprouts, 60, 72, 108; of yin and yang, 219, 224

rotation. *See* revolving

rūḥ, 14, 75

ruler *(zai* 宰*)*, 37, 38, 48, 81, 87, 100, 112, 126, 146, 147, 153–58, 162–63, 170, 171, 180, 206, 213, 226, 234; chief, 68, 81; Lord, 82, 87–92, 111, 142, 167; loyalty to, 48, 81, 154–55, 162–63; supreme *(shangdi* 上帝*)*, 80–81, 102, 133, 157, 226; *(jun* 君*)* and subject, 21, 114, 117, 121, 162, 168

Rūmī, 17, 28–29, 172

sacrifice *(zai* 宰*)*, 77, 195, 201–3; *(ji* 祭*)*, 82

Ṣādiq, Jaʿfar (d. 765), 173
sage (*sheng* 聖), 6, 8, 10, 23, 51, 61, 77–79, 90, 93, 98, 111, 134, 147, 160, 174, 175, 199, 200, 216, 225; vs. commoner (ordinary), 98, 104, 146, 174–75, 195, 199, 217, 225; embodiment of, 99, 160, 200, 202; governance of, 76, 78, 146; great, 54, 67–70, 174; Utmost (= Muhammad), 11, 16, 21, 24, 48–52, 54, 74–80, 83, 85, 87, 88, 101, 113, 123, 136, 141, 144, 146, 150, 162–65, 182, 199, 201, 202, 212, 217, 232; and worthy (wise), 8, 51, 54, 66, 70, 90, 96–99, 104, 126, 128, 133, 141, 146, 148, 152, 160, 163, 164, 170–72, 174, 175, 182, 189, 191, 193–95, 199, 202, 207, 210, 217, 230
Ṣāḥib ibn ʿAbbād, 237
sameness (*tong* 同), 38, 85, 99
sangang 三綱, 117
sanqing 三清, 87
Satan, 110, 127, 229. *See also* Iblis
saving, 146, 197; (all) people, 87, 92, 204, 218
scent, 67, 70, 82, 114, 137, 171, 230
scholars, 36–38, 67, 71, 80, 81, 89, 99, 101, 102, 108, 138, 161, 172, 182, 198; various, 36, 109, 111, 130
seasons, waning and waxing of, 47, 115, 205, 214; autumn, 62, 180, 237; spring, 62–63, 188; summer, 45, 62, 67; winter, 45, 62
secret (*ji* 機), 45–46, 57, 67, 105, 107, 113, 125, 127, 136, 140, 199, 204; of creation (transformation), 59, 70, 116, 118, 121, 142, 155, 221, 228; of recognition, 70, 76, 110, 138; mysterious, 58, 76, 110, 127, 142, 149, 201, 228; of predetermination, 63, 108
seducing (*you* 誘), 57, 209, 226
seed (*zhong* 種), of Former Heaven, 18, 60, 72, 108; and flowers and fruit (and trees), 11–12, 17–18, 48, 58, 60, 72, 75, 88, 89, 102, 103, 107–8, 111, 117, 128, 140, 156, 166, 174, 176, 180, 191, 196, 223, 225, 234; of the Non-Ultimate, 111, 144; one, 41, 72, 88, 154. *See also* flowers
seeing (*jian* 見, *guan* 觀), 59, 90, 108–10, 200; and hearing (and smelling and speaking), 45–47, 70, 78, 86, 103, 113–14, 137, 144, 167, 186, 202, 209–10, 237; with the heart, 111, 174; the Lord, 140, 152; without eyes (and ears), 46, 86
self (*zi* 自, *ji* 己, *nafs*), 22–23, 47, 146, 167, 169, 177, 190, 193, 202, 207, 213–14; coming to be by, 142–43; conquering (overcoming), 22–23, 25, 58, 130, 144, 146, 162–64, 170–71, 187, 194; individual, 105, 107; as mother of myriad things, 144, 200; private, 105, 109; of the Real, 118; reliance on, 59, 177, 215. *See also* knowledge, recognition
self-admiration (*ʿujb*), 190, 193
self-being (*jiyou* 己有), 177
self-determination (*ziyong* 自用), 86, 95, 109, 121, 129, 134, 146, 162
self-nature (*zixing* 自性). *See* nature
self-power (*zineng* 自能), 46, 166
self-single (*danling* 單另). *See* One
self-so (*ziran* 自然), 54, 72, 77, 99, 143, 147, 196, 208; mandate of, 200, 201, 207; principle of, 44, 63, 65, 97, 197, 222–23
selfishness (*si* 私), 58–59, 64, 85, 109–10, 140, 162, 206, 207, 218; selfish desire, 91, 219, 231
selflessness (*wuji* 無己), 109–10, 163, 176–78, 192. *See also* no-self
sense perception, 16, 41, 94. *See also* eyes, seeing
sentient beings (*zhongsheng* 眾生), 87, 92, 94

servant (*pu* 僕, *yi* 役), 82–83, 157, 162, 165, 168, 169, 182, 195, 203, 204, 218–19, 227; of the body, 114, 126, 151; (*'abd*), 19, 23, 108. *See also* Lord

serving (*shi* 事, *feng* 奉), 54, 187, 220; heaven, 82, 148; the Lord, 70, 80, 97, 157–59, 183, 195; parents, 155, 158–59, 206, 217; through prayer, 149–50; the ruler, 157–58; self, 213; the Supreme Ruler, 80–81, 133, 157, 226

settling and arranging (*anpai* 安排), 69, 127

severity (*wei* 威), 52, 53, 57, 179, 189

sexual relations, 122–23

shadow (*ying* 影), 43, 63, 108, 111, 120, 153, 177

Shahadah (*shahāda*), 7, 141

shallowness (*qian* 淺, *lou* 陋), 39, 83–84, 155, 220, 221, 228; and depth, 38, 89, 104, 112, 174

shame (*chi* 恥, *kui* 愧), 36, 39, 51, 58, 69, 84, 124, 141, 143, 150, 151, 163, 166, 170, 194, 205, 211, 212, 231

Shang 商 Dynasty, 61, 76, 98, 131

Shang Jun 商均, 98

Shang Zhou 商紂, 119. *See* Zhou of Yin

Shaqīq Balkhī, 165, 175

Shariah (*sharī'a*), 25, 27, 78, 190

She Yunshan 舍蘊善, 237

shen 身, 42; *shenti* 身體, 42

shen 神, 13

sheng 升, 212

sheng 聖, 6

shengwen 聲聞, 94

Shennong 神農, 7, 132

shengse 聲色, 41

Shiblī, 172–73, 229

Shijing 詩經, 80

Shu Qi 叔齊, 61–62

Shujing 書經, 80

Shun 舜, 60, 77, 80, 98, 161–62, 228; Canon of, 180

sickness. *See* disease

ṣifāt dhātiyya, 46; ṣifāt fi'liyya, 46

signs, 70–71, 78, 82, 188, 198, 220; mandate of, 76–77; (*āyāt*), 69

silence (*mo* 默, *ji* 寂), 54, 186, 216, 223. *See also* perishing

silk, 90, 146, 239; brocade, 151, 178, 181, 233, 237

similarity (*si* 似), 51, 79, 133, 186; lack of, 41, 44, 54, 86, 87, 96, 106, 119, 144, 237

sin, 58, 91, 119, 124, 129, 160, 162, 167, 168, 180, 189, 193–94, 209, 211, 235, 238

sincerity (*cheng* 誠), 20, 58, 77, 129–30, 145, 160, 168, 187, 202, 225, 235; of heart, 97, 175–76, 183, 196. *See also* intention

Sirhindī, Aḥmad, 85

slave, 64, 168, 219

sleep, 56, 66, 73, 124, 126, 139, 168, 169, 179, 185, 196–98, 232; and wakefulness, 104, 116, 225, 233

small people (*xiaoren* 小人), 184, 189, 213, 221. *See also* profound

smelling. *See* seeing

social stability, 19

soil (*tu* 土), 107, 123, 157, 167, 175, 182, 220, 221–22, 235; as element, 43–44, 47, 49, 53, 54, 74; as origin of man, 55, 127, 129, 221–23

solicitude (*ci* 賜), 56, 146, 214, 236; merciful, 71, 148–50, 164, 188, 195, 213; personal, 152; real, 16–17, 70–73

Solomon, 67–68

Song 宋 dynasty, 38, 80, 102, 226

soul (*hun* 魂), 125, 227, lower soul (*po* 魄), 209; (*nafs*), 22, 25, 103, 105, 229; levels of, 22; rational, 14, 105

sound (*sheng* 聲), and color (scent), 41, 45, 54, 67, 70, 82, 114, 137, 188, 198; and hearing, 94–95

specters (*guai* 怪), 48

speech (*yan* 言), 44–45, 77, 86, 90, 94, 188, 196–98, 217; divine, 46, 235; right, 6, 26, 196–98
spirit (*shen* 神, *rūḥ*), 13–14, 25, 42, 50, 51, 54, 74, 75, 91, 103, 110–16, 119, 126, 129, 133, 197, 203, 209, 211, 221–22, 236–37; (= jinn), 46, 50, 51, 57, 59, 72, 75, 78, 79, 86, 96, 105, 113, 116, 121, 124–29, 155, 158, 191, 193, 196; Muhammadan, 74, 78; vegetal, animal, and human, 14, 42, 75; evil spirit (*guisui* 鬼祟), 157, 227, 235–36. *See also* body, form
spiritual (*ling* 靈), 14, 18; awareness, 51–54; clarity, 56, 142, 199, 207, 222; mandate of, 16, 113; nature of, 14–15, 17, 19–20, 42–43, 49, 109–15, 124, 146, 182, 224, 236. *See also* human
spot (*dian* 點), one, 54, 87
śravaka, 94
states (*aḥwāl*), 25
station (*maqām*), 24–25
stillness (*jing* 靜), 45, 78, 187, 198, 216. *See also* movement
stone (*shi* 石). *See* metal
strength (*li* 力), 76, 100, 109, 124, 125, 126, 129, 130, 157, 168, 219
stuff (*zhi* 質), 49, 85; and vital-energy, 41, 65, 97, 102, 117
subject, 129, 225; and ruler (lord), 19, 21, 65, 117, 121, 144, 156, 157, 162, 230
submission (*fu* 服), 99, 201
substance (*ti* 體), 53, 73, 84, 112, 186, 187; clear, 231; and function, 11–12, 42, 45–46, 74, 79, 89, 91, 98, 105, 118; root, 45, 51, 68, 74, 93, 105, 230. *See also* body
subtlety, subtle (*miao* 妙), 13, 17, 41, 51, 54, 59, 69, 86, 92, 108, 110, 111, 115, 128, 138–39, 144, 224, 230; of the body, 76, 89, 90, 133, 142, 143, 186, 207, 224; and color, 54,

110, 145; function, 127, 149; Gate of all, 16, 24, 74, 97, 117, 140, 141, 154; of the human, 125, 206; of the heart, 70; of nature, 86, 87; principles, 233; of the Real, 45, 57, 79, 142, 144, 188, 236, 237. *See also* clarity
success, 57, 122, 131, 160; and failure, 49, 110, 133, 157, 177, 200, 209, 215, 221
suchness (*ran* 然), heavenly, 71, 77, 142; root, 25, 41, 45–48, 91, 92, 94, 103, 119, 146, 188, 224; undifferentiated, 52, 152, 171
suffering, 38, 58, 64, 66, 68, 92, 148, 151, 159, 168, 170, 180, 181, 187, 189, 195, 199–200, 214, 215, 217–18, 222, 223, 227, 231, 233; ocean of, 140, 203; of afterlife, 185, 194, 235, 238, 239
Sufism, 3–4, 22, 28
ṣuḥba, 173
Sui 隋 Dynasty, 211
sun, 120, 153, 155, 183, 185, 200, 228, 236; and moon, 44, 47, 58, 69, 115, 125, 136, 138, 147, 175, 186, 206, 232–34; and stars, 52–53, 55, 65, 72, 92, 147
Sunnah (*sunna*), 25
sūra, 13
sustaining (*chi* 持), 73, 116, 150–52, 166, 205; movement-stillness of (*weichi* 維持), 46–47
sympathy, 168, 204, 216

Ṭabarī, 132
Tablet (*lawḥ*), 86
Tahāwanī, 45
Tai 泰, Mount, 236
Tai Zong 太宗, 205
Taibai 太白, 212
taiji 太極, 10
taint (*ran* 染), 43, 45, 83, 91, 93–94, 97–98, 106, 130, 140, 151, 174, 196, 198, 231, 232, 235

takhalluq bi akhlāq Allāh, 21
taking (*qu* 取), and putting aside, 97, 176, 178–79, 204, 213
talent (*cai* 才), 44, 65, 131, 137–39, 170, 188, 212, 233
Tang 湯, 131
Tang 唐 Dynasty, 205, 211, 212, 226
taqdīr, 59
Tariqah (*ṭarīqa*), 25, 78
Tathagata (*rulai* 如来), 92–94
tathātā, 140
tawḥīd, 6, 9–19, 12, 13, 20
teaching (*jiao* 教), Three, 2, 5–6, 24, 141, 226; true, 36, 37, 39, 42, 48, 49, 53, 69, 70, 76–78, 83, 95–97, 99, 102, 121, 122, 128–33, 137–39, 141, 143–46, 153, 154, 159, 160, 171–72, 181, 192, 196, 199, 202, 206, 207, 209, 222, 228, 229; (various, other), 64, 67, 72, 77, 83, 89, 92, 95–97, 99, 120, 133, 147, 180, 226, 227
theater (*xichang* 戲場), 182, 230, 233
things (*wu* 物), 53; appearance of, 50; myriad, 41, 42, 44, 47, 49, 62, 85, 87–92, 95–96, 99–101, 111, 119–20, 124, 156, 176, 189, 191, 201, 205, 221, 222, 230, 232, 235; beginning of myriad, 50, 75, 87, 96; Lord of myriad, 87, 89–91, 97. *See also* heaven, human
thought, thinking (*nian* 念, *si* 思), 68, 73, 93, 100, 123, 127, 128, 131, 133, 162, 163, 175, 181, 188, 219, 234, 238; of the heart, 94, 125, 159, 191, 237
Thread (*guan* 貫), One, 63
threshold, honorable, 86, 233
Throne (*'arsh*), 75, 86
thunder, 63, 125, 178, 179, 210
Thusness (*zhenru* 眞如), 24, 140–41
ti 體, 11, 42; *yiti* 一體, 84
tian 天, 43
Tianfang 天方 (天房), 35, 36, 131–33, 223, 228

Tiantai 天台, 205
time, 41, 50, 53, 55, 62, 72, 116, 143, 179, 218; accidents of, 107, 234; great value of, 198, 210, 232. *See also* moment
tiqiao 體竅, 56
Tongjian 通鑒, 82
tongue, 46, 56, 70, 86, 113, 114, 137, 145, 151, 186, 196, 217. *See also* mouth
trace (*ji* 跡), 46, 90, 92, 127, 131, 153, 193, 202
transformation (*hua* 化), 17, 24, 53, 71, 78, 79, 87, 99, 100, 117, 120, 121, 137, 146, 154, 170–71, 207, 208, 214, 216, 222, 229; and begetting, 74, 79, 97, 101, 106, 121, 140, 143, 177; creative, 44, 47, 49–59, 65, 72, 74, 79, 81, 87–91, 95, 100, 101, 105, 115, 116, 118, 119, 124, 128, 129, 133, 143, 146, 148, 149, 153, 157, 163, 167, 168, 175, 176, 188, 195, 200, 205, 206, 208, 213, 220–21, 226, 233, 235; great, 59, 62–63; self-, 142, 171
transgression (*qian* 愆, *weihan* 違犯), 8, 67, 118, 130, 150, 151, 158, 162, 165, 168, 194, 195, 211, 214, 220, 227, 235
transmigration (*lunhui* 輪回), 223, 226–29. *See also* wheel
transmission (*chuan* 傳), 37, 44, 70; by classics, 50, 81, 131; of mandate, 76, 78, 125, 130, 189; real, 35, 49, 53, 76, 79, 82, 83, 128, 131, 133, 136, 144, 199, 201; wrong, 143, 228
travel, traveler, 43–44, 54, 56, 63, 114, 116, 120, 125, 146, 153, 172, 205, 214, 218, 225, 230–33
tree (*mu* 木), 62. *See* seed
Tripitaka (*sanzang* 三藏), 94
true, truth (*zheng* 正), 64, 67, 68, 106; attaining, 84, 106, 124, 128;

guiding to, 37, 78, 110, 148, 177; and falsehood, 37, 83, 131, 133, 135; losing, 174, 191; utmost, 8, 71, 134, 139. *See also* awareness, learning, people, teaching, way
Tu Weiming, 20, 26, 29
tuili 推理, 105
turbid (*zhuo* 濁), 54, 127, 211. *See* pure
turning (*yun* 運) and moving, 54, 56, 149, 207

'*ujb*, 190
Ultimate (*ji* 極), Great, 10–12, 41, 48–49, 53, 57, 58, 74, 79, 81, 87, 117, 121, 140, 141, 154, 198, 207, 221; Human, 10–12, 23, 50, 58, 71, 79, 116–18, 121, 125–29, 204, 207; Non-, 10–12, 48–49, 51, 53, 57, 58, 74, 78, 79, 87, 97, 111, 117, 121, 141, 144, 146, 148, 153, 154; Three, 10–12
understanding, 72, 91, 116, 135, 140, 144, 161, 192, 205, 211
undifferentiated (*hun* 渾), 43, 75, 85, 101, 103, 139; suchness, 52, 152, 171
unique (*du* 獨). *See* One
unity, exclusive and inclusive, 13. *See tawḥīd*
universal (*pu* 普), 120, 225; compassion, 64–65, 166
universe (*yuzhou* 宇宙), 29, 78, 79, 83, 90, 97, 111, 114, 130, 138, 149, 175, 206, 213; ('*ālam*), 13
uprightness (*zheng* 正), 50, 64, 124, 184, 187
utensil, 90, 91, 119
Uways Qaranī, 141

variations, 62, 65, 71, 97, 119; myriad, 41, 70, 84
vegetables (*su* 素) and meat (*hun* 葷), 206–8
veneration (*chong* 崇), 68, 75, 109, 112, 160, 176

violence, 61, 100, 151, 169, 170, 174, 210, 211
virtue (*de* 德), 60, 67, 78, 106, 114, 127, 128, 130, 133, 141, 150, 155, 170, 181, 183, 193–95, 213, 222, 228; (clarifying) clear, 20, 70, 97–98; meritorious, 190, 235; original, 77, 106; of the way, 136, 151–52, 159, 178, 180, 190–92; perfect, 107, 183; real, 123, 192, 193; virtuous deeds, 73, 106, 150, 152, 175, 191; virtuous people, 64, 122; virtues (*faḍā'il*), 21, 25
viscera (*zang* 臟), five, 47, 49
vital-energy (*qi* 氣), 41, 65, 117, 122, 129, 155; and blood, 151, 168, 170; and nature, 102–3; and principle, 17, 38, 49, 97 102
void (*xu* 虛), 65, 66, 85, 100

waḥdat al-wujūd, 85
wāḥidiyya, 13
wakefulness. *See* awakening
Wang Daiyu 王岱輿, 1–9, 35–38; Addendum (*Shengyu* 剩語), 32; *Great Learning of the Pure and Real* (*Qingzhen daxue* 清眞大學), 1, 8, 20, 74; *Real Commentary on the True Teaching* (*Zhengjiao zhenquan* 正教眞詮), 2–6, 8, 32–33; *The True Answers of the Very Real* (*Xizhen zhengda* 希眞正答), 8, 34
Wang Mang 王莽, 67
Wang Yangming 王陽明, 155
water (*shui* 水), 63, 90, 97, 104, 106, 112, 146, 178, 211, 218; and dust, 53, 224; and fire, 47, 53, 95, 173, 200, 224, 226, 228; and fish, 100, 113, 118, 208; flow of, 91, 137; and ice, 85, 96; living, 137, 238; as mirror, 90, 112, 121; and ocean, 96, 144; and plants, 138, 140, 166, 197, 198, 218; pure and turbid, 97, 104, 114, 123, 156, 218; and soil,

water *(continued)*
  54, 127, 206; salt and fresh, 56, 97. *See also* wind and water
way *(dao* 道*)*, 24–25, 38–39, 42, 47, 62, 70, 71, 83, 89, 101, 103, 116, 124–26, 134, 136, 140–41, 151, 154–55, 162–63, 178, 180, 192, 194, 195, 203, 232; of being and nonbeing, 24, 140; of the Buddha, 68, 226; of Confucianism, 38; cultivation of, 70, 96, 109, 196–200; in Daoism, 71, 89, 99; expansion of, 124, 125; of following nature, 15, 101, 103, 109; of friendship, 171–76; of heaven, 162–63; human, 38, 111, 120, 133, 140, 146, 162–63, 202, 213; of husband and wife, 121–22; of Islam, 8, 37, 84, 88, 134, 146, 147, 177, 189, 209, 223, 225; of justice, 167, 170; principle of, 36, 146, 172, 199; teaching of, 47–48; True, 49, 64, 66, 67, 71, 76, 95, 104, 109, 129, 135, 137, 140, 151, 155, 160, 163, 189, 190, 192, 195, 196, 202, 207, 221–22; Ultimate, 37, 152; utmost, 48, 78, 84, 88, 130, 180, 189, 221, 225; virtue of, 136, 151–52, 159, 178, 180, 190–92
wealth *(fu* 富*)*, and nobility, 60, 62, 64–67, 71, 107, 116, 118, 136, 140, 142, 151, 153, 155, 159, 178–79, 181, 194–95, 218–19, 230, 231. *See also* poverty
Wen, King 文王, 76, 98, 119
wheel *(lun* 輪*)*, 99, 147
wife *(fu* 婦*, qi* 妻*). See* husband
will *(zhi* 志*)*, 62, 63, 97, 98, 142, 163, 184, 199; of the heart, 84, 151, 159, 233, 238. *See also* free will
willful. *See* intention, nature
wind *(feng* 風*)*, 43–44, 47, 53, 91, 95, 125, 129, 174, 192, 217, 230; and water, 219–23; and waves, 180, 210
windlass *(lulu* 轆轤*)*, 228, 229

wine *(jiu* 酒*)*, drinking of, 63, 209–12, 237
wings *(yi* 儀*)*, two, 41, 79, 121
wisdom *(zhi* 智*)*, 21, 52, 146, 150–51, 170, 181, 188, 194, 228; great (true), 56, 135, 152, 176, 185; as human root, 56–57, 88, 108–10, 119–20; and intelligence, 41, 108, 146, 150, 151, 188; man of (wise), 48, 85, 90, 108, 135, 137, 156, 172, 178, 179, 195, 203, 211; sages and wise, 96, 104, 175, 182, 195, 197, 213, 221, 231, 232
witness, bearing *(zuozheng* 作証*)*, 48, 84, 141–42
wo 我, 53
woman, beautiful, 107, 112, 189; and man, 19, 56, 121–24, 133–34, 207
womb *(bao* 胞*, tai* 胎*)*, 69, 199, 206; and eggs, 142, 143
wood *(mu* 木*)*, 53, 224
workman, 43, 143, 194
world, worldly *(shi* 世*)*, 151, 156, 160, 164, 185, 190–92, 194, 198, 207, 210, 215, 234, 235; abandoning, 166, 178; vs. afterworld, 64, 66, 72, 100, 112, 128–29, 167–68, 178, 180–83, 219, 222, 224, 226, 229–39; earthly, 57–58, 229–32, 234; honor and disgrace, 65–67, 234; matters, 166, 195; people of, 96, 109, 110, 120, 128, 152, 156, 158, 163, 166, 169, 171, 172, 175, 177, 178, 181–83, 188, 189, 193, 194, 199, 205, 211, 213, 215, 216, 219–22, 225, 226, 231, 232; 207; three, 234. *See also* afterworld, governance
worship *(bai* 拜*)*, 68, 145, 147–50, 154, 155, 158; of buddhas, 96, 148, 157; of heaven, 82, 96; of the Lord, 97, 147–50, 156–59, 162–63, 166; propriety-worship, 147, 149–50, 157

worthy (*xian* 賢), 8, 38, 98, 137–38, 141, 151, 164, 208, 211; sayings of, 111, 137, 163, 164, 174, 216, 231, 232. *See also* sage
wrong (*fei* 非). *See* right
wu 物, 53
wu 無, 10; *wuji* 無極, 10; *wuxin* 無心, 24; *wuxing* 無形, 10
Wu 武, Emperor, 211
Wu Ding 武丁, 76
Wu Zixian 伍子先, 4

Xia 夏 Dynasty, 98, 131
Xiahui 下惠, 61–62, 98, 119, 123
Xiao Chen 蕭琛, 211
Xizi 西子 (Xi Shi 西施), 107
xiantian 先天, 10
xin 心, 23
xin 信, 21
Xin 新 Dynasty, 67
xing 形, 10, 53
xing 性, 14; *xingjue* 性覺, 42; *xingling* 性靈, 14, 42; *xingming* 性命, 7; *zixing* 自性 22
Xingmi zhenyuan 省迷眞原, 84
Xun 勳, 228
Xunzi 荀子, 101

yang 陽, 43. *See* yin
Yang Guang 楊廣, Emperor, 211
Yang Huo 陽貨, 98
Yang Huaizhong 楊懷中, 32–33
Yang Xiaochun 楊晓春, 84
Yang Zhu 楊朱, 101
Yangzi 楊子, 101
Yao 堯, Emperor, 60, 80, 98, 162, 228
yi 義, 21
Yi 夷, 61–62
Yi Yin 伊尹, 98
Yijing, 41, 43, 67, 69, 80, 84, 181
yimana 以媽納, 70–71, 73, 78

yin 陰 and yang, 43, 49, 57, 65, 79, 82, 115–16, 121–22, 124, 133, 139, 142, 154, 200, 207, 214, 219–21; roots of, 224
yiti 一體, 84
yong 用, 11, 42
Yu Zhengui 余振貴, 32–33
Yuan Ming 淵明, 212

zai 載, 69
zaohua 造化, 47
Zhang Zai 張載 (1020–77), 100
Zhang Zhong 張中, 84–85
Zhao Can 趙燦, 7
Zhao Wu 趙武, 203
zhen 眞, 1, 24–25; *zhenci* 眞賜, 16; *zhende* 眞得, 76; *zhenming* 眞命, 76; *zhenru* 眞如, 140
Zheng Yingsu 鄭應驌, 32
Zhengzhu mojie 證主默解, 84–85
zhenri 朕日, 54
zhi 智, 21
zhi 質, 41
Zhiyi 智顗, 205
Zhou 周, Duke of, 67, 80; dynasty, 61, 76, 98
Zhou of Yin 趙殷 (= Shang Zhou), 98, 119
Zhou Dunyi 周敦頤, 10; *Diagram of the Great Ultimate*, 81
Zhu Yuanzhang 朱元璋, 35
Zhu Xi 朱熹, 10, 80
Zhuangzi 莊子, 62
Zhuge Liang 諸葛亮, 220
Zi Gong 子貢, 101, 202
zixing 自性, 22
Ziya 子牙, 76
Ziyang 紫陽, 80
ziyou 自由, 59
Zizhi Tongjian 資治通鑒, 82
zuhd, 178

www.ingramcontent.com/pod-product-compliance
Ingram Content Group UK Ltd.
Pitfield, Milton Keynes, MK11 3LW, UK
UKHW041930140426
5217IPUK00014B/409